Henry Jones

A Critical Account of the Philosophy of Lotze

Henry Jones

A Critical Account of the Philosophy of Lotze

ISBN/EAN: 9783337236601

Printed in Europe, USA, Canada, Australia, Japan

Cover: Foto ©Thomas Meinert / pixelio.de

More available books at **www.hansebooks.com**

THE PHILOSOPHY OF LOTZE
THE DOCTRINE OF THOUGHT

PUBLISHED BY
JAMES MACLEHOSE AND SONS, GLASGOW.
𝔓ublishers to the 𝔘niversity.

MACMILLAN AND CO., LONDON AND NEW YORK.
London, - - - *Simpkin, Hamilton and Co.*
Cambridge, - - *Macmillan and Bowes.*
Edinburgh, - - *Douglas and Foulis.*

MDCCCXCV.

A CRITICAL ACCOUNT OF THE
PHILOSOPHY OF LOTZE

THE DOCTRINE OF THOUGHT

BY

HENRY JONES, M.A.

PROFESSOR OF MORAL PHILOSOPHY IN THE UNIVERSITY OF GLASGOW
AUTHOR OF "BROWNING AS A PHILOSOPHICAL AND RELIGIOUS TEACHER"

GLASGOW
JAMES MACLEHOSE AND SONS
Publishers to the University
1895

This Book
IS DEDICATED
BY ONE OF HIS PUPILS
TO THE MEMORY OF
A Great Teacher
JOHN NICHOL

PREFACE

In this volume I attempt to give a critical account of Lotze's exposition of the nature of thought. That exposition forms, for Lotze, a part of a larger undertaking. Before he could proceed to his main endeavour, and give a metaphysical account of the nature of Reality, it seemed to him necessary to clear the ground of false pretensions set up for thought, partly by the scientific men of his day but mainly by Hegel and his followers. For these writers, as he understood them, had identified thought with reality, and converted the rich and living world of concrete facts into a fixed system of abstract categories. Lotze, therefore, subjects thought to a most searching analysis, with a view of discovering what in reality is its nature and what, if any, are the limits of its powers.

He finds, in the first place, that thought is not an ontological principle. It does not constitute reality, but represents it—more or less inaccurately. Thought mirrors the world of being, produces an image or ideal reflection of it in man's consciousness. That ideal representation of reality we call truth; but the world of truth, though it may correspond to the real universe, does not constitute it or any part of it. Thought is thus simply a function of man's intelligence.

In the second place, it is only one function amongst several others. There is more in mind than thought, and the processes of thinking do not exhaust our intelligent activities. Besides thinking, there are feeling and volition, elements of mind neither less original nor less essential than thought. Nor are the processes of sensation and perception and imagination to be identified with thought without inaccuracy and confusion. For these deal with the individual and the concrete, while thought is exclusively occupied with what is universal and abstract. Thought conceives, judges, and reasons, and besides this it does nothing further; and the conceptions, judgments, and reasonings which it produces are only relations *between* the phenomena of mind.

In the third place, these functions which are allowed to remain for thought, it performs only with the help of the other intelligent powers which we have named, and upon which thought is entirely dependent. Some of these powers, such as sensation and perception, furnish thought with its material or content; and others, such as "faith," or "the feeling which is appreciative of worth," provide it with its ideal, its impulse, and its criterion, and they give the only guarantee of the validity of its conclusions. When thus provided with the material on which it has to operate, and with the ideal which it has to realize, thought can rearrange the given data in accordance with general laws, grouping the phenomena of experience in classes, and connecting them in an order of sequence or simultaneity which is necessary. But its function is wholly and exclusively formal; all that it does is to rearrange, substituting a rational, or ideally necessary, for a contingent connection between mental phenomena.

In the fourth place, the systematic world thus created by thought from the data supplied to it, is purely ideal. It is a world of ideas, and not a world of things. There are no things called classes in the outer world of reality; there are none which can be called subjects, and none which can be called predicates, and none which correspond to the copula; nor are reasonings which connect ideas to be confused with causes which connect real objects. The products of thought are not even *similar* to anything which exists in the sphere of reality. Nor are real things in any way responsible for them, for they take no part in their creation. Things do not conceive, nor enter into classes, nor range themselves as subjects and predicates, premisses and conclusions. These arrangements are mere products of thought, and they constitute a world of their own which is at no point in contact with that real world which they in some way represent.

In the last place, the results of thought would not be recognized even as representing reality were thought the only intelligent power which man can exercise. For the knowledge *that* things are is due to other mental functions; furnished with the facts, or intelligible data, thought may proceed to show *what* they are, to reveal their meaning or ideal significance. But the meaning of a thing is never that which it is, but only that which it *appears* to be when translated out of the sphere of reality into that of ideality. And even that meaning which thought extracts is no true or direct representation of objects as they really are. For thought is not immediate, but discursive and indirect. It never reveals what an object is in and of itself, but it shows whether it is like or unlike, equal or unequal to, or otherwise *related* to other objects, which, in turn, are just as little apprehended in themselves, or as they are. The core of reality in the individual thing entirely escapes the grasp of thought. An intuitive or perceptive intelligence might give us that inner core in things, and *re*-present that impervious personality which constitutes the inner essence of intelligent beings. But our intelligence is not intuitive; it is discursive or reflective, condemned to creep from one fact to another, instituting relations *between* them, but absolutely incapable of seizing the real being of any one of them. Thought is not, therefore, constitutive even of intelligence *as such*. It is rather an indirect and devious process, of which man is obliged to avail himself, in order to make up for the absence of an adequate perceptive intuition with which, for some unknowable reason, man is not endowed. Thought is, therefore, a symbol of man's mental incompetence, as well as his only means of acquiring such knowledge as is possible for him.

Now, if this view of thought be true, consequences of the most important kind follow from it. In the first place, the power of that idealistic reconstruction of belief which has so strongly influenced the modern mind is entirely broken. Thought, instead of being the substance of things seen, and the principle which lives and moves in all objects of all intelligence, is only a part, and a comparatively insignificant and dependent part, of man's mental equipment. Hence the work of metaphysics must be done over again from the beginning. Philosophers must seek some other ontological principle, more adequate than thought to the being and to the explanation of the exhaustless and ever-changing content of the real world. And, in the second place, the theologians who had all along striven against the reduction of God, the soul of man, and the world into logical processes of thought and mere pulsations of an impersonal reason, may now take new heart. For, side by side with, nay, dominant over, the merely formal and systematizing thought, there is room and need for that intuitive perception, that immediate consciousness, which alone makes us aware of reality—supersensuous no less than sensuous. The accent and emphasis must now fall, especially in spiritual matters, not upon the power which rearranges the content of our experience and can do nothing more, but on those activities which supply us with that content. The experience itself is more vital and valuable than any exposition of it which thought can afterwards give. Hence, for those thinkers who have accepted *simpliciter* the results of Lotze's exposition, thought is, comparatively speaking, of little importance. And we have—in Germany only as yet—a new theology which trusts the heart against the head, and which, having removed the data of the religious life from the sphere of a thought that is only formal, can regard its operations with complete indifference. Reason has nothing to do with religion, though it may have with the theology which explains it.

But Lotze's investigation of thought has had other and more valuable consequences. It has led modern writers to investigate the nature of thought for themselves, with the result that, particularly in this country, there has been a remarkable development of logical theory on Lotze's own lines. I refer more specially to the logical works of Mr. Bradley and Mr. Bosanquet, to whom I express with great pleasure deep obligations. This development of Lotze's position seems to me to issue in its refutation; and there are indications that the main contribution of Lotze to philosophic thought, the only ultimate contribution, consists in deepening that Idealism which he sought to overthrow.

It has been my endeavour in this volume to justify this conclusion in detail. That is to say, I have tried to lay bare the movement of Lotze's exposition, so as to show not only that it refutes itself, but that it indicates in a new way the necessity for an idealistic construction of experience. For if Lotze had been strictly faithful to the view of thought which he sets forth, and which he attributes to Idealists, he would have found it incapable of performing that poor remnant of its functions which he allows it to retain. In order to get his formal thought to produce any results, he is constrained to find each of its products one by one in its material. Hence, what he exposes to our view is a kind of pseudo-dialectic by which, on the failure of one form of abstract thought after another, he has recourse to its content. Each fresh appeal to the content gives to formal thought a fresh start, and the possibility of thinking at all is thus, by implication, shown to lie in its material. The very helplessness of formal thought at once indicates that *such* thought is a logical fiction, and bears witness to the ideality of its content. On his own showing the material dominates thought and expresses *itself* in thought. In this way, therefore, Lotze leads us from a formal to a constitutive, from a subjective and "epistemological" to an objective and ontological view of thought. That is to say, in expounding the conditions of its activity he yields *a tergo*, and as an unwilling witness, an idealistic conception of the world.

This conception cannot, however, be fully justified without investigating reality itself. By following Lotze's exposition I have in this volume raised questions which can be answered only by a further inquiry which is directly and undisguisedly metaphysical. I propose, therefore, to endeavour to meet some of these problems, so far as it is in my power, in another volume dealing with Lotze's metaphysical doctrines, in which, I believe, he corroborates the Idealism he sought to refute in his backward process from thought to reality, by an opposite process from reality to thought.

HENRY JONES.

The University,
Glasgow, *February*, 1895.

CONTENTS

CHAPTER I
THE MAIN PROBLEM OF LOTZE'S PHILOSOPHY — PAGE 1

CHAPTER II
GENERAL VIEW OF LOTZE'S DOCTRINE OF THOUGHT — 37

CHAPTER III
THOUGHT AND THE PRELIMINARY PROCESSES OF EXPERIENCE — 73

CHAPTER IV
THE THEORY OF JUDGMENT — 119

CHAPTER V
LOTZE'S DOCTRINE OF INFERENCE AND THE SYSTEMATIC FORMS OF THOUGHT — 173

CHAPTER VI

EXAMINATION OF LOTZE'S ASCENT FROM SUB-
SUMPTIVE TO SYSTEMATIC INFERENCE - - 223

CHAPTER VII

THE SUBJECTIVE WORLD OF IDEAS AND THE SUB-
JECTIVE PROCESSES OF THOUGHT - - - 268

CHAPTER VIII

THE PRINCIPLE OF REALITY IN THOUGHT AND ITS
PROCESSES - - - - - - - 324

THE PHILOSOPHY OF LOTZE

CHAPTER I

THE MAIN PROBLEM OF LOTZE'S PHILOSOPHY

IT is an unmistakeable mark of greatness in a man that he irresistibly attracts the attention of thinkers and makes the task of endeavouring to comprehend him inevitable. He may not claim such attention at once. He may for a time be a voice in the wilderness, and the message he utters may travel in the void. If he be a philosopher he must, as a rule, wait for the age that can comprehend him. The truths which he leaves as an inheritance to the world generally fall in the first place into the hands of rival schools which divide the heritage between them, each of them seizing a mere aspect of his doctrine, and, while following it out into its abstract consequences, sacrificing the principle which gave it vitality. The true heir of the inheritance appears in him who is able to collect together the scattered and conflicting aspects and to grasp them in their unity.

But the greater gods appear rarely. Vital revolutions of human thought are not frequent. Many must labour to understand the thoughts of the few. And, amidst the conflict of opposing systems, we must welcome those men who co-ordinate the truths though they may lack the strength to combine them. For, although co-ordination merely shows the need of an ordering principle without revealing what it is, and sets the problem rather than solves it, it nevertheless places us at the point of view from which alone solution is possible.

Such, I believe, is the service which has been done in recent times by Hermann Lotze. Without either the originality or the constructive power that brings reformation through revelation and heralds a new age with a new truth, he nevertheless commands the homage of our time. It is doubtful if any writer on philosophy has occupied so much attention in recent years as Lotze. And the modern developments of philosophy and religion, both in this country and in Germany, are so marked with his influence that the task of comprehending his significance cannot be easily or wisely set aside.

It cannot be denied that circumstances more or less fortuitous in character have combined with the intrinsic worth of his writings to lend them importance. He has received from translators such particular favour that all his greater works are in the hands of English readers. He has given a popular, as well as a scientific exposition of his views, and thus helped materially in making them a common possession; and he is intelligible to an ordinary reader. He gains also in all these respects from his contrast to his predecessors in Germany, of whose thoughts he is a vendor; and he gains still more by the impression—which the student of the earlier German metaphysicians often misses—that he is a "sound" thinker both as to matter and method. Instead of their speculative boldness, he has substituted an exposition of details which is extraordinarily careful, a cautiousness which often amounts to hesitancy, an admirable habit of arguing questions on both sides, and the still rarer merit of admitting the limitations of his own theories, and the cogency of other views with which he has little sympathy; so that he seems to sit free from his own system.

But it need hardly be said that no combination of such extraneous circumstances could of itself account for his influence. His power over the age springs from the fact that he is dealing with problems which it recognizes as vital, and his popularity from the fact that he solves them in a manner which, on the whole, accords with our convictions. For, unlike his predecessors and the majority of his contemporaries, he does no violence to the views of ordinary educated persons on any of the graver matters of morality or religion. On the contrary, he seems to have restored to us possessions which Kant and his immediate followers had made insecure, and which the Materialists and the Pessimists had rendered untenable. In the service of these convictions he has, at least for the time, stemmed the tide of Idealism and given pause to that ambitious Monism which seemed to have confused the old boundaries of thought, mingling together nature and spirit, good and evil, things and thought, the human and the divine. In the same interest he has also "stayed the Bacchic dance of the Materialists," who had occupied the place left vacant by the spent Idealism. So that it is no matter for surprise that some readers of philosophy, and, more especially, theologians of a reflective type should consider that they owe it to Lotze above all others that, after the reign of chaos, there is once more "a firmament in the midst of the waters, dividing the waters from the waters." To many such he is, if not the last refuge, the latest hope.

Nor is he of little value to the few who are more interested in the pursuit of truth than in the defence of convictions already acquired. That is to say, the writings of Lotze demand the attention of men whose interests are philosophical rather than directly ethical or religious. This is true, although he can scarcely be said to have looked upon the world from a fresh point of view, or erected a new system. Indeed, he rather set himself to show why the reflection of the world of reality in a philosophical theory is an aim that transcends the powers of man, and sought to cool men's ardour for new systems. So far from deriving all things from a single principle, there is scarcely any writer of his magnitude who leaves his students in such doubt as to his regulative thoughts. He rarely gives utterance to decisive convictions; when he does, he generally admits that he cannot prove them—particularly if they are positive—and he often seems to contradict them in other parts of his writings. His caution, his care for details, his obtrusive fair-mindedness, have obscured his main conceptions. It is difficult to say whether he is an Idealist, or Realist, or both; and he has, quite naturally, been taken for a Materialist, for a champion of Orthodox theology, and also for an enlightened Agnostic. Hartmann, his best critic, tries to make out that Lotze never says a "Yea" without a "Nay"; some, even of his followers, admit that he has no system — his centre like his circumference being everywhere.

But though Lotze's thoughts lack the unity of a system explicitly governed by a single principle, they have that other unity, which is frequently not less suggestive and valuable, that comes from being occupied with one problem. He is by no means a mere eclectic, or gatherer of simples. His contributions to special departments of philosophy have been too weighty, and his criticism of certain metaphysical doctrines too penetrating, to be the outcome of an unsystematic mind. Sporadic thought could not wield the power he has shown; and the magnitude of his influence proves beyond dispute that his speculation has one impulse and one aim. That aim has been obscured, partly by the number of the one-sided theories held in his day, and devoted to the development of abstract views with all of which he had some sympathy, and partly by the predominance of the critical over the constructive tendency in Lotze's own mind.

Erdmann, who estimates Lotze very highly, says that "the reader of Lotze must make up his mind to find much which appeared to him indisputable truth described as uncertain, and, in the same way, much which he held to be indisputably false represented as at least possible." Now, the faculty of rendering disputable what seemed certain is the distinctive mark of the genuine critic. He suspends our decision, he assists our progress by first seeming to retard it; he forces thought to turn back, so to speak, for aspects of truth that have been neglected during the excitement that comes with the consciousness of advance. With the necessity and directness of instinct the critic sets himself in antagonism to the aggressive movements of the systematizing thought of his day, and protests against the tendency to superinduce on the wealth of phenomena a rash and abstract simplicity.

We find these characteristics on almost every page

of Lotze's writings. Like the true critic, he escapes the contagion of both of the great modern enthusiasms, and endeavours to limit at once the scientific and the idealistic interpretations of the world to the spheres within which they are respectively valid. While rejoicing in the conquests of modern science, he is "filled with distrust of its importunate persuasiveness"; while sympathizing deeply with the spiritual view of the world which Idealism seeks to establish, he has the strongest antipathy to its over-confidence and a keen sense of its difficulties and of the existence of facts which refuse to be fitted into its system. Yet he is not a sceptic, except in the older and better sense of the term. His interest is not in negation. "Man," he says, "must make the best of what he has, and not decline valuable knowledge merely because it does not offer him the whole truth which he wishes to know." Unlike the sceptic, Lotze believes where he cannot prove, and finds experience itself to be richer than any theory of it. His antagonism to the generalizations of science, and especially to Idealism, in which, as I believe, lies the key to his significance, has its roots in positive convictions which, as he conceived, have been either ignored altogether or mutilated in order to be fitted into systems. In fact, he sets himself *against* the two great constructive movements of modern thought *on behalf of the contents of the ordinary consciousness.*

This double attack ultimately resolves itself into

a single one. His conviction that "the fundamental ideas of Physical Science are inadequate, disconnected, and frequently inconsistent" could only be justified by subjecting them to philosophical criticism. For it is only when a science aspires to be a metaphysic, and seeks to make its principles universal in their application, that its inadequacy is revealed; the ultimate justification or refutation of the constructive hypotheses of science is the task of philosophy—or, if the phrase is less displeasing, of a science of first principles. Besides this, Lotze possibly divined a truth which is ever becoming clearer, that there is a close affinity between natural science and Idealism, that modern science when it understands itself is idealistic in temper and tendency, and that the attempt of philosophers to establish a universal synthesis by means of the principle of evolution differs from the work which is done by men of science only in the extent of its sweep and in the breadth and generality of its results. It is not Idealism with its spiritual construction of the world that is at war with the inner spirit of science, but the scepticism which, in our day, conceals its true nature under the names of Dualism and Agnosticism. Hence the interest of Lotze's strictures on both of these modern movements, his attempt to limit the spheres within which they are cogent, centres round his criticism of Idealism.

Lotze's opposition to Idealism was based not so

much on his antagonism to its positive doctrines as upon his antipathy to its *system*. It would not be strictly true to say that Lotze adopts *each* of the main tenets of Hegel while rejecting the *whole*, but such a statement would be a fair summary of his general attitude. His view of Nature, Man, and God is not fundamentally different from that of Hegel, but he strenuously criticizes Hegel's attempt to reduce them all into pulsations or dialectical movements of a single principle of thought. To the essentially critical spirit of Lotze, a system, simply because it is a system, seems to tyrannize over its component parts. The reflective characteristic of modern thought, manifested in science no less than in philosophy, seemed to him to raise universal conceptions to such a despotic position that it was no longer possible to assign their due place and rights to the rich contents of the world and to the endless variety of its particular phenomena. His philosophy is a persistent defence of perception against reflection, of the concrete particular against pale and vacant general ideas; it is a powerful protest against injustice to the individuality and uniqueness which he found at the core of every real fact. Thought, with its abstract conceptions and unsubstantial universals seemed to him poor and thin as compared with the facts and events of the real world; every general law appeared to him to fall short of reaching the core and essence of anything actual. How much more, therefore, must a system of general laws—such as a philosophy must be—fall short of the infinite variety of the facts of the world within and without man, and the endless play of its events.

It is thus easy to see how the Idealism of Hegel, which was at once the most recent and the most bold attempt to exhaust the contents of the world of objects by means of thought, should draw upon itself the most uncompromising opposition from Lotze. It seemed to him to reduce the world to a "solemn shadow-land" of general conceptions, to convert the infinite variety of its chances and changes into a system of logical notions at once empty and ruled by necessity. In a word, Idealism appeared to him to be an attempt to establish a universal mechanism, which was not the less fixed and relentless because it was called "spiritual." "On such a view," he says, "individual, living minds really count for nothing in history; they are but sound and smoke, their efforts, in so far as they do not fall in with the evolution of the Idea, have no worth and significance in themselves, their happiness and peace are not among the ends of historical development. The course of history is as the great and awful and tragic altar on which all individual life and joy is sacrificed to the development of the Universal Idea of Humanity."[1]

It is this opposition to system that distinguishes

[1] *Mikrokosmus*, Bk. VII., chap. ii.

Lotze's criticism of Idealism from that of such writers as Schopenhauer and Hartmann. In the case of these latter writers the criticism of Idealism is preliminary to an attempt to erect a new system. Starting by rejecting the "Panlogismus" of Hegel, and by denying that thought could perform the constructive functions attributed to it, they then assigned to it a subordinate position, and sought to derive it and its activities and products from some more fundamental ontological principle, whose materialistic nature they disguised by calling it the "will" and the "unconscious." Instead of the "self-conscious spirit" of Hegel, they set on the throne a blind power; instead of a system whose principle is intelligence, they established a mechanism to which ideas and the consciousness which produced them were more or less contingent, and completely unfortunate, additions.

The constructive efforts of these philosophers have rendered their attack on Idealism comparatively harmless, at least so far as the popular and theological consciousness is concerned. They have diverted attention from the weaknesses of Idealism and centred it on their own systems, which, being materialistic, have all the defects of Idealism in addition to their own; which are weak in their logic, and which violate in a new way the current moral and religious convictions of the modern world. But Lotze enjoys the immunity from attack which is always the peculiar privilege of the pure critic;

for no camp can be burned till it is pitched somewhere, and no opponent can be overthrown till he takes up some position of his own. In this fact, I believe, is to be found the true secret of the impression that Lotze has made on both German and English thought. Far from contributing a new rival system of his own, his effort culminates in re-establishing popular ethical and religious convictions, purifying them only of their grosser contradictions. Not that Lotze's agreement with the broad opinions of the ordinary consciousness is in itself a defect. On the contrary, I should say that *primâ facie* it is a grave argument against a philosophy that it contradicts the principles which the world has found valuable in practice. In one respect at least, common sense is truer than any philosophy, and serves as its criterion. And it is a positive achievement for a philosopher to be "orthodox," provided his orthodoxy is philosophical. For he has not to invent the world of art, or morality, or religion, but to understand it. He comes neither to invent nor to destroy, but to fulfil; he rises above the fundamental convictions of mankind not by rejecting, but by comprehending them.

But he *must* comprehend them; and to comprehend them means that he holds them in a manner fundamentally different from the ordinary consciousness. He must not only acknowledge the different aspects of the truth, he must also bring them together by revealing within them the operation of a single principle of unity and simplicity. He may, like the ordinary consciousness, maintain the necessity of nature, and the freedom of man, and the omnipresence of God; he may give man all his own way which is essential to morality, and God all His own way which is essential to religion, and thus permit both these forces which mould the higher destinies of mankind to exist together. But he must also strive to reconcile them. Truth for him must not be a thing of aspects and phases merely; he must not agree with the common consciousness in its fragmentariness. This, I believe, is the cardinal defect of Lotze. He spares no effort to expose the errors and omissions of the systems which he criticizes, and he thereby performs a service whose value it would be hard to estimate too highly; nevertheless he not only leaves the difficulties where they were, he also directs his main attack against the very attempt to resolve them into a higher principle. He has exercised, and exercised with uncommon power, the function of a mere critic; but he has failed to escape the implicit dogmatism which always lies in wait for the mere critic. For the mere critic is always dominated by an unconscious conservatism which only makes a show of passing its convictions through the crucible of doubt. While seeming to pursue truth, he is really engaged in defending what he has from the first taken to be indubitable. This, as I shall try to show, is what Lotze has done in appealing from the systems of philosophers to experience. His justification for doing so lies in the fact that practice is and will remain wider than theory, and that the world is greater than our best construction of it. But the appeal must be made on behalf of that construction, and the facts of experience must be regarded as problems, and not as truths already known and certain. Otherwise philosophy has abdicated its function in favour of the dogmatism and fragmentariness of common sense. There is thus a higher service to truth than that of gathering up its fragments; it is not enough that "there was a noise, and a great shaking, and the bones came together, bone to his bone." There must be "breath in them"; and the primary business of philosophy is, after all, to be the witness to this breath and life, to find an expression for the One which pervades all the manifold differences of phenomena and makes the world a unity. The philosopher who is satisfied with exposing the abstractness and inconclusiveness of earlier systems may effectively point out the labour that remains to be achieved by others, but he does not perform it himself. But Lotze, in so far as he has confined himself to criticism and the restoration of ordinary convictions, will not give rest to any, except to those who find in the failure of philosophies an excuse for taking traditions for truth and for giving up the endeavour of the intellect.

It may seem to be a hard saying "that Lotze

has set himself against the constructive movements of modern thought *on behalf of the contents of the ordinary consciousness,*" and it certainly demands both justification and limitation. Taken absolutely it is not true. For the critical tendency which predominated in him was itself guided by the consciousness of a single problem which ordinary experience seems somehow to solve, although philosophy has not been able to reveal the principle which brings the solution. That problem is the reconciliation of reasoned or systematic knowledge with " the unscientific consciousness of spiritual reality which is expressed in religion and morality."[1] It is the problem which vexes the modern spirit and constrains it to reflection. And it is this fact —that Lotze has avoided the one-sided developments of abstract views, placed himself at the point of collision of the primary interests of human life, and thereby taken upon himself our burden— which at the same time gives him the sway he exercises over our time, and puts him in the line of succession from Kant.

For that problem was, of course, first stated by Kant, and the main features of his statement remain unchanged to our own day. He had found that human experience was divided against itself, and that human reason, in the endeavour to interpret it, was called upon to consider questions which it could not decline, and which it could not

[1] See Caird's *Critical Philosophy of Kant*, Vol. I., p. 41 *ff.*

answer. It could not decline them because they sprang from the very nature and essence of rational experience, and it could not answer them because every answer it could furnish did violence to the material on which it was directed, converting the unconditioned into the conditioned, the infinite into the finite, the real into the phenomenal. Experience contained elements which at once challenged knowledge and transcended it; and reason, in its attempt to meet the challenge, seemed to fall into intolerable contradictions. Kant was, therefore, constrained to examine "the pretensions of pure speculative reason" to deal with the practical interests which hinge upon the supersensible ideas on which morality and religion rest. The result of the examination was to deprive it of these pretensions. "*I must, therefore, abolish knowledge to make room for belief*" is his strong expression of the immediate results of his First Critique. And although he found in his Second Critique another "absolutely necessary use of pure reason—the moral use," which promised to restore to us the possessions to which man as a purely cognitive being had no right, and although in his Third Critique he came still nearer the unification of the elements of experience which seemed at first irreconcilable, the history of modern thought amply shows that the solution he offered was incomplete.

A commentator speaking of Lotze has remarked that "he never went back to Kant," implying thereby that he had no need to do so, because he was from the first engaged in the same manner with the same difficulties. Nor is there any doubt that Lotze's speculative effort derived its original impulse from the same contradiction between natural knowledge and spiritual beliefs, and that it was guided throughout by analogous views as to the nature both of human thought and of the experience which thought has to comprehend. Those who are fortunate enough really to know Kant have little need of Lotze. But to most students of philosophy there can be hardly any better help to the understanding of Kant than the study of Lotze. None betray the vulnerable points of a master's doctrine so surely as his devoted disciples, and hardly any single writer shows more clearly than Lotze does the unsatisfactory character of the Kantian compromise between faith and reason. And besides, Lotze was able to study Kant's thoughts in the light of the labours of those who succeeded him. Hence, although the problem remains the same, and, in its main features, the solution also, the processes by which that solution was attained are deeply modified by both of the great movements of thought which had only begun to appear in Kant's day and in Kant's own writings, namely, the Scientific and the Idealistic movements.

One of Lotze's works, his *Mikrokosmus*, while, owing to its popular form it has of all his writings the least strictly scientific value, has the double merit for his students of being the completest expression of his general views, and of revealing most clearly the motives and convictions which guided his speculative endeavour.[1] In the opening paragraphs of that work Lotze indicates with considerable accuracy the problem which he had set himself to solve, and the purpose which in the main was dominant throughout the whole wide range of his speculation. "Between spiritual needs and the results of human science there is," he says, "an unsettled dispute of long standing. In every age the first necessary step towards truth has been the renunciation of those soaring dreams of the human heart which strive to picture the cosmic frame as other and fairer than it appears to the eye of the impartial observer." These convictions, springing from the heart, have from one point of view, as he proceeds to show, little claim to be "set in opposition to common knowledge as being a higher view of things." They are only "indefinite yearnings ignorant of their goal"; and "though they have their source in the best part of our nature," they are infected by doubts and reflections and subject to the "influences of transmitted culture and temporary tendencies," and even to "the natural changes of mental mood which take place in men,

---

[1] An article on "Philosophy in the last Forty Years," published in the *Contemporary Review*, January, 1880, and, republished in Lotze's *Kleine Schriften*, Vol. III., has considerable value for the second of these reasons.

and are different in youth from what they are after the accumulation of manifold experiences." It cannot, therefore, "be seriously hoped that such an obscure and unquiet movement of men's spirits should furnish a juster delineation of the connection of things than the careful investigations of science, in which that power of thought, which all share in, is brought into action." We might, therefore, conclude that we must give up belief to make room for knowledge. But, on the other hand, the renunciation of these beliefs in response to the demands of systematic cognition is impossible without distorting and maiming experience in its essential features, and without stultifying the very purpose to attain which such a renunciation is made. For even if truth were attained by such a process, and even if that truth were not partial but complete, it would have, thus set by itself as the sole ideal of human effort, little value. "If the object of all human investigation were to produce in cognition a reflection of the world as it exists, of what value would be all its labour and pains, which could result only in vain repetition, in an imitation within the soul of that which exists without it? What significance could there be in this barren rehearsal—what should oblige thinking minds to be mere mirrors of that which does not think, unless the discovery of truth were in all cases likewise the production of some good, valuable enough to justify the pains expended in attaining it?"[1] If, on the one hand, the yearnings of the heart, "the spiritual demands," cannot be satisfied unless their objects are real, and if our beliefs have no right to convince unless they are true; on the other hand, the mental picture even of these objects, if it could be attained, would be nothing but a subjective imitation of their reality, and would have no innate worth. "Taking truth as a whole, we are not justified in regarding it as a merely self-centred splendour, having no necessary connection with those stirrings of the soul from which, indeed, the impulse to seek it first proceeds."[2]

Animated by this double conviction Lotze resists, on the one side, the tendency to "cling with immediate belief to that view of the world, which seems to have its truth corroborated by its consonance with our wishes." He will not "put science as a whole on one side, as if it were a maze in which cognition, detached from its connection with the whole living mind, has become entangled." He refuses, that is, to extrude the intellect on behalf of the spiritual convictions that arise from the heart. But, on the other side, he resists with even greater earnestness the other tendency more prevalent in his day, of renouncing as unreal everything that is not capable of being assuredly known or is not susceptible of systematic exposition and proof. He will not allow man "to revel in this faith of the world of feeling," nor will he agree

[1] *Mikrokosmus*, Introduction.   [2] *Ibid.*

with "the deification of truth." Neither is he content with the common compromise by which men endeavour to reap the advantages both of an uncritical faith in the facts of the supersensible world and of the systematic knowledge of the world of sensible realities. The difficulty cannot be evaded by "taking part in both worlds and belonging to both, yet without uniting the two"; nor "by following, in science, the principles of cognition to their most extreme results, and allowing oneself, in practical life, to be impelled in quite other directions by traditional habits of belief and action." "We can never look on indifferently when we see cognition undermining the foundations of faith, or faith calmly putting aside as a whole that which scientific zeal has built up in detail. On the contrary, we must be ever consciously endeavouring to maintain the rights of each, and to show how far from insoluble is the contradiction in which they appear to be inextricably involved."[1] For the rights of each, if only they are understood, will prove inalienable; and the conflict between them, as long as one aims at extinguishing the other, will therefore be endless. For *rights* are immortal. "The old contradictions rise again to battle; on the one side is the knowledge of the world of sense with its stores of exact truth and the persuasive force of perceived facts, ever on the increase; on the other side are the divinations of the super-

[1] *Mikrokosmus*, Introduction.

sensible, scarcely sure of their own content and hardly susceptible of proof, but sustained nevertheless by the recurring consciousness of their necessary truth, and still less susceptible of refutation."[1]

But Lotze is convinced that "the contest between the two is an unnecessary torment which we inflict upon ourselves by terminating investigation prematurely," and "it is this conclusion which he desires to establish." His aim is "to adjust the relation between our cognition and our spiritual needs," and he is not hopeless of success; for their opposition is not due to a final untowardness and contradiction in human nature, but to the distortion of their true relation during the course of human development, and to the elevation of each in turn at the expense of the other. He does not desire to abolish knowledge to make room for faith, nor faith to make room for knowledge. His watchword, rather, is, as he says, to "maintain the rights of each"; to render unto Caesar what is Caesar's, and unto God what is God's. And, on the whole, as we shall show, the point of view from which what is Caesar's is *also* God's lay beyond the horizon of his speculative vision. He was content to restore the disturbed balance, and to delimit the territories of faith and knowledge.

It is possible that such a purpose, even if it were achieved, cannot be regarded as satisfactory from either the speculative or the practical point

[1] *Mikrokosmus*, Introduction.

of view, and that the impulse to unity and wholeness is as imperious in the sphere of faith as it is in that of knowledge. For the division between faith and reason, which thus sunders into two parts our cognitive experience, is analogous to that which cleaves our moral nature. Just as man's moral ideal stands over against and condemns his actual achievement, so belief, with its prophetic indication of a higher truth that is merely divined, confronts and condemns as inadequate the narrow region of his assured knowledge. The *moral* ideal which condemns the actual is generally recognized as also inspiring it, and the poorest moral victory is felt to be in some dim and devious way the triumph of the supreme good. In consequence, the unity of the ideal and the actual is seen to be deeper than their division, and the former, though never realized, is always in course of realization. But, in the case of the *theoretical* life of man, this deeper unity has been overlooked by Lotze and many others; and the difference between belief and knowledge has been magnified and hardened into irreconcilable opposition. The sting of the contradiction which comes with the consciousness that the divined truth is not known, but "is given, and yet *not* given," as Lotze puts it in his earlier Metaphysic, has not been recognized by him as itself a witness to the unity of man's rational nature. He ignored the fact that the torment of a divided intellectual life could not arise except for the organic filaments which indicate that what is being rent asunder is whole and one. And consequently, instead of endeavouring to discover those principles which, while seeming to transcend experience, still constitute it, making one world of the two regions of belief and knowledge, he sought to balance their claims. Instead of regarding faith as always anticipating knowledge, as holding insecure posts with an advanced guard in a foreign land, pending its permanent occupation by reasoned knowledge, he sought to confine faith and reason each in a domain of its own, and to make some things into objects of belief, and others into objects of knowledge.

If there are principles of unity in the whole of our experience, and if these are discoverable by philosophic methods, Lotze's attempt to compromise must be regarded as having failed. Nevertheless the failure to reach a unity on the part of one who clearly recognized the initial antagonism of the parts, may be far more valuable and ultimately constructive than a theory which grasps a unity at the expense of the differences. Contradictions are always living and suggestive; abstract unities are dead and barren. And it is no small honour to Lotze that, in an age which was given over to abstract constructions of man and the world, he stood almost alone, protesting against the rash haste which secured unity by sacrificing its content. From this point of view he has been compared by some of his sympathetic critics to Rembrandt and Rousseau; for he, like them, led the way from artifice to art and nature, looked man and the world in the face, and, in consequence, found in them a wealth of content in comparison with which the theories so confidently advanced in his day were unreal and empty. He preferred the antagonisms of reality to the hollow peace of empty consistency; and he appears amongst his contemporaries in the *rôle* of one who protests on behalf of man and nature, in the whole compass of their many-sided existence, against the abstract conceptions of them which were then in vogue. And this attitude is always characteristic of Lotze. Reality and theory were, to him, contrasted as the living and the dead. In the realm of the former he found "innumerable activities," "unfailing movements," an inexhaustible content; while the limited region of knowledge was "a solemn shadow-land of unchangeable ideas," "the imperturbable repose of universal but empty relations of thought." And, whether he considered the labours of the idealists or of the materialists, he found that the extent and the value of knowledge was mischievously overrated, with the result that violence had been done to the complex nature of man, who was mutilated that he might be fitted into systems. Truth had been deified, as already hinted, as if it had sovereign and innate worth; while, as his whole aim is to show, it is able only to mirror that which veritably exists. The world of ideas at its utmost can only be a barren rehearsal, or lifeless copy, of the real world. Its value is derived and not native; it shines only in a borrowed light; the ultimate significance and worth of what we know consists merely in its subservience to "what we have to do, and what to hope." Theory exists for the sake of practice, the intellect is rooted in the heart, the true has its foundations in the good, and Metaphysics in Ethics.

Students of Kant will not miss the analogy between Lotze's view of the relation of Metaphysics to Ethics and Kant's transition from the speculative to the practical reason. The latter supplies in the moral law, the reality, the "*factum*" or "*quasi-factum*" which gives a ποῦ στῶ to the ideas of God, Freedom, and Immortality, which all experience presupposes, but which, apart from the immediate deliverance of the moral consciousness, would hang empty in the upper air of the transcendent. But, although the conception is Kant's, and the principle of reality offered by Lotze is attained by him in Kant's way, the modern movement of thought had rendered it necessary to give it a new exposition. The difficulty and the need of reconciling the contents of the religious and moral consciousness with natural science had become much more acute, partly on account of the growth of natural science and partly on account of the influence which Kant himself had exercised. The lesson of the First Critique, and of that Critique alone, had been taken to heart by one important section of the thinkers of Lotze's early days. That lesson, so long as it remains uncorrected by what Kant taught further in his Critique of Practical Reason and the Critique of Judgment, is negative. It placed the objects of reason, in which morality and religion centre, beyond the reach of knowledge, and it confined first the cognition and then the interests of man to the sphere of sensible facts. For the ideas of reason, so long as they remained unrealizable thoughts, could not command the allegiance of mankind. They might be called things-in-themselves, and even be set up as ideals which all knowledge presupposes, but so long as they could not be known, or verified, they would be allowed to remain in their empty elevation, while the endeavours of man turned into another channel. It is true that the things-in-themselves had for Kant a double meaning, sometimes standing for the realities which lie behind the objects of sensuous experience, sometimes for the realities which transcend that experience. In this respect real natural objects and the objects of our moral and religious consciousness may seem to stand on the same level, being both unknowable. But there lies a deep difference beneath this surface resemblance. In the case of natural objects Kant restores to us under the name of "phenomena" all that he refused to us under the name of "noumena," whereas the supersensible "noumena," while enjoying a superior dignity as opposed to the objects of sensuous experience, are set apart in empty sublimity above man's knowledge. The immediate effect of the Critique of Pure Reason when taken as a complete expression of Kant's views was, therefore, to direct intellectual endeavour to the world of natural phenomena, which were practically none the worse for being *only* "phenomena"; and to relegate to a faith that could not be knowledge the whole world of supersensuous reality. "A strong current of Naturalism set in, in which Lotze himself seems to have been at first caught when he gave himself to science. And this Naturalism, which maintained, to begin with, an attitude of mere indifference towards the unknowable supersensuous reality, passed easily into a Materialism which denied it. Natural science and its methods were extended over the whole region of intelligible existence, and what science could not know, could not be."

But whether we attribute it to the natural bent of Lotze's spirit towards art and literature and religion, or to his early religious training, or to the influence of Weisse, he was early in revolt against these Materialists, and his first service to philosophy was to expose the inadequacy of the categories which they employed, and to show that, side by side with Science, there was room and need for Philosophy. It is not without something of the bitterness of a convert that he says in his earliest Metaphysics, "In these days almost more time is given to the deification of science than to the solving of its problems," "These extravagant expectations so little satisfied, so much deceived by the results of science, have generated the aversion to the employment of pure thought." So, as Edmund Pfleiderer says, "Lotze raised once more the standard of Philosophy out of the dust in which it was trodden, and taught those who came after him to have courage and to trust themselves." His antagonism to the pretensions of natural science to deal with all the phenomena of human experience, and "his distrust of its importunate persuasiveness," remained with him to the end. But he did not recoil from science without learning from it. He was taught by his own experience at the dissecting table to respect its methods and to trust, in their own legitimate region, its slowly-elaborated results, although he had at the same time the painful conviction that it was, and must for ever remain, silent regarding those objects which are most worth knowing. It remains one of the best achievements of Lotze that he vindicated for the understanding its own undeniable region of activity.

But another movement, certainly not less significant in itself nor less powerful in its influence in Lotze's day, had issued from Kant: I mean, the idealistic movement. "When Lotze finished his studies," says Dr. Caspari, "most of the academic chairs were held by Hegelians. No prominent man could then enter into the holy places of philosophy who had not been stimulated by Hegel; and, although there were already schisms and divisions in the Hegelian school, still so great was the glitter of his thoughts that few dared to contradict what seemed false in them. To refute Hegel in a radical way, it was necessary to live within the power of his fundamental ideas, and work a way through his chief doctrines. This the disciples of the opposed schools of Herbart, Fries, Benecke, and others failed to do. Hegel and his disciples were, indeed, sharply called to task by them, points of view fundamentally different and antagonistic were opposed to his, but Hegel's own point of view was not actually overturned. Lotze was, historically speaking, the first among modern investigators who, in a psychological, epistemological, and philosophical sense, laid bare the secret of the deceptive power of Hegelianism and at the same time, in the most fundamental manner, refuted it. '*Man darf mit vollem Rechte sagen: Lotze hatte Hegel überwunden.*'"

Whether Lotze's victory over Hegelianism was complete or not, it is certain that the desire to refute Hegelianism was a determining element in his philosophic career. For he found in it, and in the most aggravated form, the same vicious tendency that roused his antagonism to the pretensions of natural science, namely, the tendency to fit all things, with whatever violence, into one system of thoughts, and to deify the intellect and its products. And his very respect for the methods and results of science, so long as it confined itself to its own proper region, deepened his antagonism to Idealism. "Bred," as he tells us, "in the traditions of the Hegelian school, which believed itself to have explained all the particular facts of the world's history as independent consequences of a single general principle"; and, as a philosopher, necessarily sympathizing with its attempt to unify experience, he had the deepest aversion to its method and results; for it seemed to him to have turned its back upon the world of facts, and lost itself in the region of empty thoughts. He shared with his age the hunger for facts, and the aversion to the generalizations of *a priori* speculation which had driven his contemporaries to seek satisfaction in natural science. It was with a "prejudice" against pure thought that, as he tells us, "he entered upon the lively philosophical current of his youth." And that distrust of thought he himself attributes mainly to the influence of Hegel, from which the mind of Germany was gradually emancipating itself during his youth. In fact, the *Stoff-Hunger*, the yearning for the real, or at least the palpable and the particular, under whose impulse the thought of Lotze's day threw itself upon the natural world of perceptible facts and events, and which seemed to be the direct and necessary consequence of confining the German people to "the thin Hegelian diet" of abstract and ambitious Idealism, had complete possession of Lotze. If his positive attitude was determined for him by Kant, his negative attitude was determined for him by Hegel, as is evident whether we have regard to his logical, metaphysical, psychological, moral, or even some of his religious views. To Hegel was partly due both his recourse to natural science, and his consciousness of its inadequacy and of the delusory character of its pretensions outside the sphere of nature. Hegel's abstractions, as he considered them, drove him to the individualism of Herbart, and drew him away from his intellectualism. It inspired his psychological researches, and generated his respect for the empirical data which they yielded. Above all it was the recoil from Hegel that produced both his affinity to and his difference from Leibnitz, and strengthened his adherence to Kant—especially to the Second Critique, leading him to endeavour to base Metaphysics upon Ethics, and to subordinate "The True" to "The Good."

The relation of Lotze to Hegel on one side and to the pure Naturalists on the other, and his attempt to correct the errors of both by recourse to the teaching of Kant, make Lotze a most interesting figure in the history of philosophic thought. He appears before us, from the beginning of his career, as a highly complex phenomenon, representing in a remarkable way the multiplex elements which are in constant conflict in modern life. And for all its diseases he prescribes one sovereign remedy. For reflection had taught him that the apparently opposite defects of the science and philosophy of modern times spring from the same cause. In both cases alike, reason, or the faculties of mere cognition, had been mischievously overrated. Both disciplines had awakened extravagant expectations that cannot be realized by human knowledge. It had been forgotten "that intellectual life is more than *thought*." "Much goes on within us which our thinking intelligence follows and contemplates only from without, and whose peculiar content it cannot exhaustively represent, either in the form of an idea, or through the union of ideas. He, therefore, who is animated by the conviction that real existence is not impenetrable to the mind, cannot with equal confidence assume that thought is the precise organ which will be able to comprehend the real in its innermost essence. . . . I recall the multitude of those who maintain that they experience that which is highest in the world, perfectly intellectually, in faith, in feeling, in presentiment, in inspiration, and who yet acknowledge that they do not possess it in knowledge. . . . All science can, of course, only operate with thoughts, and must follow the laws of our thinking; but it must understand that in all the objects it occupies itself with, and especially in that highest principle of all which it presupposes, it will find matter which, even if intellectually it were apprehended quite perfectly, could yet not be exhausted in the form of an idea or a thought."[1]

But Hegelianism put its whole trust in thought. "That philosophy," he tells us, "sought to lay bare, by its dialectical method, the whole contents of the physical and moral world, every particular in the precise place which it occupied in the world's plan; but, of what it then disclosed, it had little more to say than that it occupied that particular place. The peculiar character with which every separate part of the whole filled its place in the system remained a superfluous circumstance which was little considered, and was counted incapable of being explained; and the essential thing in every fact and phenomenon consisted in its repeating as the Nth or $N+1^{th}$ example in the total series of all things real, one of the few abstract thoughts which the *Hegelian* method announced as the deepest sense of the world."[2]

Lotze never loses sight of this error of Idealism, and he was so possessed with the conviction of its viciousness that he regarded it as the cardinal defect of the great philosophers of Greece. It is scarcely too much to say that the main endeavour of his life was to refute it. There is no form of the distinction between knowledge and reality which he neglects to emphasize. He sets Logic and Metaphysics so apart that it is more difficult to relate

[1] *Kleine Schriften*, III., pp. 453, 454.   [2] *Idem*, p. 454.

them to each other at all than to identify them. He is never weary of repeating that thoughts are not things, although they may be valid of things; and his world of ideas or of knowledge stands apart from, though it is in some way connected with, the world of things. And even within that world of knowledge he endeavours to draw a distinction between the work of thought and that of our other faculties of cognition. He represents the activity of thought as secondary and formal, and he throws all the emphasis upon its data. Perceptions or impressions, whether of sensible or supersensible facts, whether derived through the influence upon our senses of the natural world, or through "divine or supersensible influence upon our interior being, by means of which intuitions of another species fall to our lot, such as the senses can never supply, and such as constitute that religious cognition which obtrudes itself upon us with immediate certainty"[1] —these alone give him his "*punctum stans*," his sure footing amidst "the wash and welter" of mere thoughts. And hence, however little he may have intended it, he rendered the activity of thought nugatory, and prepared the way for that despair of philosophy which so characterizes thought in Germany in our day, and especially religious thought. To such devoted disciples as Edmund Pfleiderer he may seem to have succeeded in establishing a "Philosophy of the Feelings," and

[1] *Outlines of Religion*, p. 4.

to have reconciled speculation with Christianity by explaining all things in terms of "Love"; but to less ardent devotees his claim to respect will lie in his unconscious exposure of the Scepticism that underlies distrust in thought, and especially in the illustration that he gives of the necessity of advancing from the halting idealism of Neo-Kantism to that fuller reconciliation of the true and the real which Idealism has endeavoured to effect.

The main task of the critic of Lotze must consist in the examination of his view of the function of thought. Compared with this, the superstructure of psychological and metaphysical doctrines will, *on his system*, have only secondary interest. The value of his positive contribution to philosophy depends upon the success of his attempt to restrict the claims of thought, so as to make room for faith. We must, therefore, first endeavour to determine in what respects and for what reasons thought is regarded by Lotze as incapable of meeting the demands that have been made upon it, and then estimate the value of the other elements of experience which Lotze summons to the aid of thought in his attempt to present such a view of man and the world as is adequate to their complexity.

CHAPTER II

GENERAL VIEW OF LOTZE'S DOCTRINE OF THOUGHT

WE have seen that Lotze describes the main purpose of his philosophical investigations as the adjustment of the relation between the intellectual and the practical interests of man. He desired to restore the broken harmony of our modern life. The cause of the discord and "torment" seemed to him to lie in the attempt of the intellect to arrogate to itself supreme and exclusive dominion, and to extrude as untrustworthy those "vague beliefs and unquiet yearnings which arise from other parts of our nature," even though these parts were "the best," and though the objects to which these yearnings were directed seemed alone to have transcendent worth. This aggressive use of the intellect, on account of which the conflict arose—a conflict which must be endless because we cannot extinguish a part of our own nature—was characteristic alike of the votaries of science and of the idealists. Both schools sought to satisfy the manifold demands of human nature by means of knowledge alone, both treated truth as alone having independent worth, and both dealt with man as if he had no impulses, no desires, no ends except those which are cognitive. And, as against both, Lotze strenuously endeavoured to lower the claims of speculative reason, and to emphasize the existence and significance of the practical side of life, which derives its stimulus from the object of religious faith and the moral ideal. I propose in this chapter to give in outline his view of the true place and functions of human thought.

If Kant may be said to have examined reason in order to determine what we can know, Lotze may be said to have examined it in order to show what we *cannot* know. With a frankness which is as admirable as it is rare, he admits that he entered upon his philosophical career with a prejudice against, and a disposition to resist, the claims that had been set up on behalf of thought; and he suggests, what none of his readers can deny, that his after-work may be regarded as a prolonged attempt to justify his early attitude by definitely confining thought to its own proper limits. The "incitements to these doubts" of the supremacy of thought came to him mainly from the philosophy of Hegel;[1] and since his own doctrine of thought thus originally appears as a protest, it may be best understood, to

[1] See *Kleine Schriften*, Vol. III., p. 454.

begin with, in the light of that which it protested against.

It is scarcely necessary to say that Hegel, no less than Lotze, started from Kant, and with the aim of solving the problem which Kant had formulated. In one sense they both agreed in their view of the final results of his philosophy. They found in it "pairs of opposites which Kant could neither separate nor reconcile. Sense and understanding, necessity and freedom, the phenomenal and the real self, nature and spirit, knowledge and faith" stood over against each other, opposed and yet related.[1] Lotze regarded this antithesis as final, and, as we have seen, endeavoured to establish harmony by separating the antagonists and dividing the realm of reality between them. But Hegel regarded the opposition between them as itself a witness to a deeper unity, a unity whose nature is most fully expressed in the second terms of this opposing series. He sought, therefore, to "refer nature to spirit, necessity to freedom, the phenomenon to the noumenon: to show that spirit is the *truth* of nature, that freedom is the *truth* of necessity, that the noumenon is the *truth* of the phenomenon."[2] And by their "truth" Hegel meant their *reality*. That is to say, he resolved reality into spirit, or, to quote his own phrase, he regarded "the real as the rational."

Now, so long as Lotze is criticising Hegel, and

[1] Caird's *Hegel*, p. 122.   [2] *Ibid.*, p. 124.

not developing his own metaphysical views, he represents Hegel as endeavouring to identify reality with the thoughts that arise in the human consciousness, or with the system of knowledge in which these thoughts in some way or other cohere. And Hegel's doctrine that the real is the rational seemed to him to mean that the real consists in the movements and the products of our thought. Nor is it possible to deny that there are expressions in Hegel which are *susceptible* of this interpretation. "Everything we know," says Hegel, "both of outward and inward nature, in one word, the objective world, is *in its own self the same as it is in thought*, and thought consequently expresses the truth of the objects of perception." "In modern times a doubt has for the first time been raised in connection with the difference alleged to exist between the results of our thought and things in their own nature. This real nature of things, it is said, is very different from what we make out of them. The divorce between thought and thing is mainly the work of the Critical Philosophy, and runs counter to the conviction of all previous ages, that their agreement was a matter of course. The antithesis between them is the hinge on which modern philosophy turns. Meanwhile the natural belief of men gives the lie to it. In common life we reflect without particularly noting that this is the process of arriving at the truth, and we think without hesitation, and in the firm belief that thought coincides with thing. It marks the diseased state of the age when we see it adopt the despairing creed that our knowledge is only subjective, and that this subjective result is final. Whereas, rightly understood, truth is objective . . . The whole problem of philosophy is to bring into explicit conciousness what the world in all ages has believed about thought."[1] And what the world has believed is, that the objects of our thought are things and not mere ideas, that the truth expresses their essential being, and that the real is the ideal. When reflection comes in, this simple faith in the identity of thing and thought is destroyed—and reflection *must* come in. Then it is seen that "what reflection elicits is a product of our thought, and that the products of our thought are subjective, and it is assumed that they are *merely* subjective. But this assumption is regarded by Hegel as only "half of the truth"; the true thought, the universal, he holds to be so far from being *merely* subjective that it is "the essential, true, and objective being of things."

At this point lies the parting of the ways between Hegel on the one side and Lotze and many others of Hegel's critics on the other. They would regard the rift between thought and its objects, which reflection reveals, as final; and if, in order to avoid the Scepticism which seems to lie in wait for such a view, they postulate correspondence between our

[1] *Logic:* Wallace's Translation, first Edition, § 22.

subjective ideas and the things to which they point, they throw no light upon that principle of unity in virtue of which alone such correspondence is conceivable. The world of ideas and the world of objects, sensuous and supersensuous, are represented as mutually exclusive; no *real* element, no *ontological* principle connects them, but the former "represents ideally," or "symbolizes" the latter across the void. Hegel would press through the difference which reflection reveals, to the unity which manifests itself in the activities of both the subject and the object; and the thoughts which *seem* to be purely subjective he regards as the product of the reality which energizes in *both* the subject and the object. Man and the world conspire together wherever thinking takes place, and the resulting thought is the product and revelation of both, or rather of that which is greater than both because it comprehends them. But Lotze and others would stop at the stage of reflection which severs the subjective from the objective side of both the things and the thoughts. Ideality and reality are handed over respectively to the thought and to its objects; so that thought is ideal *only*, and objects are real *only*, or thought is ideal without being real, and its objects are real without being ideal. And these thinkers are consequently left with the difficult task upon their hands of discovering or inventing a connection between the ideality and reality which they have thus separated.

The importance of the issues, alike for our speculative and our practical interests, will justify the attempt to follow carefully the effort of Lotze to establish this view.

Lotze goes with Hegel so far as to admit that the first attitude of human thought is one of immediate and entire trust in itself. It directs itself upon objects without further ado. "The first attitude of the mind can never be doubt; it begins always with entire confidence in all its perceptions." But this confidence is due to mere ignorance, and to the absence of all analysis. It is not that a complete scepticism ensues with the beginning of reflection, or that things are held to be "in fact quite different from what they necessarily appear to us," but that we distinguish between things themselves and the mental appearances. The idea is still held to be true of an object, but it is now distinguished from the object; and although the question *whether* any reality exists and corresponds to our thoughts is not raised, the assumption *that* it corresponds needs now to be justified, and philosophy comes in to show *how* it corresponds. In a word, the assumption with which the ingenuous consciousness sets forth, that things and ideas are the same, is discredited. We discover that the objects of thought are phenomena of consciousness and not real, external objects; and our problem henceforth is to show not how ideas can *be* things, for that is impossible, but how they can be *true* of things.

Lotze starts, then, by presupposing the pure ideality of thought. This, the first discovery of reflection, is regarded by him as an ultimate truth. To him the contrast is final between the conception of an independent world of things and our own world of thoughts. "All we know of the external world depends upon the ideas of it which are within us; it is, so far, entirely indifferent whether with Idealism we deny the existence of that world, and regard our ideas of it as alone reality, or whether we maintain with Realism the existence of things outside us which act upon our minds. On the latter hypothesis as little as the former do the things themselves pass into knowledge; they only awaken in us ideas, which are not things. It is, then, this varied world of ideas within us, it matters not where they may have come from, which forms the sole material given to us, from which alone our knowledge can start."[1]

This, then, is the first limitation to which Lotze would subject thought. Its material consists of ideas, which are purely subjective whatever their origin may have been; and although its products may be true of things, they are themselves not the things of which they are true. Thought is a subjective activity, and subjective also are its data and its results. We cut ourselves free from reality in thinking, however we may afterwards explain the validity of the representation of reality which thought furnishes.

[1] *Logic*, II., § 306.

We might at first sight be led to consider that the failure of knowledge actually to reach over to reality, and identify itself with it, is a special defect that attaches to the knowledge of man. But it is not so. "We may exalt the intelligence of more perfect beings above our own as high as we please: but so long as we desire to attach any rational meaning to it, it must always fall under some category of knowledge, or direct perception, or cognition, that is to say, it will never *be* the thing itself, but only an aggregate of ideas *about* the thing. Nothing is simpler than to convince ourselves that every apprehending intelligence can only see things as they look to it when it perceives them, not as they look when no one perceives them; he who demands a knowledge which should be more than a perfectly connected and consistent system of ideas about the thing, a knowledge which should actually exhaust the thing itself, is no longer asking for knowledge at all but for something entirely unintelligible. One cannot even say that he is desiring not to know, but to *be* the things themselves; for, in fact, he would not even so reach his goal. Could he arrive at *being* in some way or another that very metal in itself, the knowledge of which in the way of ideas does not content him; well, he would *be* metal, it is true, but he would be further off than ever from apprehending himself as the metal which he had become. Or supposing that a higher power gave him back his intelligence while he still remained metal, even then, in his new character of intelligent metal, he would still only apprehend himself in such wise as he would be represented to himself in his own ideas, not as he would be apart from such representation."[1]

In this passage the distinction, or even the ontological severance, of knowledge from the realities known is represented as the characteristic and essence of knowledge wherever we may find it. It implies that perfect knowledge, say God's, is still only knowledge, only an image, or replica, of the world of being.

Now, such an ultimate distinction between thoughts and the real objects of thought has generally been made the ground from which the failure of knowledge is inferred. It has been assumed that if knowledge is subjective it cannot be true. But, Lotze argues, this assumption is entirely unjustified. "Since knowledge must be subjective in every case, the proof of such a subjective origin of our knowledge can, for that very reason, neither decide for nor against its truth; and he who believes that it decides against it, only takes the first step in the error which idealist views carry out more extensively."[2] In Lotze's view, the condemnation of knowledge on account of its subjectivity springs in reality from a false theory of its nature and purpose. It is presupposed that knowledge aims at *being*,

---

[1] *Logic*, II., § 308.
[2] *Kleine Schriften*, Vol. III., p. 466.

and not merely at representing its objects; but this presupposition is doubly absurd. For, in the first place, it is impossible that ideas can *be* things. As long as the law of identity holds, one thing cannot possibly *be* another; one idea cannot *be* another idea, any more than it can *be* the thing of which it is an idea. And, in the second place, if by some kind of miracle knowledge were to make this transition from itself so as actually to become its own object, it would *ipso facto* cease to be knowledge. It would be sunk and lost in undistinguished and undistinguishing existence. For knowledge is a relation *of* ideas *to* reality, and relation implies difference. Delete the difference, and the relation which knowledge is, is extinguished. It cannot, therefore, be the aim and purpose of knowledge to become or to be its own object. Nothing can aim at its own extinction, nor realize itself by ceasing to be. And if either knowledge or morality seem to aim at a perfection in which they would cease to be, that seeming is false, and it implies that *we* have set before them an end which is not their own. The false end which we have set before knowledge, and the false criterion by reference to which we condemn it, are easily exposed: we have assumed that its goal is to exist *as* things, instead of to be "*valid of*" things. Hence the division between knowledge and reality is, ontologically speaking, complete; and thought is entirely confined within the ideal sphere.

And yet this conclusion needs to be qualified in a way to do justice to Lotze's view. He does not mean to say that knowledge falls into some sphere outside of reality: it is manifest that everything is real, even false knowledge and mere illusions. Ideas, as psychical phenomena, are events which occur, and in that sense they are as real as any other events. But *as events* they are not knowledge, and "their content, so far as we regard it in abstraction from the mental activity which we direct to it, can no longer be said to occur, though neither again does it exist as things exist; we can only say that it possesses Validity."[1] As knowledge our ideas may be true, but they are not real in the sense of having existence. "Truth belongs to existence, but it does not as such exist," says Dr. Bradley. "It is a character which indeed reality possesses, but a character which, as truth and as ideal, has been set loose from existence; and it is never rejoined to it in such a way as to come together singly and *make* fact. Hence truth shows a dissection, and never an actual life."[2] "Our principles may be true, but they are not reality."[3]

This, then, is Lotze's first step in reducing the pretensions of thought. Even if thought receives the widest extension of meaning and is regarded as equivalent to the whole of our intelligent ex-

---

[1] *Logic*, II., § 316.   [2] *Appearance and Reality*, p. 167.
[3] *Principle of Logic*, p. 533.

perience, it is not to be considered as co-extensive with and constituent of reality. It is only a subjective fact, symbolic, representative, or valid of the world of real things and events. "It is only by misunderstanding," as Mr. Bradley says, "that we find difficulty in taking thought to be something less than reality."

But Lotze proceeds to limit the pretensions of thought still further. Thought is not all reality, as Hegel believed; it is not even co-extensive with our intelligent experience. "The nature of things," says Lotze, in a decisive manner, "does not consist in thoughts, and thought is not able to grasp it. Yet, perhaps, the whole mind experiences in other forms of its activity and passivity the essential meaning of all being and action. Thought, thereafter, subserves the mind as an instrument for bringing what is experienced into that connection which its nature demands, and for making that experience the more intense the more thought masters this connection."[1] That is to say, we might conceivably *experience* "the essential meaning" of all things, but we cannot *think* it. Experience does not consist entirely of thoughts. All reality, as we know it, must manifest itself as our experience; but thought is only one of several elements that enter into the constitution of experience. We have other ways of attaining truth than that of thought. Lotze cites with complete approval "the multitude of those

[1] *Mikrokosmus*, Bk. VIII., chap. i., § 8.

who maintain that they experience that which is highest in the world, perfectly intellectually, in faith, in feeling, in presentiment, in inspiration, and who yet acknowledge that they do not possess it in knowledge." It is a grave error "to look upon knowledge as the sole portal through which that which constitutes the essence of real existence can enter into connection with the mind. . . . Intellectual life is more than thought."[1] Thought, in a word, is only a single part, or element, or faculty of mind, occupying a restricted place amongst several others, which co-operate with it in the production of the contents of our intelligent life. And, apart from the prime error of identifying thought with reality, philosophers have not in anything strayed more mischievously from the truth than in representing all the processes of cognition as processes of thought. Lotze believes, as we shall see in detail in the next chapter, that thought is to be distinguished from sensation, perception, memory, and all the associative processes without which it would neither have material on which to operate nor the power to act upon it. But even if we take thought in its broadest sense, as including these activities, we are not entitled to give it the sole, or even the supreme dominion in our theoretical life. We have no right, in fact, to follow the example of the Idealists, and either to ignore the function of feeling and will in knowledge, or to merge them in the process of

[1] *Kleine Schriften*, Vol. III., pp. 453, 454.

thinking. Even if we were to regard man, as they did, as a being who is merely cognitive or contemplative, and as if he had all the complex needs of his nature satisfied with knowing, we should not be able to account for even that limited mode of existence if his only intellectual instrument were thought. There are elements in our cognitive experience which thought cannot yield. The unique consciousness of pleasure and pain is no product of thought, nor are the numerous emotions that give variety and interest to our inner life. "The living forces which living faith in God beholds, the sensuous impressions that perception yields, are all equally inaccessible to thought: we *experience* their content, but we do not possess them by means of thought. What is good and evil can as little be *thought* as what is blue or sweet. It is only after *immediate feeling* has taught us that there is worth and worthlessness in the world, and taught us, too, the gravity of the distinction between them, that thought can develop out of this experienced content, signs which enable us to bring a particular fact under these universal intuitions. Is the real living nerve of righteousness to be found in conceptions? . . . Love and hate, are they thinkable? Can their essence be exhausted in concepts?"[1] Idealism, he goes on to show, so far from being able to reduce these phenomena into thoughts, "has never succeeded in showing that thought is the most

[1] *Mikrokosmus*, Bk. VIII., chap. i.

essential element in spirit, nor that thinking about thought, or the pure mirroring of itself on the part of a logical activity, is what is highest in thought." The uniqueness of the feelings and emotions, their absolute irreducibility into mere conceptions, indicate that they have another origin than thought. They spring from "the capacity of experiencing pleasure and pain which is original in the soul," and which is not explicable in terms of thought. For although we cannot regard the soul as composite, after the manner of the older psychologists who divided it into quasi-independent faculties, and although we must, on the contrary, regard feeling, thought, and volition as inseparable elements in every psychical activity, we cannot ignore the difference between them, nor derive the one from the other. Feeling never passes into thought, nor thought into volition. Nor is there any necessary connection between them, either in the way of subsumption or of causality —or, at least, none that the human intelligence can discover. "It is possible that even divine intelligence would find nothing in the conception of knowledge alone that should necessitate feeling to issue out of it." Nor does the conception of thinking in any way imply volition or explain it. It is perfectly possible to conceive beings who could know, and find neither pleasure nor pain in the operation; who could feel without knowing; who could both know and feel without willing. No doubt, that is not our case; and, no doubt, "what we know as three is, nevertheless, but one in the being of the soul." "Perfect intelligence would see the whole nature of the soul in every one of its manifestations, and discern its unity amidst the difference, but we must be content with merely postulating that unity, and remember that, while we see a plurality of capacities, unity of being is a fundamental attribute of the soul."[1] In this manner Lotze resists the attempt to regard cognition as the sole origin even of our cognitive experience, and tries to show that "a cross section of any conscious phenomenon" or activity would reveal the presence of elements derivable only from feeling and volition.

But he is not content to place feeling on the same level as thought; he would subordinate the intelligence to the emotions in a manner analogous to that in which Schopenhauer and Hartmann would subordinate it to a merely active principle. And nowhere is the revolt of Lotze against what has been called the Panlogismus of Idealism more evident than in the emphasis he lays upon the function of feeling in our intelligent life.

"If," says Lotze, "it was an original characteristic of spirit to present its own changes to itself in thoughts as well as to experience them, it belongs to it in a manner equally original, not only to apprehend them, but, by means of pleasure and pain, to become aware of the *worth* which they have."[2] The apprehension of the value of objects in

---

[1] *Mikrokosmus*, Bk. II., chap. ii.   [2] *Ibid.*, chap. v., § 8.

terms of pleasure and pain is, for Lotze, *the* characteristic of feeling. That value, he proceeds to show, that is, the pleasure or the pain which objects bring in their relation to the self, depends upon their tendency to stimulate the soul in harmony with, or against, the nature of the self, so as to assist or arrest its development. Pleasure, in fact, is the consciousness of the successful development of the powers of the soul in its interaction with objects; pain, of disturbance and arrestment "consequent upon its being stimulated by objects in a manner contrary to the natural course of its activity." Upon this relation of objects to the self, feeling alone can pronounce; and thoughts can neither yield, nor corroborate, nor correct, nor retract its deliverances. For the judgments of cognition and those of feeling deal with different materials: the former with the manifestations of objects, or the qualities which they show in their relations to one another; the latter, while silent as to the qualities of objects, deals with their value in their relation to us. Knowledge finds its goal in Truth, feeling in Supreme Worth, or the Good.

Now, as we have already partly seen, the Good is for Lotze a higher category than the True; the main purpose of his philosophy is to vindicate for the aesthetic, moral, and religious ends of life a position not only co-ordinate with, but superior to, that of Knowledge. The Good comprehends and exhausts the meaning of the True. It is *ex vi termini* a supreme end, while truth has only derivative worth as means to the good. The work of the intelligence in rehearsing in the mirror of the mind the content of the real world would be vain and worthless apart from the practical purposes which knowledge subserves. Hence feeling, as the only source of the judgment of value, or as alone capable of apprehending what is good or the opposite, takes precedence of cognition. In the first place, it is the source of the impulse to know; for we desire truth not because it is *true* but because it is good. "It is not a necessity of thought that thought itself should be possible," Lotze tells us in his *Logic*. Thought derives its necessity from the practical ideal. In the second place, feeling guides knowledge as well as inspires it. In other words, it supplies the cognitive, or the subsidiary, as well as the practical or supreme ideal. And it does this because it is the power from which issues our sense of harmony. Being the source of our consciousness of harmony it dominates the sphere of art. "It is the basis of the imagination from which are born the works of art, and which enables us to comprehend all natural beauty; for this creative and re-creative power consists in nothing else than in that delicacy of apprehension which can clothe the world of values in the world of forms, or detect the happiness that is enfolded in the form." But further, feeling, as the principle of harmony, yields, although in an indefinite way, that conception of the totality of being, or the systematic wholeness of the relations of differences within a unity, which Knowledge seeks to realize in detail by tracing one by one the connections of objects with each other. Feeling, and not any intellectual principle of mere consistency, is the ultimate source of the requirement that our conception of the world should be "that of a whole and essentially complete unit, and that it should at the same time comprehend all individuals." In a word, feeling is the source of the ideal of knowledge; and with no other powers than those of the mere intellect we should neither have it nor seek it.

Feeling thus supplies experience with a positive content other than that which our cognitive faculties could yield. "In its feeling for the value of things our reason possesses as genuine a power of revelation as it has in the principles of investigation by means of the understanding, an indispensable instrument of experience." And that which it reveals is precisely that which has most value, namely, our ideals, intellectual, aesthetic, moral, and religious. No doubt the ideals with which it guides life need definiteness and articulation. "No source of revelation is less clear, nor does anything stand in greater need of a firmer basis than these assertions regarding the necessary form of the world which are only founded on the feeling of worth." The intellect must come in to explain,

But its function is only formal; while feeling, on the other hand, is the real source of "the higher views of things, which will continue to be the animating and quickening breath of all human effort."

Now, inasmuch as feeling produces the consciousness of harmony, and, therefore, the ideal of knowledge, it is also of necessity the criterion of truth. It shows from time to time, during the progress of knowledge, the degree of its inadequacy, and exposes the incompleteness, and therefore the inconclusiveness, of the system of relations set up by thought. For thought as a relating faculty is radically incapable of bringing its products into a unity. It explains everything in relation to something else, and its attempt to reach a first principle only leads to an infinite regress, in which it pursues receding conditions. The universals which it yields "speak only of that which must be *if* something else is; they show what inevitably follows from conditions the actuality of which they leave entirely doubtful."[1] Hence our thought-derived experience is as to its parts necessary, and as a whole contingent; it is a system of necessity on a hypothetical basis. And whether we seek the real meaning and essence of the individual parts, or try to discover that which converts the hypothetical whole into actuality, we must pass from thought to feeling. Thought cannot reveal the unique

[1] *Mikrokosmus*, Bk. IX., chap. i.

elements which constitute the individuality of each thing, just because it is a function of relations; nor does its necessity lie within itself, but in the aesthetic and moral facts which alone have apodeictic certainty. There would be no *logical* contradiction in regarding the highest and the best which thought could reveal as a mere thought, to which nothing corresponds; nor in the view that the system of nature which science constructs, or the idea of a perfect being to which theology points, may be nothing but empty thoughts. But it would be "*intolerable* (*i.e.*, to feeling) to believe of our ideal that while it is an idea produced by the action of thought, it has no existence, no power, and no validity in the world of reality."

"It is not out of the perfection of the perfect that its actuality follows as a logical consequence, but, without any circuitous process of inference, the impossibility of its non-existence is *immediately felt*, and all the show of syllogistic proof only serves to make the immediacy of this certainty more clear."[1] In short, the certainty that Truth is valid, that the Beautiful and the Good are real, or in other words, that our cognitive, aesthetic, moral, and religious ideals are not empty thoughts, rests on no logical ground: it is "supported by the living feeling that precisely to this, which is most perfect and greatest, it belongs to be in a perfect and complete way real."

[1] *Mikrokosmus*, Bk. IX., chap. iv.

It is usual to regard certain laws of thought as carrying within themselves an irrevocable authority, and as constituting an ultimate court of appeal in reference to both truth and reality. Such laws as those of Identity, Causality, and so on, seem to have no need of any extraneous support, and, indeed, to be incapable of it. But even these, Lotze believes, must borrow their ultimate authority from feeling and its content. "The fact that there is truth at all cannot in itself be understood, and is only comprehensible in a world the whole nature of which depends upon the principle of the Good." And that supreme Good is Love. "If this eternal and supreme Worth of Love did not lie at the foundation of the world, and if in such a case we could still think or speak of a world, this world, it seems to me, would, whatever it were, be left without truth and without law."[1] A world, that is, might be real, even although thought found in it nothing but disorder and contradiction. That which is thinkable need not exist, and that which exists need not be thinkable—for all that *thought* could show to the contrary. Thought gives us no guarantee that there may not be an ultimate discrepancy between itself and reality, and it cannot turn aside the impotence and despair of absolute scepticism. It is not "pure intelligence, whether we call it understanding or reason, that dictates to us those assumptions which we regard as

---

[1] *Mikrokosmus*, Bk. IX., chap. v.

inviolable; it is everywhere the whole mind, at once thinking, feeling, and passing moral judgments which, out of the full completeness of its nature, produces in us those unspoken first principles to which our perception seeks to subordinate the content of experience." While thinking plays its own necessary part in articulating and defining, and *in that respect* substantiating these inviolable assumptions, the ultimate basis is to be found in the conviction of their worth, and worth is estimated by feeling.

Hence the final criterion of the reality of anything is not that it accords with the laws of thought or with the idea of a complete system of experience, nor is its unreality shown by its inconsistency with such a system. There is no *contradiction* in thinking that an unthinkable world may be real, or at any rate, the contradiction is harmless. But there is *absurdity* in it. It would be repugnant to our aesthetic and moral nature, that thought should so miss its end as either to represent the real as unreal or the unreal as real. And it is this "absurdity," which is not an intellectual but an emotional phenomenon, it is this violation of aesthetic feeling or of the consciousness of fitness and harmony which is the supreme criterion of truth.[1] Feeling, therefore, is the source of the necessity which we recognize in the laws of thought. We recognize that what contradicts itself in thought cannot be

---

[1] See *Mikrokosmus*, Bk. v., chap. iv.

real, and we conclude rightly; but the authority of the law of contradiction and of thought itself is derived from feeling. Its untrustworthiness would be inconsistent with the aesthetic conviction derived from feeling that thought *must* have worth.

There is still one more consideration advanced by Lotze in illustration of the dependence of thought upon feeling to which we must allude, seeing that it turns upon a matter of fundamental importance, namely, the distinction of the self from the not-self. It is not necessary to show that human knowledge hinges upon this distinction of the subject and the object of thought, or that the whole task of knowledge is comprised in revealing the relation of these poles of experience through which alone truth and reality come to be for us.

Now the distinction of subject and object, or of the self and the not-self, is usually regarded as set up by thought; and there is no doubt that the intellect is *par excellence* the discriminating and analytic faculty; articulating the material with which experience supplies it. It distinguishes objects from one another. But the distinction between subject and object must not be confused with that distinction between objects which is only possible through the former. The difference between the subject and the object is so unique as to point to the activity of a power other than the intellect. For all the contrasts set up by thought fall into the *objective* world, and are set over against the subject which thinks; so that even the self, in so far as it is known, is an object. And even if we were able completely to represent ourselves in thought, still that would be a representation of the thinker, and not the thinker himself, and we should not identify ourselves with that representation. "This perfect knowledge would, indeed, imply that our own being had become to us clearly objective—objective, however, in the sense that our own self would appear to us but one among other objects."[1] The self's intimacy with itself, as distinguished from its relation to objects of thought, the inwardness of *self*-consciousness, which is the essence of the contrast between the Ego and the non-Ego, cannot be given in thought. In attempting to yield that consciousness thought falls foul of itself, and necessarily stultifies its own process; for it can only know by objectifying, and in this case if it objectifies it defeats its end, producing the consciousness of a not-self instead of the consciousness of self.

What, then, is the source of this distinction? It arises from the peculiar *value* which each individual necessarily sets upon himself as the centre and focus of all his experience. And this value, of course, is given only in feeling. "Not as thought, but as felt in its immediate value for us, does the identity of the thinker and the thought form the foundation of our self-con-

[1] *Mikrokosmus*, Bk. II., chap. v.

sciousness, and once for all lift the distinction between us and the world beyond all comparison with the differences by which it discriminates between one object and another."[1] For this purpose the simplest feeling serves, while "the consummate intelligence of an angel, did it lack feeling," would utterly fail to give the consciousness of the self *as a self*. "What we know, do, and suffer does not exhaust our ego . . . we find ourselves, on the contrary, in the general mood of our feelings, in the temperament which differs in each of us." The intellect can present the self to itself, and may define and even deepen the contrast between the self and the not-self; but both the self and the contrast must in the first place be *given* by feeling as facts, before the intellect can present them. Self-consciousness, therefore, is a datum of feeling.

The conception that thought depends upon a foreign source for its data lies at the root of the whole attempt of Lotze to limit its powers. It leads him, in fact, to share the material of thought between feeling on the one side, and sensation on the other. Feeling supplies it with the ideals which inspire and guide knowledge, and which express, although indefinitely, the harmonious totality of experience; and sensation supplies it with the material out of which is elaborated our world of sensuous objects. And, as we shall see hereafter, thought,

[1] *Mikrokosmus*, Bk. II., chap. v.

even when thus supplied, is not able to carry out by itself the work of converting the data of knowledge into actual knowledge. Feeling must give it its impulse and the ultimate criteria of truth and error; and an "unconscious psychical mechanism" must prepare beforehand the sense-given material by a preliminary elaboration of it. The consequence is that thought is reduced into a purely formal function, which merely re-arranges a content given to it from without, and which, even in that re-arrangement, is led by ideals which do not issue from itself but from feeling.

The general attitude of Lotze towards thought, which it is my object in this chapter to illustrate, may be better understood if we compare it for a moment with that of Kant.

It is evident that thought, on Lotze's theory, is dependent upon feeling, as the "understanding," on Kant's, is dependent on "reason." In fact, it may be said that he has endowed feeling with the functions of reason, and reduced thought to mere understanding, making it occupy an intermediate place between sense and reason, and cutting away from it both the highest and the lowest forms of consciousness. We have seen already that he makes feeling yield one by one the three ideas which Kant attributed to reason, namely, the Self, the World, and God. To these ideas of feeling, if such a phrase is allowable, he gives precisely the same function as Kant gave to the ideas of reason. They are ideals which knowledge strives to attain, they regulate the use of thought, they point to the true content of thought which thought itself can never possess, they serve as the criterion which thought employs in distinguishing truth and error, and they give the only possible guarantee that the products of thought are not, even at their highest and completest, merely illusory subjective phenomena. It would be easy to show that the parallelism between Lotze's "Feeling" and Kant's "Reason" runs into the practical sphere as well, feeling being for Lotze the source of our moral and religious ideals. Indeed, in Book II. of the *Mikrokosmus* Lotze all but identifies feeling with Kant's "reason" in so many words: he speaks of feeling as "containing the principle of reason," and attributes to reason the essential characteristic he finds in feeling, telling us of "the inspirations of a reason appreciative of worth." In the same context he uses the term "understanding" to represent what he elsewhere calls "thought." In a word, what Kant means by asserting that we may *think* what we cannot *know*, Lotze expresses by saying that we can *feel* what we cannot *think*.

At first sight this may seem to be a harmless change of terminology. But closer examination will show that these new expressions indicate that Lotze fell away in essential matters from the Kantian Idealism, converting the cleft *within* the intelligence, which characterizes the Kantian doctrine, into a cleft *between* the intelligence and the emotional faculties. The implicit dualism in the doctrine of Kant would be eliminated if the intellectual powers, whose highest form is reason, could be made consistent with themselves, a task which was attempted by Fichte, Schelling, and Hegel. The dualism in Lotze's doctrine can be eliminated only by the completer subjugation of the intelligence to feeling, which, as the subsequent history of Philosophy has shown, leads to the despair of Philosophy itself, and to an attempt to base our intelligent and practical life on those "immediate intuitions of the heart," which arrogate to themselves the name of "faith." In a word, he paved the way to a deepening of the dualism of Kant into an explicit Scepticism, and thereby showed indirectly that the true line of the development of Kant's doctrine is that which was adopted by the Idealists, and which Lotze in his *logical* theories so strenuously resists.

The opposition of Reason and Understanding by Kant led to the contrasts of the phenomenal and noumenal, nature and spirit, to which we have already alluded. Kant himself felt that it was only by tempering the opposition between them that either truth or goodness could be saved. He endeavoured, therefore, to bring reason down from its isolation and to relate its *datum*, or *factum*, to the phenomenal world by using the latter as a "*typic*" and *in*directly filling the noumenal world with its content. Kant's immediate successors sought to mediate further between these powers, and to make the understanding and the reason interpenetrate; and Hegel endeavoured to complete the process by representing the understanding as a stage in the self-evolution of reason—the stage, namely, in which reason, on its way from implicit to explicit, or from abstract to concrete, unity, is employed *primarily* with relation, distinction, difference, beneath which that unity was always operative. But such ways of mediating between the powers that co-operate to constitute our intelligent experience are not possible on Lotze's view. There is no way of making a transition from cognition to feeling, and the judgment of reflection differs *toto coelo* from the judgment of worth which Lotze attributes to feeling. We are left with the parts of the intelligent life in our hands, and bidden still to believe in its unity, while all rational grounds for such a belief are taken away from us. That is to say, if the soul still is a unity, it is not a unity conceivable on Lotze's theory; and he really summoned up belief not to anticipate but to contradict his own conclusions. He makes no attempt to show how one of the powers of the mind can be inspired by the ideals, guided by the principles, employed upon the data supplied by another. And in his criticism of transeunt action in his Metaphysics, and of the conception of the possibility of a relation *between* things, he shows us sufficient reason why such an external relation between thought and feeling is impossible. No single principle can under-reach the differences as he expounds them; nothing can fill up the interstices between feeling and thought.

The dualism of Lotze's view will become further evident when we consider the relation between sense and thought. On the doctrine of both Kant and Lotze sense gave a discrete *manifold*, and the task of thought was to relate it; and, on the theory of both, that manifold was *given* in the sense of being supplied from without. Kant tempered this opposition also; he used the imagination to mediate between sense and understanding, and if he still retained for the manifold an extraneous origin and —in the characteristic of pure difference—a nature foreign to thought, he deprived it of all significance. When the contributions of the understanding were withdrawn from sense, little remained besides the name. Later idealists, appreciating Kant's progressive attempt, sought to make sense and thought, perception and conception, completely relative to each other, and to show that the sense-given material carried within it from the first those principles of unity which, at higher stages of consciousness, became more and more evident. They denied that the *datum* is a mere manifold, and conceived it as implicitly rational. Instead of the hard contrast of sense and understanding they regarded sense as in process of evolution, and the lowest form of consciousness, which is always rational, as passing into a reason which comprehends itself. The conception of the *datum* of knowledge as rational carried with it the idea of the real, which reveals itself in sense, as rational, and led to a completely idealistic view of the world.

Lotze is not ignorant of the impossibility of bringing the purely relating activity of thought to bear upon the purely discrete data of sense. But instead of endeavouring to modify these opposites through the conception at which Kant was reaching, that each implied the other, and that the pure universal and the pure particular are nothing but logical abstractions, he sought to interpose between them an "unconscious psychical mechanism" which prepares the sense material for thought. He is obliged to endow this "unconscious mechanism" with the functions of thought, as we shall see, but so resolute is he to reduce thought to a formal power that he will not definitely recognize these functions as elementary activities of thought. He ends with the most distinct contrast between them, making thought a faculty which deals with universals only, with connections or relations, and looking elsewhere for the particulars, the points on which to hang these relations. So that, in this respect also, the dualism of Lotze is more complete than Kant's, and he attributes more to sensation and perception, and less to thought or the understanding.

Thus Lotze, in opposing the tendency manifested by both scientific men and idealists, to exaggerate the functions of thought in knowledge, strips the reflective intelligence on both sides. He hands over the original data of thought to pure sense, and the first elaboration of them to an "unconscious psychical mechanism"; and he hands over the ideals which inspire and regulate knowledge to feeling. Before thought proper enters the field the unconscious mechanism has already built up the world as it appears to the ordinary consciousness, and supplied "the conception of the cosmos." The processes of sensation, perception, and association in its various forms, however analogous they may be to those of thought, are still not attributed to thought in this sense of the term. It "comes in afterwards, and takes cognizance of relations which it did not by its own action originate, but which have been prepared for it by the unconscious mechanism of the psychic states."[1] Nevertheless, with all this extraneous assistance from the nether side, thought, if left to itself, would still remain helpless. Feeling and its consciousness of worth must give it the impulse to do its work, present it with the ideal of harmony which it is to pursue, supply it with the criterion of its truth, guarantee its principles, and fill its otherwise empty forms with the value which alone renders them adequate to reality. Thus he makes ample amends for the "deification of thought" from which he recoils. Thought, *taken by itself as he takes it*, has nothing of its own to think about—sense must supply the content; even if thought had a content of its own it could not

[1] *Mikrokosmus*, Bk. v., ch. iv.

even try to think—the impulse to know must be awakened by feeling, and we desire truth only as means to the good; if by some chance thought did try to think, it has no ideal of its own to regulate its endeavour, but must borrow it from the emotional consciousness of harmony; having borrowed its ideal, thought can neither reach it nor know whether it has reached it or not—the criterion of truth is immediate feeling; even if thought did reach the ideal it could not convince any one that the only truth which it has in its power to offer is not a subjective and illusory phantasm to which no reality corresponds—faith must guarantee that thought has worth, and feeling alone can apprehend that worth.

It is amply evident that if this be thought we cannot avoid Lotze's conclusion that "Intelligence is much more than thought." We cannot regard it as the dominant function even in the creation of our intelligent experience, far less can we identify it with the principle of reality, as the Idealists have done. It remains to be seen whether thought, thus shorn of its pretensions, is capable of performing any function whatsoever; or whether it is not, on the contrary, a helpless residuum, an abstract remnant found by analysis and set up as an independent entity, rather than a faculty really possessed by any intelligent being.

To determine this question we shall have to inquire whether Lotze has not simply transferred to feeling processes which must be regarded as processes of thought, obliterating his own distinction between them, and endowing feeling with the powers of both sense and reason. In other words, we must examine his treatment of feeling. But before doing so, we shall endeavour to follow him in his exposition of the processes which still remain to thought.

CHAPTER III

THOUGHT AND THE PRELIMINARY PROCESSES OF EXPERIENCE

WE have seen how Lotze attributes to feeling on the one side, and to an unconscious psychical mechanism on the other, processes which are generally regarded as belonging to thought. We have now to follow his exposition of the functions which thought is still allowed to retain.

There are one or two notable similes which recur in Lotze's writings, and which are very suggestive of his general view of the nature of thought and of the place it fills in our intellectual life. He regards thought as a means to knowledge, and compares it to a "tool" which the mind employs in order to attain it. Now, a "tool" suggests the idea of an artificial contrivance employed to overcome some initial defect or weakness; and although I would not willingly press a metaphor unduly, I believe that ample evidence exists in Lotze's writings to show that he considered thought to have only this secondary and external use. In other words, he does not regard thought as of the essence of mind, or as constituting the vital element in intelligence. On the contrary, he conceives minds which have no need of employing the processes of thought, and constantly refers to thought as something which derives its necessity and its use from the peculiar character of the human mind, and especially from the peculiar position in the world which man is originally made to occupy. "The forms and laws, since it is *man* who, by means of them, is to arrive at the truth, must attach themselves to the nature and stand-point of man; and accordingly they must have peculiarities which are comprehensible only from this fact, and not from the nature of the 'Things' which are to be known."[1] To understand the "tool" we must consider the workman who is to use it and the material on which it is to be employed, for, as he tells us, "a tool must fit the thing and it must fit the hand." Such consideration may bring to light that peculiarity of intellectual constitution which makes thought necessary for man, although it may not be necessary for other intelligent beings.

This peculiarity is illustrated by Lotze through the help of another recurring simile. A mind,—presumably like God's, or an "archangel's,"—"which stood at the centre of the real world, not outside individual things, but penetrating them with its

[1] *Outlines of Logic*, 5.

presence," would stand in no need of thought. "It could command such a view of reality as left nothing to look for, and would, therefore, be the perfect image of it in its own being and activity." That is to say, reality would immediately reflect its image on such a mind, or such a mind would know the truth of things by an immediate act of intellectual intuition. But that mind is not man's. "The human mind, with which alone we are here concerned, does not thus stand at the centre of things, but has a modest position somewhere in the extreme ramifications of reality." And it is precisely this original eccentric position of man's mind which makes thought necessary. "Compelled as it is to collect its knowledge piece-meal, by experiences which relate immediately to only a small fragment of the whole, and thence to advance cautiously to the apprehension of what lies beyond its horizon, it has probably to make a number of circuits, which are immaterial to the truth it is seeking, but to itself in the search are indispensable."[1] These circuits are the mediate relations which thought employs. Being incapable of knowing a fact directly we infer it from another, or we compare it with another, or we classify it, or we relate it to others by means of judgment. By employing these methods we arrive at truth, or at least at such truth as is given to man to know; but yet they are all symbols of our imperfection,

[1] See *Logic*, Introduction, § ix.

indirect means whereby we make up to some extent for our inability to know intuitively and reach the nature of reality at once. Had we been placed "at the centre of things," or been born upon the mountain top, to use another of his metaphors, we might have commanded at once the view of the broad expanse of being. But, as it happens, "Every one who desires to enjoy the prospect from a hill-top has to traverse some particular straight or winding path, from the point at which he starts up to the summit which discovers the view."[1]

From this conception of thought as a *means*, or a *tool*, which man has to employ in the absence of the power to know the truth directly, there follow the most important consequences. In the first place, thought, like all mere *means*, derives its only value from its reference to the end for the attainment of which it is used. And we thus arrive once more, and by a new path, at Lotze's way of subordinating thought to other faculties. But, in the second place, the activities of thought, like those of all mere means or tools, have no interest *in themselves*, and its products have no *immediate* value. They are significant only in their reference to *us*, and they give us no direct clue to determine the nature of reality. "The act of thinking," says Lotze, "can claim only *subjective* significance; it is purely and simply an inner movement of our minds, which is made necessary to us by reason of the constitution

[1] *Logic*, § 345.

of our nature and of our place in the world."[1]
"All the processes which we go through in the framing of conceptions, in classification, in our logical constructions, are subjective processes of our thought, and not processes which take place in things."[2] This business of thinking is apparently our own and private, and the real world stands aside from it as having nothing whatever to do with it. It awaits the issue of these processes without itself giving them any guidance, or otherwise taking part in them. Starting from a certain point—some eccentric position—in the real world, we creep our way by the help of the relating activities of thought towards the centre. "By a process of movement from point to point we arrive at a determinate objective relation," and get the view from the hill-top. But "the particular movement chosen neither is, nor yet copies, the way in which *this* (the objective or real) relation itself arose or now obtains."[3] And just as the real world takes no part in the thinking process, so the results of that process, the conceptions, classifications, judgments, and influences, are not copies of reality, nor do they in any way represent really existing facts or events. "The *content* of knowledge which is expressed through these forms of thought has no Real significance." Thought produces general conceptions, but there is no general plant, or general

[1] *Logic*, § 345. [2] *Ibid.*, § 342.
[3] *Ibid.*, § 345.

animal, amongst existing objects.[1] Thought classifies objects in an ascending order; but "this horse was not to begin with animal in general, then vertebrate in general, later on a mammal, and only at the last stage of all a horse."[2] Thought forms judgments, combining two ideas by means of a copula, but objects are not related to one another as subjects and predicates. Thought infers conclusions from premises; but real things do not exist in a series of major and minor premises and conclusions. In short, all these products of thought are artificial. They correspond to nothing whatsoever in the real world, and do not in the least reveal to us the nature of reality. They are only means to knowledge, indispensable to *us*, but issuing neither from the real world nor from the essential nature of mind, as mind. They are our devious paths to the mountain-top, or to use his other favourite metaphor, they are only "a scaffolding which does not belong to the permanent form of the building which they helped to raise, and must be taken down again to allow the full view of the result." It is not *thought* which gives us such reality as we know, and what thought gives us is not real.

This double separation of thought from reality seems to defeat the very object of thought, which is to enable us to know reality. For if reality yields no guiding principle to the process and is totally unlike each and all of its results, if, in other

[1] See *Logic*, § 342.   [2] *Ibid.*

words, thought is thus a purely subjective, merely human instrument, it is difficult to see how it can assist in the attainment of objective truth. In a word, Lotze's view seems at once to involve absolute Scepticism. But that is by no means Lotze's intention. The fact that thought and its products are mere *means* and have no value or truth in themselves does not, in Lotze's view, justify us in denying to them the value and significance which they have in so far as they serve to attain their end. And he strenuously insists that they *do* enable us to attain their end; the tool *is* fitted to the thing and to the hand, the paths *do* lead to the hill-top, whence an "*objective*" view is obtained, the scaffolding does enable us to raise the edifice of knowledge. No doubt the laws and forms of thought are subjective and formal, and they are not to be taken as laws and forms of things; nevertheless they are not "mere results of the organization of our subjective spirit without respect to the nature of the objects to be known." That is, they have after all *some* reference to reality, and we should apparently qualify what has just been said about their *pure* subjectivity. Nor are they *merely* formal. "They are, rather, 'formal' and 'real' at the same time. That is to say, they are those subjective modes of the connection of our thought which are necessary to us, if we are by thinking to know the objective truth."[1] *How* they can be real

[1] *Outlines of Logic*, § 5.

as well as formal, how the processes which are thus subjective *can* have "respect to the nature of the objects to be known and give an 'objective' view," are questions which gave Lotze much trouble. But *that* they do so, or in other words, that thought because it is subjective is not therefore invalid is one of his most invincible convictions.

If we keep in mind both of these views of Lotze we may be able to follow the windings of his exposition of thought, an exposition which, I am tempted to say, is the most valuable of all the contributions which he has made to philosophy, and which has had the deepest effect upon subsequent speculation both in Germany and in this country. The key of his position lies once more in his relation to Idealism on the one side, and on the other to the positive interest he always felt, and which he took pains to justify, in the ideals of our cognitive, and especially of our moral and religious life. He wished, in fact, to strike a middle path between the Scepticism which severs knowledge and reality, and the Idealism which seemed to him to identify them. Like Bunyan's pilgrim in the Valley of the Shadow of Death he walked along "a pathway that was exceeding narrow, and was the more put to it"; for on the right hand was "a very deep ditch," and on the left "a very dangerous quag, into which, if even a good man falls, he can find no bottom for his foot to stand on." Our task henceforth is to follow

Lotze's exposition of the processes of thought, and especially to observe how, *while denying the presence and activity of the principle of reality in man's thinking, he still attributes value and validity to its results.*

To the question, "What is the specific function of thought?" Lotze gives a clear answer. It is "to reduce the coincidence of our ideas to coherence" by exhibiting the ground, or reason, or principle of their combination. It converts an associative into a reflective experience. An examination of the contents of an individual's consciousness would bring to light two kinds or degrees of knowledge, springing from the different ways in which the ideas that it contains are combined with each other. First, there are ideas which are contingently connected. They have simply happened to come together in an individual's experience, owing to the peculiar position in which he is placed from time to time, and they may come together again; for one idea excites another, so as to produce trains, or, as Lotze says, "currents of ideas." "If we knew the permanent characteristics of a single particular soul, if we had a view of the form and content of its whole current of ideas up to the present time, then, the moment it had produced a first and a second idea on occasion of external irritants, we should be able to predict . . . what its third and fourth idea in the next moment must be. But in any other soul whose nature, past history, and present condition were different, the same first and second idea, developed at this moment by a similar external irritant, would lead with a similar necessity in the next moment to an entirely different combination."[1] That is to say, the connection between the ideas is not, strictly speaking, a connection *of* the ideas; they are brought together, not by anything within themselves but by some accidental circumstance in the psychical history of the individual; they are coincident, not coherent. Such a current of ideas gives "rise to many useful combinations of impressions, correct expectations, seasonable reactions," and it may "correspond with fact." But the question of truth or untruth does not arise in connection with purely associated knowledge. These ideas have happened to arise and to be connected, and nothing more can be said about them. But, in the second place, there are ideas which have a right thus to come together; there are combinations of them which claim to have validity for every consciousness, so that if certain ideas are entertained, certain others are regarded as *necessarily* following from them. And the specific work of thought is to bring this necessity to light as a principle of coherence between the ideas themselves, and therefore as independent of, or rather as exercising a regulating and determining authority over, the in-

[1] *Logic*, Introduction, § ii.

dividual consciousness. "The thinking mind is not content to receive and acquiesce in its ideas as they were originally combined by casual coincidence, or as they are re-combined in the memory; it sifts them, and where they have come together in this way it does away with their co-existence; but where there is a material coherence between them, it not only leaves them together but combines them anew, this time, however, in a form which adds to the fact of their connection a consciousness of the ground of their coherence."[1] Thought thus performs "a surplus work over and above the mere current of ideas." "It always consists in adding to the reproduction or severance of a connection in ideas the accessory notion of a ground for their coherence or non-coherence." "The peculiarity of thought, which will govern the whole of our subsequent exposition, lies in the production of those accessory and justificatory notions which condition the form of our apprehension."[2] Lotze further explains his view by contrasting the human with the presumable animal consciousness, in which, though there are trains of ideas suited to the ends of its life, there are no thoughts in the specific sense of the term, and, therefore, no universal knowledge, and no distinction between truth and error.[3] The distinction is too familiar to need any more words.

[1] *Logic*, Introduction, § iii.   [2] *Ibid.*, § vii.
[3] See *Outlines of Logic*, § 4; *Logic*, Introduction, § vii.

But a question immediately arises as to the nature of the relation that exists between the associative and thinking forms of consciousness. Are we to regard the two as distinct; or does the former pass into the latter through the gradual evolution of its contents? Does thought *produce* the principles which give coherence to the contents of our experience, or does it only *discover* them in that experience? Is the original datum of thought a genuine manifold with no inherent connections, or is there in truth no such thing as a manifold, but only what *appears* to be a manifold, because the principles of unity within it are latent or merely implicit? Until this question is answered it is manifestly impossible to distinguish clearly the datum from the product of thought, or to determine how far thought is subjective. I find Lotze's answer very ambiguous, if I may not say inconsistent. He opens his exposition, both in the larger **Logic** and in the *Outlines*, by insisting upon the necessity of preliminary intellectual processes which shall prepare its material for thought. Such a view is implied in the passages already quoted, in which Lotze defines the specific function of thought as "reducing the coincident into coherence," or as generating "accessory or justificatory notions" or "grounds" "*in addition* to the mere current of ideas." "From mere impressions, in so far as they are nothing more than our affections (moods, that is, of our feeling), no logical connection is to be established; but each individual impression, in order to be capable, in the logical sense, of being combined with another into a *thought*, must be already apprehended by the spirit in such a quite definite form as renders this combination possible."[1] If the states of consciousness that follow the external irritants "are to admit of combination in the definite form of a *thought*, they each require some previous shaping to make them into logical building-stones and to convert them from *impressions* into *ideas*."[2] This seems to be sufficiently explicit: thought is not able to grasp the impressions as they are first given, and certain processes, which Lotze regards as carried on by a psychical mechanism, must interpose between the universals of thought and the particulars of sense. In Book v., chap. iv., of the *Mikrokosmus* and in § 20 of his *Logic* he gives these preliminary processes in detail. First, there are "the direct sensations caused in us by the outer world." Secondly, there are "the forms of grouping to which the mechanism of the inner states gives rise, and by which these impressions are combined into the image of a universe." How this is done we cannot tell, though "in scientific thought we may guess how our psychic activity arranges in time and space the manifold of impressions." Thirdly, "with equally unconscious necessity arise in us ideas of things in general,"

[1] *Outlines of Logic*, § 6.   [2] *Logic*, § 1.

—something we may call sense-conceptions, or universals of sense. Fourthly, "there are comparisons and distinctions given directly in perception," which "may become more distinct with the aid of conscious reflection," but which "must be left to the unconscious mechanism of our nature to produce." Into all these "consciousness enters *afterwards* and takes cognizance of relations which it did not by its own action originate, but which have been prepared for it by the unconscious mechanism of the psychic states." From the same point of view he represents "the current of our ideas as a series of events which happen in us and to us according to universal laws of our nature," while he represents thought as "an activity which our mind exercises in reacting upon the material thus supplied."[1] "We do not deny that, *apart from thought*, the mere current of ideas in the brute gives rise to many useful combinations of impressions, correct expectations, seasonable reactions; on the contrary, we admit that much even of what man calls his thought is really nothing but the play of mutually productive ideas."[2] It would be easy to multiply quotations illustrating the view that a mechanical and associative form of intellectual activity prepares beforehand the contents of experience, building them up into a coherent image of the world.

But when we come to examine these processes we

[1] See *Logic*, Introduction, §§ iii. and iv.   [2] *Ibid.*, § vii.

find not only that they are identical with those of thought, but definitely attributed to thought by Lotze himself. In the *first* place, it is thought which seizes upon the state of consciousness, or the event or change in consciousness, and gives it significance, converts it, in fact, from a mere mental occurrence or *impression* into an *idea* which refers to an object. It "objectifies the subjective," as he says, and thereby produces at the same time a meaning for ideas and an object to which they refer. And, since the essence of ideas consists, not in their mere existence as states of consciousness, but in their having meaning or objective reference, it is plain that ideas, as such, cannot be said to exist at all except as products of distinguishing thought. In the *second* place, it is thought which endows the objectified state of consciousness, or meaning, with some kind of independent existence. For thought "cannot simply distinguish it from an emotional mood of its own without accrediting it with some other sort of existence, instead of that which belonged to it as such a mood." Thought "reifies," as Dr. Ward says, this aspect of the state of consciousness, making the symbolic reference into a 'this,' individual object. But, in the *third* place, thought in producing from the psychical state a 'this' something, necessarily invests it with some characteristic or other which serves to distinguish it from another 'this,' or particular object. That is to say, thought yields the qualities of intelligible objects. In the *fourth* place, thought, when it has thus created a number of such substantial entities with their adjuncts, places them in some kind of relation to each other, so as to constitute a system. And, as a result of all these processes, the world of perceptions comes to be conceived as a world in which there are "things as fixed points, which serve to support a number of dependent properties, and are connected together by the changing play of events."[1] The results of these operations of thought are embodied for us in the primary differences, or parts of speech: the substantive gives the object, the adjective its quality, and the verb the changing relations into which objects enter. They indicate three fundamental "concepts which are indispensable for our judgments of reality," and therefore three fundamental operations or forms of thought. For all reality whatsoever must present itself either as a thing having independent existence, or as a quality, or as a change or event.[2] Not, however, that the actual world necessarily exists in these forms, but that the intelligible world, the world as it seems to us, has this appearance; for it could not appear to us at all except under these forms.

In this analysis[3] the world as it appears to the ordinary consciousness, so far from being generated by processes anterior to thought, is shown to be from its first foundation the creation of thought;

[1] *Logic*, § 7.   [2] *Ibid.*, § 316.   [3] *Ibid.*, § 2 *ff.*

and the associative consciousness, instead of being preliminary to and a condition of the reflective or thinking consciousness, is shown to be impossible without it. It is thought which converts an impression into an idea, a psychic event into an intelligible object; it is thought which gives objectivity and quality and relation. Its activities enter into all the other mental processes; and sensation and perception, together with all our associative powers, so far from being preliminary and independent, must be regarded as either identical with, or essentially related to, thought. The distinction between the "receptive" and the active or reconstructive parts of mind is rescinded; for we find the presence of the activity of thought everywhere generating intelligible objects, their qualities and their relations. The datum of thought has sunk from an "image of a cosmos" into sequent states of consciousness that, apart from thought, could never constitute an intelligible world, for they are not *ideas*, but meaningless changes in the state of the soul.

The discrepancy between these views is not removed by distinguishing between "thought in general" and "thought strictly so called," or "logical thought," or between the proper and the preliminary activities of thought. For it would still remain true that, according to the second view, the psychical mechanism and "the play of ideas," whether unconscious or not, cease to be independent and preparatory, and are themselves directly due to the discriminating activities which ultimately build up our reflective view of the world. And thought, instead of being confined to the task of converting coincidence into coherence, is represented as the author of the elements which coincide and of the relations in virtue of which they form any kind of system. In a word, a purely associative consciousness is denied, and thought is made completely dominant in the intelligible world.

But no sooner is this consequence seen than the spontaneity of thought in which it posited, qualified, and related its objects is again withdrawn; and Lotze, in his account of the "second operation" of thought, makes it once more receptive. Thought, which seemed to produce objectivity itself, by a translation of a state of consciousness into an object having meaning, is obliged to find all that it needs in the material. We are told that "the action of thought consists merely in interpreting relations, which we find existing between our passive impressions."[1] Thought does not *make* its objects, nor their qualities, nor their relations; it finds them. It is purely reactive, and for each of its particular reactions it must find an appropriate stimulus in its material. Thought does not, for instance, make the idea of red or blue, neither does it make the distinction between them, or the common element in virtue of which distinction is possible. "It cannot be said that we have the idea of red as red only

[1] *Logic*, § 9.

when we distinguish it from blue or sweet, and only by so distinguishing it; and, again, the idea of blue as blue only by a similar opposition to red. There could be no occasion for attempting such a distinction, nor any possibility of succeeding in the attempt, unless there were first a clear consciousness of what each of the two opposites is in itself."[1] The facts are *there* in the impression, so is the distinction between them. Following out this conception, that thought must find what it makes, Lotze proceeds to constitute the world of sense into a complete analogue of the world of thought, so that the latter may be furnished with all it needs, and have its formal character maintained intact. There are even *universals of sense* provided, in order to occasion those of thought. "The *first universal* is the expression of an inward experience which thought has merely to recognize, and it is an indispensable presupposition of that other kind of universal which we shall meet with in the formation of conceptions." To discover any common element in red and yellow "we must have an immediate sensation, feeling, or experience of the connection which exists between red and yellow, of the fact that they contain a common element; our logical work can consist only in the recognition and expression of this inward experience. The first universal, therefore, is no product of thought, but something which thought finds already in existence."[2]

[1] *Logic*, § 11. [2] *Ibid.*, § 14.

In a similar way Lotze proceeds to show that differences of quantity within universals are *given* to thought *in the matter of sense*. "The judgment '*a* is stronger than *b*,' is, indeed, as a judgment, a logical piece of work; but that which it expresses —the general fact that differences of degree do exist in the same matter, as well as the particular fact that the degree of *a* exceeds that of *b*—can only be experienced, felt, or recognized as part of our inward consciousness." Feeling, or experience, gives it first, and thought starts from this prepared material. The same applies "to the manifold matter of ideas, the systematic order of its qualitative relationships, and the rich variety of local and temporal combinations": "they belong to the material which serves thought in its further operations, and *must be given it to start with*."[1] In short, there must be in the matter of thought something which by its likeness solicits the specific acts of thought; there must be differences to call forth the thought of differences, similarities to call forth similarities, relations of quantity, quality, degree, temporal and special combinations to call forth the like. "Thought is a recognition of facts, and adds no other form to them except this recognition of their existence. Thought can make no difference where it finds none already in the matter of the impressions; the first universal can only be experienced in immediate sensation; all quantitative

[1] See *Logic*, § 17.

determinations, to whatever extent thought may develop them by subsequent comparison, always come back to an immediate consciousness of certain characteristics in the object matter."[1] In this way the same series of processes seem to be repeated upon two different levels, once by feeling, or experience, and once by thought. There is, however, this important distinction between them, namely, that while the processes of thought are possible only on condition that they have been already performed by the psychical mechanism, the latter can be carried on and completed without thought, for, as we are told, they "must be given to it to start with."

Now, seeing that the world of thought has so complete a counterpart in the lower world of sense, it might seem difficult to find any reason for the emergence of the thinking activities. Can it be regarded as anything better than *a useless repetition?* Lotze answers by indicating a second important distinction between them—namely, that thought, in addition to the given facts of experience and the connections between them, supplies the reason or ground for them. The presence of the *ground,* in virtue of which qualities are combined in an object, is the distinguishing mark of the concept, which is the first product of thought proper. In an *image* which, on Lotze's view, could be produced by the associative intelligence,

[1] *Logic,* §§ 19, 24, etc.

or by the psychical mechanism, qualities coincide and constitute a kind of whole; but this coincidence is merely contingent. The combination is due to the fortuitous experiences of the individual mind, and it has no justification in fact. It may be valid, or it may truly represent the actual combination of qualities in an object; but it may not. In fact, the question of its validity does not arise at this stage. The combination simply happens to be in consciousness, and it may contain elements which are really quite incongruous. But with the concept, *i.e.*, with the first specific product of thought, there arises a regulative principle which sifts the elements already present, rejects the irrelevant, and even makes possible the prediction of elements not yet experienced. Both the image and the concept, being units of experience, contain something which combines, that is, some kind of a universal in which the parts are held together. But the universal in the image "comes to us without logical effort as a simple fact of observation in our mental life"; while the universal in the concept "we do produce by logical effort," though not without the help of the first universal.[1]

From this there issues a third distinction between the image and the concept. The universal in the former does not really dominate the particulars which it combines; that is to say, the combining elements, being externally superimposed upon the

---

[1] See *Logic*, § 24.

content, leave it unchanged. But the universal which appears in the concept comprehends the content and systematizes it by relation to itself, making the differences into species within the whole. So that the "concept" or unit of the thinking consciousness is radically different from the "image" or unit of the associative consciousness. For when the particulars become species of the universal, they also become *instances of* the universal, and lose their mere particularity; whereas those of the image remain particular, and their combination is external as well as contingent. The concept is, therefore, a universal which combines *universals*, while an image is a universal which is itself empty, and simply allows the particulars to lie within it side by side. In the *image* of a piece of gold, for instance, the specific colour, yellow, is in some way joined with a particular weight, malleability, size; and in the image of a piece of copper another particular colour is joined externally to another particular weight, size, etc. But, in the *general conception* of gold or copper or metal, the qualities that are combined are themselves general; and they are combined in accordance with a form or principle which determines that connection and makes it valid for all possible instances. The concept, which is the first product of thought proper, is thus universal through and through. Its elements are universal, and they rest upon a ground or principle in which alone their combination is intelligible. This product, therefore, is guided by a necessity which, at the same time, makes it valid for every human consciousness, and makes it representative of the objects of thought as they must be, in order to be intelligible at all. We attain, in fact, the curious result that while the universals of sense which we *observe*, and which are *given* in the material, may or may not be true, seeing that they are purely contingent upon the individual's experience, the universals which thought makes and which presumably are not in the material, are regarded as necessarily valid for everyone. That is to say, thought *observes* what may not be in the material, and *makes*, after observing, what is necessary in order that the material may be intelligible!

Now if, at the conclusion of this exposition, we endeavour to discriminate between what thought makes and what is supplied to it in its data, so as to comprehend the function it performs in our intelligent life, we find that the task is an exceedingly difficult one. According to one view so much is supplied to thought that nothing is left to it except to "sift" the rich content of perceptive experience and rearrange it, without in any way adding anything to it except the reasons for its combinations. Thought, on this view, is formal and receptive, and its only work is that of reflection. It presents the old world over again, but in the new light of an ordering principle. According to the other view it is only through the intervention of thought that there are either ideas or an intelligible world at all. It arrests the shifting panorama of subjective states of consciousness, objectifies and fixes them so as to give them meaning, and then relates them into a systematic world of knowledge. On this view everything, except the absolutely meaningless subjective data, is due to the spontaneous activity of thought. In other words, thought, instead of being receptive and formal, is essentially constructive, the cause on account of which alone there can be either ideas or objects, or connections between them.

Nor is the contradiction removed by making these apparently spontaneous activities once more depend upon analagous stimuli in the matter and data of sense. It is only reiterated. If whatever is done by thought in the way of analysis or synthesis can be done only because each analytic and synthetic act is prompted by differences and common elements provided by immediate perception or inner experience, then we must return to that anterior experience all that we have just taken from it. The only element which thought retains as entirely its own, and which does not seem to have its counterpart in the associative world, is the reason or the ground for the coherence. And the only element which is definitely excluded from thought is the manifold, the change in the state of consciousness which thought has from time to time to objectify. But if we apply consistently the idea which led Lotze to find for each of the activities of thought a parallel in the sphere of sense, we should have to postulate the existence in the matter of sense even of these grounds or reasons; for, as we are emphatically told, all that thought can do is to react, and every reaction demands its own special incentive. Lotze did not apply the idea consistently; he leaves it quite doubtful whether thought *makes*, or *finds*, these grounds or reasons; or, rather, he adopts the one view or the other according to the necessities of the moment.[1]

Now, if we bear in mind the middle position which Lotze wished to maintain between Idealism on the one hand, and Scepticism on the other, we shall discover that no other way was left to him, except this of first attributing all to sense,

---

[1] Lotze quite explicitly refuses to identify the principles of pure thought with the principles which constitute the real world, or which connect real objects. For instance, he entirely separates the intellectual grounds or reasons for a fact, from the causes which bring it about. What I am referring to here is the relation between these principles of thought and the principles which bind our experience, or world of *intelligible* objects, into a system. What Lotze leaves ambiguous is, whether in conception, judgment, and inference we *reveal* connections already present in and constitutive of our perceptive knowledge, or whether these processes bring about new and therefore artificial universals, necessary for us in *interpreting* experience, but not necessary for the *existence* of experience.

and afterwards attributing all to thought, and, finally, of attributing it to thought only because it was already in its material. The *see-saw* is essential to his theory; the elements of knowledge, as he describes them, can subsist only by the alternate robbery of each other. If thought is merely formal, and all its processes are one by one determined by an anterior psychical mechanism, then there results, in everything but the name, the Associationism and the consequent intellectual and moral Scepticism which Kant refuted simply by showing that all these earlier processes involved thought. If, on the other hand, the very objectivity of things and the first possibility of their having any existence, qualities, or relations, is due to thought, then we are on the verge of the Idealism which found nothing in the world except thought. In other words, thought becomes constitutive and not formal. Lotze was well aware of both of these dangers, and he directs his main endeavour to the attempt to make thought effective and its functions real, while stopping short of making it constitutive. Having discovered that thought cannot draw distinctions and form connections unless both distinct objects and their common element are immediately given to it in perception, or feeling, or inner experience, we might have expected him to take the further step and to say simply that these objects and their common element exist in virtue of thought. That is to say, we might expect the simple conclusion that because the higher is possible only if it also is in the lower, therefore it *is* in the lower, and the lower is only an elementary form of the higher.

But that step, simple as it is, would have transformed his view of both thought and reality: it would have made the former constitutive and the latter rational. Except for the fact that the manifold is given, and that what is given is on Lotze's theory a manifold, the real and the ideal would be completely identified. Instead of taking that step, Lotze rests satisfied with asserting the *similarity* between the differences and universals of sense and those of thought. He cannot venture to identify them like the Idealists, and he cannot show how the latter can issue from the former. The world of sense and the world of thought correspond point by point, and each analytic or synthetic act of thought has its own proper incentive in sense; but Lotze does not try to furnish any reason for this correspondence and mutual adaptability. If he had supplied such a reason the worlds of thought and sense would have become species in a universal, to use his language; or different stages in the evolution of a single principle of reason, to use the language of idealism. But he conceals from himself and his readers the necessity for seeking this deeper principle by practically denying the existence of any *process* in the associative, or lower world of knowledge. "The universal marks in the simplest case require no special logical work of thought for their origin, but arise out of the *immediate impression* without our logical assistance. That 'green,' 'blue,' 'red,' for example, have something in common is a matter of *immediate experience*. . . . So, too, differences of magnitude are immediately perceived as true."[1] "The 'first universal' comes to us without logical effort as a simple fact of observation in our mental life, and just for this reason it can be applied in building up this second universal, which we do produce by logical thought. That the yellow of gold, the red of copper, and the white of silver are only variations of a common element which we proceed to call colour, *this is a matter of immediate sensation*."[2] But how can these be *immediate*, if, as Lotze has told us, the original datum of sense is a subjective state of consciousness which, apart from the activity of thought, would have no objective reference whatsoever? Does Lotze mean that the world of objects related in space and time is given to us at once without any process of intelligence, so that we have only to open our eyes, so to speak, in order to get it? Put thus broadly, we must answer in the negative. It was impossible for him to go back to the naïve position of Locke, in spite of his insistence upon the efficacy of "immediate" sensation, impression, perception, or experience. The work done by modern psychologists, not to mention that of Kant, had blocked the way by revealing the poverty of the supplied material and the

[1] *Outlines of Logic*, § 13. [2] *Logic*, § 24.

significance of the work done upon it by the intelligence. So he escapes the difficulty by calling these truths "immediate," that is, by attributing them dogmatically and unanalytically to "inner experience," and by making their *results* so similar to those of thought as to enable them to excite its activities one by one.

The ultimate cause of Lotze's vacillating and inconsistent account of the relation between thought proper and the preliminary processes of intelligence lies in a double hypothesis, which, when applied to the facts of our intelligence, proves to be unworkable, but which, nevertheless, he cannot give up without admitting the main contention of the Idealists. This hypothesis is that knowledge consists of two elements which are so radically different as to be capable of being described only by defining each negatively in terms of the other: these elements are the pure manifold or differences of sense and a purely universal or relative thought. Unable to admit at once that such elements can in no wise be brought together, or to adopt either a pure Associationism or a pure Idealism, he endeavours to mediate between them. When that mediation is examined, however, it turns out that it consists in endowing each alternately with the characteristics of the other. That is to say, when he comes to consider *how* the manifold can be combined into systematic knowledge, it turns out that what is given to thought is anything but a manifold: it is, on the contrary, the varied world of perception, with its objects distinguished in quantity and quality, and related to one another in space and time. And when he comes to consider how thought which is merely formal can combine particulars, he has to admit that it is not formal, but constitutes its object by endowing a state of consciousness with objective reference, and "reifying" it. Both the manifold and thought change their character in his hands; but that does not lead him to examine his assumption, or to define anew either the datum of knowledge or thought which is its instrument. From the fact that pure thought and the manifold of sense pass into each other, and that the one proves meaningless and the other helpless in its isolation, he did not draw the conclusion that they are only aspects of one fact, correlates mutually penetrating each other, distinguishable in thought and for purposes of investigation, but not separable as existences. In other words, he did not recognize that he was endeavouring to substantiate abstractions, and make mere logical remnants do the work of an intelligence which is never purely formal, upon a material which is nowhere a pure manifold. And consequently, instead of solving any of the difficulties which Kant had left, as to the relation of sense and understanding, perception and conception, and instead of passing on towards an Idealism which attempts to resolve the contrasted factors into stages in the evolution of reason, he simply made the difficulties of the Kantian theory more manifest, and showed with new clearness the need of the transition into some form of Idealism. He has thus helped indirectly to show that thought and its data cannot in this way be set in direct antagonism to each other if knowledge is to be the issue of their interaction. He unconsciously teaches by his contradictions that knowledge, however elementary and sensuous, or advanced and reflective, always presents the same characteristic of combining form and matter, and that its object is always *both* real and ideal. At the earliest beginnings, thought is there making sense possible. In its highest developments in systems of science and philosophy, the elements of sense are there, held, as it were, in solution by the universal laws and forms. Nowhere in knowledge do we find anything but a system. Both the differences and the unity may be more or less explicit; the articulation into reality and ideality, which is everywhere characteristic of intelligible objects, may be more or less complete, but they are always there. The difference between the primary and elementary data of thought on the one hand, and the highest forms of systematized knowledge on the other, is no difference in kind, analogous to that between a mere particular and a mere universal, or a mere content and a mere form ; but it is a difference in completeness of articulation. As all the organism is in the living germ, so all knowledge is in the simplest perception, and all reason is in sense. But Lotze's mechanical presupposition of thought as an instrument externally adapted to its data, leads him to do injustice to both thought and its material. In trying to correct it he contradicts himself: representing the datum now as a mere meaningless state of consciousness, and now as a world of objects related in space and time, and representing thought, now as a function of mere empty universals, and now as reaching down into and articulating the most elementary datum of sense.

We may put this matter in another way, and its importance demands the utmost care and clearness. The πρῶτον ψεῦδος of Lotze's doctrine lies in the assumption that the first datum of knowledge is the subjective state, or the change in consciousness consequent upon the varying stimuli arising from the outer world, and that the first act of thought is to objectify this subjective. His whole doctrine rests upon the psychological hypothesis that what we first *know*, indefinitely enough perhaps, is a subjective state, and that the first act of thought is to make this state in ourselves representative of an outward object. The subjective is projected, reified, posited, so as to become an object.

Now, this assumption is, in the first place, not supported by psychological evidence. It cannot be denied that a change in ourselves is antecedent to our knowledge of the meaning of that change, any more than it can be denied that rays of light must impinge upon the eye, and that certain physiological processes must take place before we can see an object. But it does not follow that we infer the existence of the seen object from these physiological changes in our brain or nerves, and from the fact that light impinges upon the eye. On the contrary, we infer these processes because we have first seen the object. The object is first given in sight, and then science discovers the conditions on which alone it could be seen. That is to say, the first in the order of events is the last in the order of interpretation ; or the first as a matter of fact is the last as an object of thought. And similarly in the case of the subjective state. That consciousness as a matter of fact must change in order that we may know the object which incited the change, does not prove that we first *know* the change in ourselves and then infer the object. On the contrary, the first in the order of events is again the last in the order of thought. What thought first gives is some sufficiently indefinite object, so indefinite an object that if psychologists are right it is not recognized as either subjective or objective, as occurring either in the self or in the outer world. Whenever we endeavour to *account* for our knowledge of that object, we recognize that it is possible only by relation to ourselves, a relation which we explain on the hypothesis of a change in our states of consciousness. But it is most important to note that what is inferred is the change in consciousness, and that the premise from which that inference starts is the fact that we already do know the object.

That is to say, we infer the subjective (in this sense of the term) from the objective; and do not infer the existence of an object from a change in the state of the subject. In the order of knowledge the objective comes first; in the order of the reflection, which *accounts* for that knowledge, the subjective change comes first. We know the objective in part before we know the subjective, the world before we know ourselves; and our knowledge of ourselves is due to our return from the world in the way of reflection. In other words, the subjective appears to us as subjective only because we have analyzed the reality which we first know into two elements. The reality first given to us indefinitely, opens out upon us into differences, and sunders into the primary distinctions of subjective and objective. But we are not entitled, on account of the fundamental character of this distinction, to forget or deny the unity of the reality in which the distinction takes place; nor is there any justification for fixing a complete gap between the subjective and the objective, and compelling thought in some unknowable way either to *objectify* the former or a part of it, or to leap blindly from the one world into the other, from the sphere of mere subjective states to that of external facts corresponding to them. I should say that no modern psychologist would deny that the first fact in the order of events is a change in the state of consciousness; for obviously, if there is no change in our state, there is no need of endeavouring to account for it, either by postulating the presence of an object that incites the change, or otherwise. But no modern psychologist would admit that the first thing known, say, by an infant, or by the unsophisticated consciousness in any of its forms, is this subjective state. The relation of the known object to the subjective state is the discovery which the psychologist makes, and the history of early philosophy shows us that it took a long time to make that discovery. Indeed, we might cut the knot at once by stating that the event of knowing, like every other, must take place before its interpretation, and that therefore the *relation* of the subject and the object is prior to the distinction between them which the process of interpretation brings to light. But Lotze and many others begin with a mere state of consciousness as the first fact of experience, and then they try to escape out of themselves into an outer world.

But neglecting this objection, let us admit that the change in the subjective state not only occurs before we know an object, but that we know this subjective state first and then infer the corresponding object. What follows? That it is impossible to account for the fact that an object corresponding to this change of state should ever reveal itself to us, and that, if we begin with the purely subjective, we must end there. Lotze, as we have seen, speaks of thought as objectifying the subjective. He admits, indeed, that the objectified state of consciousness is not an outward fact in the sense of a real thing in space and time; and asserts, on the contrary, that the objectified states of consciousness which constitute our system of experience, though they are "valid of" the world of real objects, do not constitute those objects. From this, of course, it follows that the intelligible world is only a phenomenal world, and that feeling and faith must, on his view, come to the assistance of thought in order to give to that world its worth and validity. But that is not the point I wish to press just now. What I wish to show is, that this process of objectification is unintelligible and impossible. Lotze himself nowhere explains this extraordinary process of seizing upon a mere change in consciousness, flinging it, or a part of it, into a sphere in which it can confront the self as a not-self, and endowing it with a quasi-independent existence. Nor is it explicable. A change in consciousness is in itself, to begin with, an occurrence and nothing more. It is not an idea, any more than a change in the state of the brain is an idea—until thought objectifies it. But such objectification is impossible, *unless we confound an event with a known event.* If it is a known event it is already an outward object, *in* the self if we please, but distinguished from the self, and therefore as outward as a change in the position of Jupiter. Both the psychic change and the change in the position of the planet are in consciousness as known, and I should say also that they are both parts of the self, except that I should have to turn aside to justify the statement. In any case there is no need of objectifying a *known* event. But there is no possibility of objectifying an *unknown* event; at least it seems to me obvious, on the ground that what is unknown is for it non-existent, that thought cannot deal in any way with the unknown. This remarkable process of objectifying a state of consciousness is mythical.

But the same supposed process receives another expression. The subjective state is made to *symbolize* outward facts. Psychical states, we are told, both occur and have meaning, *i.e.*, they are events that either have or acquire the power of symbolizing something other than themselves. An idea has two sides: it is, as an existing fact, a change of state in the individual's consciousness, but as having meaning it is also a symbol of an object. And the essence of an 'idea' is this power of symbolizing. Here also we have, though in a less crude form, the conversion of a subjective fact into an object of thought, or the translation of what is at first merely real into what ought to be merely ideal, if the writers were thoroughly consistent.

There seems to me to be something unusual in this use of the term "symbol." Ordinarily, symbols presuppose the facts symbolized, derive their significance *from* them, and are explicable only in their light. But in this case the event, a state of consciousness, symbolizes something which is not originally there to be symbolized, points to an object which does not as yet exist, and indeed becomes that object in the act of pointing to it, thereby adding an ideal side to its own pre-existing real one. This is a strange, and, I believe, an impossible process. It is certainly impossible if the state, or change of consciousness, is a mere event, and not already the new knowledge of an object. Events symbolize nothing, whether they be psychical or not, until they are known; but if they are already known they are already objective and ideal, and are themselves, on this phrasing of it, symbolized. The psychical events or ideas are, further, supposed to symbolize something other than themselves; for, as real events, ideas are said to be subjective facts, while their *meaning* is an object. And we are told that a thing never is what it means. But I cannot believe either of these assertions. For a change of consciousness, whether as an event not known at all but as a simple change, or as a known event, is not subjective. Nothing whatsoever is subjective if we can indicate or speak of it. The purely subjective is as completely beyond our reach as the purely objective. In fact it is only because it is already an object of thought that we can call it subjective; for we present it *to* ourselves, and therefore distinguish it from ourselves, although we at the same time regard it as a part of the history of ourselves. But in strictness, it is impossible to speak or think of a state of consciousness as purely subjective, for the very act of doing so makes it an object, or a part of that reality from which we never escape, and which embraces both the world and ourselves. The state of consciousness, like every other possible object of thought, is both subjective and objective; it is a real thing, which is also intelligible or ideal. We do not begin with the subjective, therefore, unless we begin with that which is *ex vi termini* not an object of thought. But perhaps what is meant is that the change or state of consciousness belongs to ourselves, and not to the not-self. If so, I do not deny its subjectivity; but I would assert that my arm, or eye, or purse, or wife, or child, or my next-door neighbour and my enemy are subjective in precisely the same sense; for if there is any philosophic attempt more futile than another, it is the attempt to shut a part of reality within and a part of it without the self. My interest in my own states of consciousness as facts belonging to me may very likely be stronger than my interest in other facts belonging to me; but the difference is only one of degree. Everything that I can possibly know, or have an interest in, is, in one sense, mine, or subjective; but it is also at the same time not *me* in the exclusively subjective sense, but my object. Since the Ego potentially includes the Universe, everything is in one sense subjective. In knowing it I am only knowing myself, and yet I am all the while knowing it as an object. It is presented *to* me, and therefore objective; it is presented *by* me, and therefore subjective. The ideal and the real side, the fact and its manifestation in thought, are inseparable. We cannot begin with the subjective, and do not need, therefore, to objectify it; for in order to begin at all we must already have an object.

But supposing we admit that we begin with the psychical event and then make it *mean* something, can it mean something other than itself? Is it true that a thing never means what it is, and that reality and significance, the fact and the ideal content, never coincide? I think not. Against the bare assertion that a thing never is what it means, I would set the question, "Is a thing ever anything *except* what it means?" I am aware that every finite object does mean something else in the sense that in order to explain it we have to seek its meaning *in* something else.[1] If I want to understand a I trace it to b, and b to c, so that the meaning of a is not in itself but in b, and the meaning of b is in c, and so on. But, on the other hand, the meaning of a which I find in b is at the same time regarded by me as the reality of a; and if the meaning of a is not in itself—as it is not if a be finite—neither is the reality of a in itself. In such circumstances I say not only a means b, but that b is the reality of which a was the appearance;

[1] More strictly in *everything* else.

and, so far as I endeavour to express my complete thought or to give the whole meaning of *a*, I cease to speak of *a* except in its relation to *b*. I do not see how we can escape this conclusion unless we are to regard the process of knowledge as a self-stultifying one, which in pursuing truth turns its back on reality. No doubt an idea seems to point to something other than itself, and the psychical occurrence, as an occurrence, is not that of which it is an idea. But if I wish to know what that psychical occurrence is, I try to explain it, just as I would try to explain any other event, by looking for its conditions. And the explanation of that psychical occurrence would be found, not in the external object to which it points—for as an occurrence it points to nothing—but in the conditions psychical and other from which it has sprung. If, on the other hand, I abstract from the idea its psychical occurrence, then nothing whatsoever remains to have the meaning—*except an outer object*. That outer object, if I know any psychology, I recognize as standing in relation to me, or as having a subjective side. And if my psychology is false, I substantiate that subjective side of the object, endow it with a quasi-independent existence, oppose it to and then sever it from the object, and give all the ideality to the former and all the reality to the latter. What is meant by saying that an idea has meaning can only be that the object shows itself to be ideal; but every attempt to make the idea, as idea, show itself as real must fail. Nor would any one make the attempt of finding reality for ideas except for the psychological assumption, which psychology itself cannot justify, that we first know the subjective and then the objective. But I must insist that ideas, in so far as they are objects of thought, are both subjective and objective, and in so far as they are not objects of thought they are as good as nothing. They do not need to be "objectified," because they are objects already; and they have meaning, like all other things, just because they are objects interpretable through their conditions by the intelligence. Both "objectification" and "symbolization" are psychological inventions, designed to meet the insurmountable difficulty which springs from assuming that we know the subjective occurrence otherwise than in the attempt to explain the conditions under which its reality has made itself manifest to us. The genuine object of thought, therefore, is *reality*, and reality, *pari passu* with our knowledge of it, shows itself as ideal. For, to the degree in which the relations of an object to the intelligence are discovered, to that degree its relations to the system of which the intelligence is the focus are discovered. That is to say, by revealing the relations of an object to the self its place in an all-inclusive system is revealed; and the all-inclusive system is reality.

Lotze's error in starting with the subjective state and then seeking the objective reality makes itself further evident in the difficulty, to which I have already casually referred, of collating the universals of thought with the preliminary universals of sense knowledge. That difficulty may be put in this way: How can the universals of sense, which are admittedly contingent and external, and which give nothing more than casual coincidence to their content, occasion or suggest, or otherwise lead to universals which are necessary and valid for all intelligence, which give *coherence* to the content, and which convert the particulars into species of the universal, and therefore themselves into universals? The only answer which Lotze gives is the following: "If we wish for practical purposes to ascertain in any creature, object, or arrangement, what is the line which divides what is inwardly coherent from casual accessions, we put the whole in motion, in the belief that the influence of change will show which parts hold firmly together while foreign admixtures fall away, and in what general and constant modes those parts combine while changing their relative positions in particular cases: in this sum of constant elements we find the inner and essential cohesion of the whole, and we expect it to determine the possibility and the manner of variable accretions." Vary the circumstances, as Mill would say, and note what groups hold together, and we thereby "determine the element which maintains itself in the same instance under changed conditions; for it is only the assumption that the group *a b c*, the common element in several groups of ideas, will also be found thus to maintain itself, which strictly justifies us in regarding these coexisting elements as coherent, and as the ground for the admissibility or inadmissibility of fresh elements."[1] But it is evident that observation of the elements which happen to cling together under varying circumstances cannot reveal the principle which makes them coherent. Observed coincidence can only yield coincidence; by no repetition of particulars can we ascend to a universal, and no intellectual alchemy can extract necessity from chance.[2] We must either rest with coincidence, that is, with purely associative thought, which is to give up the conception of the rationality of experience; or, by assuming a hypothesis, as science does, we must repudiate the coincidence altogether. That is to say, we must regard contiguity in space and time, chance coherence, or association, as our first attempt at systematization, and as resting upon higher categories, and ultimately upon the highest of all, namely, the supreme unity of apperception. But Lotze does not explicitly admit the presence of the principles of reason in the rudimentary data of knowledge. On the contrary, he allows associative or chance-connected knowledge to subsist side by side with reflective knowledge; and does not transmute perception into conception, or, rather,

---

[1] *Logic*, § 22.   [2] See *Logic*, § 56.

find the former to be the latter at a lower stage of development. With the problem still upon his hands of discovering the principle which at once gives the universality of truth to our knowledge and necessary coherence to facts, he passes from conception to judgment. For conception, even upon the most generous interpretation of it, only suggests that there *may be* a universal under the coincident elements of sense knowledge. But Lotze does not discover the universal in conception. And just as he fails to find it in conception, he also fails, as we shall see in the next chapter, to find it in the judgment; and he has to seek it in inference. But inference does not yield it, and he has to postulate it as an object of faith lying outside the confines of reflective thought. He has begun with the conception of the content of knowledge as a mere manifold, and of thought as purely formal; he has taken the distinction or severance of the subjective and objective as the first *datum*, and he is therefore unable to bring them together again in a principle which is deeper than their division. The only function of thought is to connect, and that function it fails to perform.

CHAPTER IV

THE THEORY OF JUDGMENT

WE have seen that Lotze represents thought as an activity which combines the contents of experience according to universal, necessary grounds. The first products of thought proper are conceptions; and conceptions are combinations of universals within a universal, or, in other words, combinations of elements which are determined by a universal in such a way as to form a necessary system of differences within a unity. The determination of the differences by the universal is regarded by Lotze as an essential characteristic of a true concept, and it is this which distinguishes the concept from a general image. A general image "subsumes" particulars under it, leaving them unchanged; a concept "subordinates" them to the universal, resolving them thereby into species of itself. The former is obtained merely by the omission of differences. The latter not only does not omit, but it transmutes the contents and systematizes the materials of experience. And concepts, as we ascend from one to another, become always more concrete. It has been the aim of philosophers to arrange the matter of knowledge under an ascending series of such concepts, so as to set up "a structure resting on a broad basis, formed by all singular concepts or ideas, growing gradually narrower as it rises, and ending in a single apex, the all-embracing concept of the thinkable."[1] Such an aim is regarded by Lotze as not capable of being realized, and that not merely because the world is great and our minds are small, but because we must necessarily arrive "not at one but at several ultimate concepts not reducible to one another." These ultimate concepts correspond to "those very meanings of the parts of speech which at the outset we found to be the primary logical elements." The concept of a *something* corresponds to the substantive, of a *quality* to the adjective, of *becoming*, or an event, to the verb, and "the rest to relation." And as we cannot resolve being, becoming, and relation into each other, nor find their roots in anything higher, "the entire structure of our concepts rises like a mountain-chain, beginning in a broad base and ending in several sharply defined peaks."[2]

Now, inasmuch as "it is not necessary that our thoughts should have greater unity or simplicity than the reality which they represent," the fact that a single supreme conception is not possible, is not

[1] *Logic*, § 33.   [2] *Ibid.*

considered as a defect by Lotze. From this point of view there does not seem to be any necessity for any forms of thought besides conception. By means of conception alone thought might go on to complete a systematic representation of the intelligible world, uniting its elements under these few ultimate concepts; these highest concepts exercising a determining power upon, and subordinating to themselves, all the lower ones. Thought might, therefore, seem to be capable of finishing the work of connecting the contents of experience according to necessary principles, by means of conception alone.

But such a conceptual view, even if it were complete, would be radically untrue of reality; so untrue that "even a perfect knowledge of the ideal world would give us little support in understanding the real."[1] It would be "an image of a fixed order," whereas reality is always changing. What "reality shows us is a changing medley of the most manifold relations and connections between the matter of ideas, taking first one form and then another without regard to their place in the system."[2] Hence, since the real world is a world of change, we require, in order to represent it, another process of thought than that of conceiving, which fixes its material in a motionless and invariable order. That process is Judgment. Judgment performs for "changeable coincidences" what conception effects for coexistent facts. The one deals with Becoming

[1] *Logic*, § 34.   [2] *Ibid.*

or change, in the same way as the other deals with Being; and both operate in obedience to the fundamental impulse towards necessary coherence which characterizes thought.

We might conclude from this that thought has two different organs whereby it performs the two different tasks of representing permanence and change, coexistence and sequence. For, as we have seen, Lotze deems it impossible either to reduce these phenomena to each other, or to find any common ground for them. But in the very next paragraph to that in which he confines Conception to the representation of a fixed order, and Judgment to the representation of change, Lotze makes conception the starting point of judgment. Judgment comes in to complete the task left unfinished by the former; for the combination which conception effected has not been logically justified. That is to say, conception, while producing coherence by means of its universals, has not shown how the universals come to be applicable to the particulars. Nothing has been revealed either in the universals or in the particulars that enables them to come together, nor has any third mediating element been shown to exist. The units of conceptions are thus, so far, mere facts which happen to be. We must, therefore, "break up these presupposed combinations again; or, if they can be justified, reconstitute them, but in a form which at the same time expresses the ground of coherence in the matter combined.

In seeking to solve this problem, the form in which thought will move will obviously be that of the *Judgment*."[1]

According to the first view judgment is introduced in order to deal with a specific aspect of reality, namely its change, conception apparently being itself able to complete a view of the world as a fixed order. According to this second view judgment is brought in to reveal the ground by which conception unifies its content. Seeing that conception does not bring to light the necessity of the coherence by revealing its principle, and seeing that in consequence the elements in the concept simply happen to cohere, and are, therefore, little better than coincident, judgment must take up its work with the specific aim of rendering the principle of connection explicit, and justifying the subordination of the contents. I do not wish here to press this inconsistency; I shall simply say that the second view is the more consistent with the general theory of Lotze.

The judgment, then, according to Lotze, is "intended to express a relation between the matters of two ideas, not a relation of ideas." It seeks to disclose not the mental medium of connection, or subjective link, but the objective element which makes one fact cohere with another. In the proposition "Gold is yellow," for instance, the idea of yellow is not represented in judgment as a property of the idea of gold, so that the idea of gold is a

[1] *Logic*, § 35.

yellow idea; on the contrary, judgment relates the facts to which these ideas point. These facts are first given in experience as simply coincident: "the relation between them is primarily no other than this, that whenever, or whenever under certain conditions, the one idea, gold, is found, there the other idea, yellow, is also found. . . . The problem of the logical judgment is to express what it is which makes this relation possible, justifiable, or necessary; and it solves the problem by exhibiting through its copula the relation between the object matters of the two ideas, a relation due to that which the ideas represent, and differing in different cases."[1] Judgment, in a word, has to bring to light an objective, and, therefore, a necessary and universal connection between facts. Hence it is evident that the whole problem of judgment turns upon the possibility and nature of this connection, that is to say, upon the copula. Its task, in a word, is to furnish grounds of connection, "accessory notions," principles of coherence, between materials which otherwise would either remain entirely separate or else be connected merely by the contingent psychical bond of association.

Now, as the whole problem turns upon the nature of the copula, it is evident that the different kinds of copula supply the principle on which judgments can be classified. Hence the ordinary distinctions of Quantity, Quality, and Modality are, in strict-

[1] *Logic*, § 37.

ness, logically irrelevant. *Quantity* refers *directly* only to the extent of the subject, and the copula is, in the first instance, of the same nature whether the whole or a part of the subject is spoken of. Indirectly, it is true, the copula is itself concerned: for where the subject is used in its whole extent there is implied that the relation of the predicate to it is universal and necessary, whereas the relation of a predicate to a part only of the subject must be contingent. But the necessity is only implied, and if the implication is developed the distinction is found to turn, not upon quantity, but upon the nature of the copula. *Qualitative* distinctions between judgments are still more easily shown to have no bearing upon the nature of the copula, and, therefore, no logical worth. For, as Lotze thinks, Affirmative, Negative, and Limitative judgments express precisely the same relation between the subject and the predicate. In the one case a certain relation is said to hold; in the other case it is denied; but the denial or the affirmation has to do, not with the connection of the subject and the predicate, but with the relation of both of them to reality. As to the *Modal* distinction, unless we either identify it with the relational one, or make it arise out of the nature of the combining element or the copula, we must regard it as expressing, not the nature of the judgment, but the psychological conditions, or other limitations, under which the judgment is made; and with these logic has nothing to do.

Judgments are, therefore, logically different only in virtue of the different kinds of connection which they establish between the contents of the two concepts which respectively form the subject and predicate. In one respect, indeed, the relation which judgment establishes is always the same; for it is always necessary and universal, never particular or contingent. That is to say, the relation is always one of coherence between the facts themselves, and never merely associative or dependent upon the subjective experience of the individual consciousness. But that necessity, or universality, or objectivity, may reveal itself in consciousness in different ways, or arise under different conditions. And Lotze, following the steps of previous investigators, finds that there are three of these conditions: one fact may include the other; one fact may be connected with another through a third fact or element which conditions them; or it may be related to another because they both fall within a system of necessarily related elements. If we take S to mean one of these facts, namely, the subject in the judgment, and P the other, which is the predicate, then we may say that these different relations are expressible in the following form: 1st, S *is* P, that is, P is already implied in S, and the relation between them is that of subsumption; 2nd, If S is x it is P, that is, P is necessarily connected with S through a condition, x; 3rd, S is either P or Q, that is to say, S having a certain specific character is confined to one of these exclusive alternatives and necessarily connected with it—which of the two is its predicate cannot be determined by judgment, and must be left either to empirical observation or to some higher form of thought, such as Inference. These forms are respectively called the Categorical, Hypothetical, and Disjunctive Judgment. Our immediate task is to follow Lotze's exposition of these forms.

Now it is manifest that, as an event in our psychical history, the Categorical Judgment comes before the Hypothetical; for we should have no occasion to investigate the condition of a connection between S and P "unless we had already had experiences of the presence of P in some S and its absence in others." And, for a similar reason, the Categorical precedes the Disjunctive. But Lotze finds a form of Judgment which is earlier even than the Categorical, or, more strictly perhaps, which displays the Categorical Judgment in the process of being formed. It is the Impersonal Judgment, whose differentia is that it gives "logical setting to a matter of perception without regarding it as a modification or determination of an already fixed subject."[1] In other words, the predicate of the Impersonal Judgment qualifies an indefinite subject. A something, which has as yet no independent content, passes into a limited and recognizable, inadequate content in a predicate. And as there are not, as yet, *two* definite and

[1] *Logic*, § 47.

fixed contents to be connected, the relation between them, or the copula, is itself indefinite. Thought has not passed from an interfused to a definitely articulated difference. But it is caught in the attempt to do so, and on that very account reveals the condition which all thought must fulfil, which is "that everything which is to be matter of perception must be conceived as a predicate of a known or unknown subject."[1] Thought begins thus with an indefinite reality, and in the attempt to make that reality definite it forms a predicate, which qualifies the subject, and thereby tends to give the subject a definite form. If we say, "It rains," "It is warm," "It thunders," we are *in process* of defining the "it," and of forming a definite S which shall have a fixed content of its own. When we have formed such a subject, and can, therefore, oppose it to, and connect it with, a predicate by means of a copula, and not till then, we have a real example of the act of judging. It is only then that the question of the nature of the copula or ground of connection between the elements of our experience really emerges. The Judgment then, for the first time, assumes the categorical form, and we affirm or deny that S is P.

But immediately we make such an assertion as 'S is P' we fall into difficulties, for we find on investigation that we have brought together things which were given simply as opposed. We have

[1] See *Logic*, § 48.

asserted identity between things which were *given* as independent. Hence this, the first step in judgment, seems to be altogether unjustifiable. "This absolute connection of S and P, in which the one is unconditionally the other and yet both stand over against each other as different, is a relation quite impracticable to thought."[1] By this Lotze does not mean that thought does not form such judgments, for that is obviously untrue, but that in making them it seems to perform an illegitimate process. And we are brought to the pass of being obliged either to reject all categorical judgments of the form S is P, or else to find some justification for them in another form of thought.

The briefest examination of the categorical judgment will serve to bring this difficulty to light. To say that S is P, or that "gold is yellow" may mean one of two things: first, that P is added to S, or yellow to gold as a new mark or element which was not at first recognized as belonging to it; or second, that the predicate P, or yellow, is asserted to have been already contained in the subject and therefore necessary to the complete conception of it. If we take the judgment in the first of these two senses it is evidently synthetic, if in the second, it is analytic. Now, it has been supposed that it is only synthetic judgments, in which we seem to add one element to another, which present any difficulty to the logicians; and,

[1] *Logic*, § 54.

indeed, that even these synthetic judgments present no difficulty unless they are *a priori*, that is, unless we have no empirical datum to enable us to make the transition from the one fact to the other. But, in truth, the possibility of *a posteriori* synthesis in a judgment is as difficult to explain as that of *a priori* synthesis. For even though experience should show us that S and P, gold and yellowness, are always connected, it only shows that they are concurrent phenomena of our consciousness; they are experienced together by us. But that they *must* be so experienced, or that there is any real and objective connection between the facts themselves, can never be given by observation; and it is the necessary and objective, and by no means the subjective or psychological connection which Logic demands. Hence, since experience cannot yield that objective coherence it cannot justify the synthetic *a posteriori* judgment. Nor is the judgment S is P any more justified if we take it in its *analytical* sense. "However much yellow may be already contained in the concept of gold, the judgment "gold is yellow" does not merely assert that the idea of yellow lies in the idea of gold, but ascribes yellowness to gold as its property; gold must therefore have a determinate relation to it, which is not the relation of identity."[1] Judgment, as Lotze insists, does not establish a connection between ideas, but between *facts*. And

[1] *Logic*, § 56.

how one fact can be the other remains unexplained. Indeed, Lotze might have gone further and said that it is altogether impossible to identify any objects given as different.

What, then, can justify us in saying that S is P? "What right have we to assign to S a P, which *is* not S, as a predicate in a categorical judgment? The answer can only be, that we have no right." Nothing can justify the categorical judgment as it stands. For thought also has its laws; and its primary law is the principle of identity which we express positively in the formula $A = A$, negatively in the formula A does not $=$ non-A.[1] And, in accordance with that law S cannot be P. It permits us, on the contrary, only to say that S is S, P is P, and S is *not* P. "*Every* predicate P which differs in any way whatever from S, however friendly to S it might otherwise be conceived to be, is entirely irreconcilable with it; *every* judgment of the form S is P is impossible, and in the strictest sense we cannot get further than saying 'S is S,' and 'P is P.'"[2] The Categorical Judgment seems, therefore, to be irreconcilably inconsistent with the law of identity. Thought which impels us to the formation of such judgments seems to fall foul of its own primary law.

But this is only seeming. For examination will show that it is what the judgment says, not that which it *means*, which is inconsistent with this

[1] See *Logic*, § 54. [2] *Logic*, § 55.

primary law. Taken as they stand, categorical judgments unite, in whole or in part, universal concepts. The subject, for instance, of "Some men are black" seems to be the universal concept "man," but the subject that is *meant* is certain individual men. "It is not left to our choice what individuals we will take out of the whole mass of men; our selection, which makes them 'some' men, does not make them black if they are not so without it; we have, then, to choose those men, and we *mean* all along only those men who are black, in short, negroes; these are the true subject of the judgment. That the predicate is not meant in its universality, that on the contrary only the particular black is meant which is found on human bodies is at once clear. . . . The full sense, then, of the judgment is, 'Some men, by whom however we are only to understand black men, are black men.'"[1] We do not connect any men with any blackness in saying that some men are black; that is to say, the categorical judgment, although it may seem to do so, does not connect universals. We connect the men who are black with a particular blackness, with men who are black with that blackness; that is, we connect definite particulars with definite particulars. The appearance of connecting universals only springs from the fact that in ordinary speech we elide the conditions or accessory notions. *S* is *P* there-

[1] *Logic*, § 58.

fore really *means* that particulars which fall within S are the particulars which fall within P; and we may express this symbolically by saying that S is P is in truth Σ is Π.

Lotze proceeds to show in a similar way that in such Singular Judgments as "Caesar crossed the Rubicon" there are *implied*, but not expressed, accessory ideas which limit the significance of both subject and predicate. It was Caesar at a particular point in his history that crossed the Rubicon once at a particular point in time. "The Caesar whom the subject of this judgment means is that Caesar only whom the predicate characterizes."[1] The S that is P is the S that is qualified by P, and the P that qualifies S is that which is itself qualified by S. S is P therefore really *means* SP is PS, or, more strictly still, perhaps, SP is SP. The categorical judgment is an identical one, because it is a connection not of universals but of particulars. "So far, our result seems to be this: categorical judgments of the form 'S is P' are admissible in practice because they are always conceived in the sense which we have called particular, and as such are ultimately identical."[2] "The judgment, as regards its matter, is perfectly identical, and, as regards its form, it is only synthetical because one and the same subject is expressed from two different points of view."[3]

[1] *Logic*, § 58. [2] *Ibid.*, § 59. [3] *Ibid.*, § 58.

But Lotze is not satisfied with this conclusion, and the reason is obvious. The act of thought in judging, as it is described by Lotze, destroys the judgment and stultifies itself. For the judgment has to express a coherence between the matter of two ideas. But if we add all the supplementary notions which were implied in it, and by means of which alone we could reconcile such a judgment with the primary law of thought, then we have no longer two ideas, but one. The whole content falls into the subject, and the repetition of that subject under the form of a predicate which is identical with it is a perfectly meaningless process. We may as well say 'S' at once, that is, try to point it out as a fact that simply *is* and is related to nothing, as say that the particulars within it are identical with themselves, or that SP is SP, or Σ is Π. For all relations of thought have disappeared with the extinction of difference. "These judgments no longer assert any *mutual relation* between the parts of their *content,* but only that this content as a composite whole is a more or less widely excluded *Fact,* and this is clearly a relapse to the imperfect stage of the impersonal judgment."[1] There results nothing but "simple or composite perceptions, and between the several perceptions, or even the several parts of each composite perception, there could be no expressible connection, such as could show their mere coexist-

[1] *Logic,* § 59.

ence to be due to inner coherence."[1] Thought, whose specific function was to reveal inward coherence between facts, has failed. What it can connect must be identical, and therefore needs no connection; what was different it cannot connect. Nothing remains as the result of the categorical judgment: experience has lapsed back into the contingent form of external association, out of which judgment was to lift it.

Since thought, in the course of the necessary process of forming judgments, thus falls into contradiction with itself, one might expect Lotze to deny either that the function of thought is to relate differences, or else that its primary law is that of identity. But he does neither; for it is not his way to examine hypotheses that have proved untenable. He returns rather upon "the accessory notions," or limiting ideas, and gives them a new interpretation. These accessory notions have, so far, been those ideas which are elided in ordinary speech, but which when expressed turned the universal judgment into a combination of particulars, "ultimately identical with one another." That is to say, if the accessory notions implied in the statement that S is P were made explicit the judgment would take the form Σ is Π, these being the particular facts that are identical. But, henceforth, the accessory notions instead of being additional limiting ideas, confining the subject and predicate to particular facts, are

[1] *Logic*, § 59.

to be considered as *conditions* of a universal and necessary connection between differences. So that these notions which have so far served to remove the difference between the subject and predicate and to produce pure identity, are now to act as principles of unity in difference, and to enable us to combine S and P without completely identifying them, and yet without violating the primary law of thought.

Hence the hypothetical judgment, in which that condition is expressed which was only implied in the Categorical, comes in to justify the process of the unification of differences. S is P is never immediately or unconditionally true, but S is P *if* it is x. Of course there may be some difficulty in conceiving that S can be x, or that $S+x$ can be P, *if the law of Identity*, as Lotze conceives it, *is to hold*. But it is not to hold any longer as the *only* law of thought. Lotze has more than one arrow to his bow. Having seen that "the principle of identity merely asserts the sameness of everything with itself, and that the only relation in which it places different things is that of mutual exclusion,"[1] and that, therefore, all apparent connections between different things are contingent and subjective, he looks round for another principle of thought. He starts with an innocent, academic, "quite general presupposition that the totality of things thinkable and real is not merely a sum

[1] *Logic*, § 61.

which coexists but a whole which coheres." If this presupposition is granted, "then the law of identity has wider consequences. The same *abcq*, with which *p* has once been found in combination, can then, according to the law of identity, never be found in combination with a non-*p*, nor can *this abcq* ever occur without its former predicate *p*."[1] Hence, if we know that *abc* is a coherent whole, and if we are "given *ab*, we know that *c* is the only new element which can necessarily accrue; if we are given *ac*, *b*, and if we are given *bc*, *a*; in other words, whichever of these elements occurs first in any case has in the second the sufficient and necessary condition for the possibility and necessity of the accession of the third. That element or group of elements to which we here give the first place appears to us then logically as the subject; that which we place second, as the condition which operates upon this subject, while the third represents the consequence produced in the subject by the condition."[2] Nor does it matter which of the elements is regarded as reason, which as the thing, and which as consequent, provided they constitute a system. "In itself, every element in such a combination is a function of the rest, and we can pass inferentially from any one to any other."[3] Lotze thinks that it does not matter for Logic whether such a system really exists; for its only task is to find coherence

[1] *Logic*, § 61.   [2] *Ibid.*   [3] *Ibid.*

between the matter of ideas, or to reveal the conditions of "the merely thinkable." The task of Logic at this point "is confined to developing the principle of *Sufficient reason*, which, no less than the principle of identity, has to be regarded as the source of our knowledge." "It has merely to show how, from the combination of two contents of thought, S and Q, the necessity arises of *thinking* a third P, and this in a definite relation to S."[1]

In order to comprehend this process of necessary connection, we must explain the nature of the law of sufficient reason, and that means something more than merely asserting that for every valid statement there must be an adequate ground. We must discover "in what relation reason and consequent stand to each other, and in what sort of a thing we may hope to discover the reason of another thing." Lotze finds that the "reason," taken in its full sense, is "completely identical" with the consequence, "that the one *is* the other." Let $A + B = C$ be the expression of the principle of sufficient reason; then, although "taken by themselves A only $= A$, $B = B$," there is no reason why a particular combination $A + B$ . . . should not be equivalent to, or identical with, the simple content of the new concept C," provided we do not take them by themselves, but as elements in a system. For, if $A + B$ is any given subject, along with the condition by which it is influenced, then C is not a "new predicate which

[1] *Logic*, § 62.

is the consequence of this subject, but the subject itself in its form as altered by the predicate."[1] Ordinarily the reason is supposed to be something different from and additional to the subject, and, in consequence, its identity with the consequent does not appear. But, if we correct this abstraction, and bear in mind that the reason is the *whole* antecedent, that is to say, is the thing *plus* the condition, their identity becomes apparent, because the former passes into the latter and becomes it. The consequent C is simply $A + B$ over again; the explosion *is* the powder at a high temperature.[2] Hence, "sufficient reason" falls, after all, within the principle of identity, or rather, it extends the principle of identity in such a manner as to render it valid of differences—provided, of course, those differences constitute a system of mutually determining elements.

But *is* there such a system ? Or, in other words, have we any right to the "quite general presupposition" we have made ? For, so far, "we were only able to show that an extension of our knowledge is possible *if* there is a principle which allows us to make $A + B = C$." We must endeavour to convert that presupposition into a certainty by revealing its grounds, unless knowledge of the unity of difference, or of a principle of coherence between phenomena, is to remain a baseless hypothesis or mere conjecture. Now the law of identity requires no deduction. We

[1] *Logic*, § 63.   [2] See *Logic*, § 63.

have "an immediate certitude" of it: "we feel immediately that it is necessary, and the opposite of it we feel with equal conviction to be impossible in thought." But the law of sufficient reason is not so advantageously placed. "We do not by any means feel it impossible to suppose that, while every content of thought is self-identical, no combination of two contents is ever equivalent to a third."[1] Neither it nor its opposite impresses us as immediately necessary. Hence it "must be considered as an assumption which serves the purposes of thought . . . and which is guaranteed by the concentrated impression of all experience."[2] The impulse of thought to convert the coexistence of the elements of experience into coherence *implies* such a principle, and an empirical fact confirms the assumption of it. The world of intelligible objects fortunately happens to be constituted in such a way that thought finds coherences, identities, and equivalences between its different elements. It might, it is true, have been constituted otherwise: that is, all its elements might have been incommensurable, without any inner coherence, and connected merely by association, or subjective experience. But its elements are not incommensurable as a matter of fact; and that matter of fact gives the most valuable, although it is only "an empirical confirmation of the principle of sufficient reason." It is admitted that *an* experience would be possible

[1] *Logic*, § 65.   [2] *Ibid.*

without any such law, whereas no experience whatsoever is even conceivable except on the basis of the law of identity. Nevertheless, *our* experience, in which elements which are different are actually combined, is not possible without both of these laws. Hence our experience confirms our assumption of the law of sufficient reason; it is proved that $A + B = C$, that the whole antecedent actually *is* the consequent. It might appear at first sight that the law of identity rendered the combination of differences impossible. But, if these differences are placed within a system, the threatened danger is averted. The principle of identity only insists that a thing shall have a content which is one with itself; it cannot exclude other contents which do not conflict with it; it relates a thing only to itself, and leaves it free to enter into any relations with other things, provided such entrance is possible on some other grounds.[1] And since experience *is* a system of differences within a unity, these other grounds are furnished. Hence thought does convert coincidence into coherence, not immediately or categorically, it is true, but mediately through the fulfilment of a condition.

But although the possibility of combining differences in a unity has been shown, it has not as yet appeared how that combination takes place. In other words, we have seen that a condition is able so to affect the subject as to make it identical with

[1] See *Logic*, § 62.

the predicate, or that *if S is x it is P*; but *how* it has that power has not been shown; we have not actually discovered a principle of coherence. "It remains to determine in each particular case, *what A*, combined in *what* form with *what B*, forms the adequate reason of *what C*."[1] We might, perhaps, discover this empirically in each instance as it arose; but that would not satisfy the demands of logic, which seeks a universal principle of coherence that would enable us to anticipate experience. "There must be at any rate *a* principle which allows us, when once the one truth $A + B = C$ is given, to apply it to cases of which experience has not yet informed us. . . . Whenever we regard $A + B$ as the reason of a consequence C, we necessarily conceive the connection of the three as a *universal* one; $A + B$ would not be a condition of C, if, in a second case of its occurrence, some casual D instead of C might possibly be found combined with it."[2] The connection of an antecedent and a consequent is, therefore, one which takes place in accordance with, or in subordination to, a rule. Any reason cannot bring any consequent; for in that case they would not be a reason and a consequent, and experience would be chaotic. Hence a reason is a reason, and a consequent a consequent, only because they are subordinate to a universal, which gives to each of them its specific character and brings about their connection. That universal has not

[1] *Logic*, § 67.   [2] *Ibid.*

been found. Hence the combination of differences, although indubitable as a fact of our experience, has not been logically justified, nor has the principle which converts coincidence into coherence been discovered. But that is as much as to say that *the function of thought is not even yet explained*; and in order to do so we must pass beyond the hypothetical form of judgment.

Now we find an example of a combination which is universal in such a judgment as "Man is Mortal," in which it is implied that "it lies in the character of mankind that mortality is inseparable from every one who partakes in it."[1] The combination in this case is not contingent. "The general judgment lets the reason of its necessary truth be seen through it"; man and mortality fall under some law which universally connects them, so that if the one is, the other is also. And yet we must not fall into the error of thinking that the universal "man" is connected with the universal "mortality." The universal "man" does not die, and no death is death in general. What is meant is that *if* any one is man he is mortal. Hence, "the general judgment is properly an abbreviated hypothetical judgment, in its full form it ought to stand—If any S is a man, this S is a mortal."[2]

But even this second statement is not complete; for we have allowed the predicate, mortality, to remain a universal. But a universal predicate—a

[1] *Logic*, § 68.   [2] *Ibid.*

mortality in general, is as little possible as a universal subject—a man in general; and universal mortality can as little attach to an individual man as a universal man can die. That which is expressed in the predicate is a universal, but what was meant is some particular instance of that universal. Hence, if we bring out the meaning of a proposition S is P and express all its implications, it will take the following form: "If any S is an M it is either p^1, or p^2, or p^3, and here p^1 p^2 p^3 mean the different kinds of a universal mark P which is contained in the generic concept M."[1] Seeing that S is subjected to a condition M, and can be P only if it is an M, that concept M acts in the way of a rule upon S, compelling it to have as a predicate some one particular form of P. "The subordination of S to M implies that S must choose its own predicate from amongst p^1 p^2 p^3, the specific forms of P."[2] Thus, at length, the effort of thought to combine the matter of ideas in a necessary way seems about to be successful. The Disjunctive Judgment which thus grows out of the hypothetical, represents thought as articulating experience into a system; for it combines an individual subject with an individual predicate. And as the particulars which it brings together are not *mere* particulars, but are instances of a universal, as they all fall under M, the connection is necessary.

Nevertheless, even the disjunctive judgment has

[1] *Logic*, § 69.   [2] *Ibid.*, § 71.

a defect. It does not connect the subject with any particular predicate, but only goes so far as to show that its predicate must have a certain character, must be, that is, some one of a number of instances of a universal to the exclusion of the others. But it gives no indication as to which is the one. The differentia of the disjunctive judgment is that "it gives its subject no predicate at all, but prescribes to it the alternative between a number of different predicates."[1] The universal does not enable the subject to grasp its own particular predicate, although it shuts it amongst others as within an enclosure. Nor can "the decision *what* p^1 or p^2 belongs to S come from the fact (which is thus far only the fact) that S is subordinate to M, for it is just because it is a species of M that it is still free to choose: that decision can only come from the specific difference by which S, as *this* species of M, is distinguished from other species of it."[2] Hence the subject must be more accurately defined than can be done by merely placing it under an M, so that when this specification is accomplished it may appear that it is p^1, and not any other, which must be its predicate. But no further kind of Judgment is available to perform this task, and we must pass on to another form of thought, namely Inference. Inference may exhibit the success of thought in producing a universal which shall make the contents of experience

---

[1] *Logic*, § 69.   [2] *Ibid.*, § 75.

cohere: so far the principle of necessary combination has escaped us.

I have considered it necessary to follow with considerable care the exposition which Lotze gives of the manner in which thought performs its function of combining in judgment. It may be possible to gain greater clearness by bringing his main points together in a summary.

So far two main steps have been taken by thought proper; one from perception to conception, and one from conception to judgment. The first step is only made possible through the sub-conscious elaboration of the original data, namely, states or changes of consciousness into individual and single but complex ideas which refer to objects. It consists in bringing into evidence the existence of principles of coherence between the material thus combined, and it either displaces the contingent by the necessary, or else shows that the contingent was really never there. It either abolishes the associative consciousness by showing that it is a stage in the growth of the thought- or reflective-consciousness, or else it leaves consciousness divided into a higher and a lower section. In either case, thought arrives at conceptions, or universal ideas; ideas, that is, whose elements are themselves universal, and are combined by a universal.

The second step from conception to judgment is taken because the impulse which led thought from the particular datum of experience to universal concepts has not yet been satisfied. The overt reason alleged by Lotze for taking this step is that concepts, serially arranged in a sort of hierarchy, could only represent a static, or frozen world, and would miss all the movement and change which is continually pressed upon us by experience. But a deeper reason than this incidentally reveals itself as he proceeds; it is that the concept has not really enabled us to see how the principle of coherence operates—how a universal can combine differences. No principle of unity has been discovered, and the uniting activity of objective thought, though present in conception, has not been logically justified. The whole and the parts fall asunder, whether we regard that whole as a constant nucleus amidst change in time, or as a universal amidst differences, both above time. It is manifestly the object of judgment to bring these together, or else to show that, and why, they are already together in the concept. For there lie before us precisely the same option and ambiguity as in the case of the perception and the conception. That is to say, just as we may conceive the conception either as something new, or as an evolution of the old, as bringing in a principle of coherence for the first time or as revealing such a principle in the perception, so we may conceive judgment either as the process whereby universals are first brought together, or as a process which reveals the universals as already combined in a universal manner in conception. According to the first view, judgment is a process which unites conceptions which have been already made, and judgment rests upon conception as a later process impossible without the first; according to the second, the concept is an implicit judgment, and in passing from the former to the latter we are following the development of a single function, rendering explicit what was present in conception from the first, and therefore basing conception upon, or what is the same thing, explaining conception in the light of judgment. Judgment on this last view would become the primary and fundamental activity of thought. But in either case, what we are trying to solve is the logical question of the possibility of making the coexistent coherent, and of the methods which thought employs in doing so. This is accomplished, in the first instance, in the Categorical Judgment S is P—the Impersonal Judgment may be set aside for the present as a merely imperfect form of the Categorical, or as the Categorical in the making. But the Categorical Judgment fails to bring S and P together. "S is not P; it only *has* P," and it remains to make really clear what constitutes this "having" which we oppose to "being."[1] It fails because the immediate identification of S and P, which the Categorical Judgment *expresses*, would violate the primary law of thought, namely, the law of identity. All we can possibly have in

[1] *Logic*, § 51.

accordance with that law is S is S, and P is P. That is, instead of making S and P coherent in virtue of a universal principle which inwardly unites them, they are allowed to remain hard, exclusive units. We can, at the very best, only associate them. Hence the categorical judgment, instead of furnishing the principle of coherence, only shows the need of it. In other words, the attempt to justify the categorical judgment logically, shows that we require a universal, or condition under which it becomes possible to make such a judgment. The universal, which was merely implicit in the concept, remains merely implicit in the categorical judgment. But the task of logic is just to make this principle explicit, to reveal its presence as constitutive in the function of thought. Now the hypothetical judgment seems to perform that task. It gives definite expression to the condition under which the universal combines the particular. Instead of S is P, which is impossible to a thought that is governed by the law of identity, we have, *If S is x, S is P*. The protasis expresses the principle of coherence between S and P, so that we seem to have succeeded in catching and fixing the Universal.

But we have not shown that, or how it combines the elements, nor exhibited the law by which it determines that S under the condition x shall veritably be P. We have only the bare assertion *that* it does so, an assertion which, as it stands, is as little justified as the categorical assertion that S is P. The *immediate* transition from S to P was proved to be impossible; we have now to justify the mediate transition through a condition. That is, we have actually to apply the condition to the conditioned, the universal to the particulars. So that precisely the same problem of finding coherence still lies before us. But its form has changed. Instead of discovering a universal we have now to apply it to particulars; or, in other words, we have to make the condition effective in distinct and different instances. That, of course, is done by experience; but it is done according to a principle, and logic has to discover that principle. The first step in this discovery is made by the Disjunctive Judgment, according to which S is, not P in general, for that is impossible, but some particular P, such as p^1, or p^2, or p^3. So that instead of the conditional judgment "If S is x it is P," we have "If S is x it is either p^1, or p^2, or p^3." We have, in other words, to subordinate both the subject and the predicate to a universal in order to bring about the coherence of their contents. We cannot combine universals, for universals cannot be identified: S cannot be P. And it is obvious that we cannot make *mere* particulars cohere. Hence our only refuge is to make the particulars examples of, or cases within, a universal. And this is done in the Disjunctive Judgment; for our S is not *any* S, but an S conditioned, an S which is an x; and our p^1, p^2, p^3, are not *any* predicates, but cases of the universal P, which, together, exhaust its content. Here, therefore, is the combination of particulars into coherency by means of universals—the thing we sought.

But our task is not finished even yet. For the hypothetical, while it combines the elements within the system which constitutes the subject S with the elements within the system which constitute the predicate P, both of which in turn fall under M, does not show what element of S is combined with what element of P. s^1, s^2, s^3 within S may go respectively with p^1, p^2, and p^3 within P; but s^1 may also go with p^2 or p^3, s^2 with p^1 or p^3, and S^3 with p^1 or p^2. The Disjunctive leaves us with this option in our hands, and affords us no further guidance. It does not define the s that is to go with p, or the p that attaches to an s. The universals fail to grasp the particulars, and s^1 is as little inwardly coherent with p^1, or p^2, or p^3 as S is coherent with P. Hence we must pass altogether beyond the judgment, which can do no more; and seek in the major and minor premises of inference the connection of the elements which will justify us in saying that S is P, or, in other words, which will actually combine the different.

Whether "thought as inference" succeeds in this task in which thought as judgment has failed we must enquire in the next chapter. I now turn to the examination of this most important and instructive part of Lotze's doctrine of thought. I have already indicated at the beginning of this chapter the inconsistency that lies in Lotze's account of the relation between judging and conceiving. He definitely states[1] that Judgment cannot precede conception, because that act of thought consists in uniting conceptions. And in §§ 34, 35 of his *Logic* he speaks as if a conceptual view of the world of thought could be completed without the aid of judgment. The need of judgment is there represented as springing from the fact that the view which conceptions arranged in an ascending order gives of the world, is an *image of a fixed order*, while the world of experience is a world which is always changing. Judgment must come in, in order to deal with this process of 'Becoming' after the manner in which conception deals with static 'Being.' Mr. Bosanquet regards the distinction which Lotze draws on this ground as practically a hasty oversight, and it is quite true that Lotze makes no use of it, *i.e.*, he does not confine Conception to Being and Judgment to Becoming. He proceeds rather to show that Judgment continues on a higher level the attempt of conception to bring the coincident into coherence; and the problem of change sinks into a case of the general problem of difference or negation. Conception had failed to reveal explicitly the

[1] *Logic*, § 8.

bond that seems to combine its content, or the manner in which it is applied to the content; and judgment seizes the material and "reconstitutes it in a form which at the same time expresses the ground of the coherence in the matter combined." On this view judgment would be implied in conception, and conception and judgment would be the same function of thought at different stages of development.

Now while admitting that Lotze in confining Conception to Being and Judgment to Becoming is only giving expression to a casual opinion which was not thought out, I must consider the inconsistency which he still allows to remain as indicative of a radical flaw in Lotze's view of the function of thought. It indicates two tendencies which are always at war in his doctrine: a conscious tendency to represent thought as formal, and an unconscious tendency to regard it as constitutive; a tendency to divide thought into sections externally or mechanically related, and a tendency to regard all its stages as the evolution of one function. It is an example of what we must continually witness in his method: he starts from a certain presupposition as to the nature of thought, finds in the attempt to trace its operation that he is obliged to treat the presupposition as if it were false, and nevertheless he refuses to abandon it. We have seen some signs of this already in the difficulties into which he falls in dealing with the associative consciousness and the first form of the reflective or thought consciousness. The datum of experience is taken, to begin with, as a manifold of sensations, and consequently the only combination of which it is capable is an external one. This first combination he attributes to a psychical mechanism, and thereby he escapes the problem of explaining how it is possible. He does not see that it is *impossible*, that a pure manifold cannot in any manner be combined, that no combining principle *can* be external, that, as he himself insists *elsewhere*, a relation which is merely *between* things is inconceivable and impracticable. Or, if we insist that he does see this,—and that also would not be difficult to prove,—we are forced to admit that he does not regard the original datum as itself carrying within it the characteristics of thought; that is to say, he does not give up the presupposition, proved untenable by his process, that thought has to deal with a manifold. To reconstitute his starting point so as to make it consistent with his results would have been to admit the truth of Idealism which makes thought think thought, and reality itself inwardly ideal.

We have also seen the same inconsistency in the second stage, that is, in the relation of the associative consciousness to conception, or of co-incident to coherent perceptions. He starts with a mere subjective bond of temporal and spatial relations between perceptions, but, in order to bring these together into concepts he has to invent objective universals between them. That is, he has to qualify perceptions by conceptions, which is to deny their particularity and isolation. He has to invent sense universals, which are identical in everything except in name with the thought universals which he has assumed to be not present. But, as before, the fact that perceptions *must* be combined into conceptions in order that knowledge may be possible, and the fact that perceptions if they are merely associated or combined externally cannot really be combined at all, do not lead him to reconstitute his starting point and deny that perceptions *are* thus singular and isolated. He allows the presupposition which has proved untenable to remain, and therefore he thinks himself still justified in holding that thought is formal and not constitutive, and that it deals with an alien datum.

We have precisely the same inconsistency in his view of the relation of conception and judgment. Conceptions are *assumed* to be isolated, and judgment has to form a connection between them. *S* and *P* in the categorical judgment have to be *brought* together; they are given to judgment in order to be connected, but it becomes clearer than ever that if they are to be connected they must have been already connected: they must have been coherent in virtue of a condition which the Hypothetical judgment reveals as present all along. And yet this does not lead Lotze to reconsider his original assumption that the terms of the judgment are first independent, or that the function of the judgment is to connect ideas. That is, he does not cease to regard the judgment as a combination of elements first given in their isolation, and then brought together by means of a copula, and therefore he is obliged to regard judging as a process subsequent to, and indeed different from, conception.

We have then to observe the difficulties into which Lotze is led by his view of the judgment as "an expression of the relation between the matters of two ideas." The first attempt of judgment, which takes the categorical form, is met with a definite *non possumus* springing from the fundamental law of all thought, namely, the law of identity. Instead of finding how S and P are united, we discovered that they cannot possibly be united in that judgment. If they were different before, they remain different. To make the one "unconditionally the other while both stand over against each other as different is quite impracticable to thought." This is obviously true, *if* S and P were originally mere differences, and *if* the law of identity excludes all difference. But Lotze does not turn back on these presuppositions. On the contrary, having failed to make S and P unconditionally one, he endeavours to make them conditionally one. For although the law of identity forbids us to say at once that S is P, we may say, nevertheless, that S is P if S is x.

But *how* can S ever be *x*? Are not the difficulties of identifying S with its own condition precisely the same as those of identifying any other two things which are given as different? Lotze virtually admits this, and instead of connecting S and P by means of a condition he drops them, and connects Σ and Π. "The true subject is not the universal S but Σ, a determinate instance of it; and the true predicate is not the universal P but Π, a particular modification of it; and the relation asserted is not between S and P, but between Σ and Π; and the relation is no longer a synthetical, nor even an analytical one, but simply one of identity."[1] In order to connect S and P, Lotze has to abandon some facts contained in the universal, and to confine himself to certain particular ones, which are known to be identical in the subject and in the predicate! He rejects the universals S and P for particular instances of each, on the ground that it was these latter which we really meant to combine. But if they are "*instances*" of universals, they are themselves universals; hence it would be necessary to analyze these in turn, if we are to find the "instances" in them which are really combinable. And the process would repeat itself *ad infinitum*. Nor would it ever succeed, nor approach success. For "instances" of universals can never be particular; and yet unless they are instances of a universal they cannot be

[1] *Logic*, § 57.

combined. Hence they either cannot be combined, or they do not need to be combined. In other words, if we have to analyze S and P into Σ and Π in order to combine them, we likewise have to analyze Σ and Π into s and p, s and p into σ and π, and still they would not be particulars; and if they were they would not combine. It is because he is uneasily conscious of this difficulty that Lotze is found to hint that we must either give up the possibility of making synthetical judgments, or else find their guarantee in "immediate perception."[1] But that is as much as to say that thought cannot produce coherence, which is its only task.

It should be evident at once that the synthesis of the elements of knowledge into a system by means of thought is impossible if the fundamental law of thought is that of *mere* identity. Lotze's conclusions seem at times to be about to force this admission from him. He does admit explicitly, as we have seen, that the law of mere identity instead of identifying things simply isolates them irremediably, defeating its own sole purpose.[2] But he does not give it up as a logical phantasm, or conceive the law of identity which thought actually employs as a law of difference as well, inasmuch as identity is meaningless and impossible except as the identity of differences. Instead of this, which would involve the repudiation of a universal *plus* differences, relations *plus* points on which to hang them, that is, the

[1] See *Logic*, § 99.   [2] *Ibid.*, § 361 ff.

repudiation of an *external* relation between the universal and the particular, the concept and its contents, the judgment and its parts, Lotze has recourse to another law of thought which is not only different from but inconsistent with the first law, as he conceives it. He attempts to escape the formalism and tautology of pure thought, as he conceived it, by subordinating its activities to the law of reason and consequent, and by *assuming* as a starting point of knowledge the systematic form of unity in difference, which the law of identity has proven to be unthinkable.

Now, I am not concerned to deny the validity of this new departure by the assumption of a system. On the contrary, the cardinal error of Lotze's view of thought seems to me to lie in the fact that it is not *originally* and *consistently* based upon the conception of system. He is driven to adopt it by the failure of the tautological view to which he is at first committed; but instead of repudiating that view on the ground that it leads to a deadlock, he endeavours to set the second view side by side with it. There are for him two laws of thought—that of identity and that of reason and consequent; there are two kinds of universals, one which proves empty and fails to combine differences, and one which only exists within a system, and which therefore permeates these differences; there are two kinds of particulars, or of thought contents, those which lie asunder awaiting combination by the act of judgment, and those which determine each other, which are *conditions* and which, therefore, are already universals, though not *bare* universals. There is nothing within the whole theory of thought more important than the distinction between these two views. "Logic," as Mr. Bosanquet has said, "is little more than an account of the forms and modes in which a universal *does* or *does not* affect the differences through which it persists. All turns on the distinction between the abstract or powerless, and the concrete or dominant universal."[1] But Lotze, while distinguishing the two, uses either of them according to his convenience, and does not see that if the one of them is the universal of thought the other is not.

The question which Lotze has to face is the possibility of making the transition from the first of these to the second; and he is not entirely unconscious of the difficulty. He raises the question of our "right to translate those supplementary additions, to which the true subject of the then identical judgment owed its origin, into *Conditions*."[2] It is interesting to observe his answer. He arrives at it, as we have seen, by the way of *assuming* that knowledge is systematic, or that it is "a whole which coheres." He finds the possibility of such coherence to lie, in the first place, in the existence of the law of sufficient reason, according to which one element is able to *determine* another, and, according to which, therefore, each of the elements is not

[1] *Logic*, Vol. II., p. 3. [2] *Logic*, § 61.

a particular but an instance of a *concrete* or dominant universal. Having made these assumptions of a system, and of a principle of sufficient reason, he is able to proceed further towards representing the process whereby the universal principle manifests itself in systematic knowledge—though, as I shall have occasion to point out, he repeatedly lapses into his original view of the universal as "abstract and powerless." But he acknowledges, to begin with, that the whole view rests on an assumption. How, then, does he justify it? *First*, by a reason which, *as he represents it*, is entirely empirical. " It serves the purposes of thought." It is useful. It is even indispensable *to us*, an essential characteristic of *our* thought. But it is not essential to thought as thought, for he finds a world of knowledge conceivable in which everything should be incommensurable, a world, that is, of associated ideas in which the concepts lie idly and peacefully side by side, no one of them conditioning or conditioned. It happens that our world of our knowledge is not such a world. It happens, too, that reality as we know it corresponds to such knowledge as issues from the conception of a system dominated by a principle of sufficient reason. But the first of these is fortuitous, and the second is a "fortunate" accident, "a fortunate trait in the organization of the thinkable world, a trait which does really exist, but has not the same necessity for existing as the principle of identity." In truth, on this view, it has not any *necessity.* Its opposite is neither unthinkable nor impossible in fact; but it *happens* to be so. It is guaranteed, no doubt, by "the concentrated impression of experience," whatever that means. But it has not "immediate certitude like the principle of identity." We do not "*feel* it immediately to be necessary, nor feel its opposite to be impossible in thought."[1] Lotze is therefore obliged, in *the second* place, to bring it into relation with the principle of identity which *has* this immediate necessity; and he calls it an "extension" of this latter principle. He endeavours to prove that it is an extension by directly identifying the subject, when qualified by the condition, with the consequent, and saying that $A + B$ *is* C. "Taken by themselves A only $= A$, $B = B$." But there dwells such efficacy in the condition, or relation between A and B, which is symbolized by the sign $+$, that $A + B$ becomes "equivalent to, or identical with, the simple content of the new concept C." "Reason and consequence are completely identical, and the one *is* the other." If it is objected that the principle of identity bars them against identification if they are different, and that if they are *not* different, we cannot distinguish them into reason and consequent, Lotze replies—"The possibility of mutual relations between what is different is not really threatened by the principle of identity, . . . it cannot exclude other contents which do not conflict with it."[2] And

---

[1] See *Logic*, § 65 *ff.*   [2] *Logic*, § 62.

this answer is quite valid. But it is valid only if we regard the principle of identity as at the same time a principle of difference. As a law of *mere* identity it cannot exclude other contents, as Lotze says; but it fails to exclude just because it has no content of its own: having no content of its own there is nothing in it to exclude or militate against anything whatsoever. Nothing can either exclude or include except that which has meaning, except a universal which is concrete. Mere identity is inconsistent with nothing, because it is itself nothing. *All* relations disappear where differences cease to exist, and amongst them that of identity itself. Bare identity thus, on Lotze's own showing, allows the whole content of experience to lie in irremediable chaos. He would allow the law, indeed, to apply to single percepts, and to ensure the consistency of an object with itself. But it is evident that it cannot do even this unless the object is absolutely simple and empty. In attempting to reduce the law of sufficient reason into an extension of the principle of identity, Lotze is unconsciously forced to do the opposite, and to regard identity as itself an implicit principle of self-differentiation. But, as before, the results into which he is forced do not lead him to reconsider his starting point; he allows the law of mere identity, and that of sufficient reason, to lie side by side in the same consciousness, and he subjects thought to two fundamental laws which, as represented by him, are radically inconsistent with each other.

But although these two laws are allowed to exist side by side they have not the same value; their authority is different in character because, as we have seen, it is different in its source. At the foundation of the validity of "Identity" there is "immediate conviction," "the *feeling* of its necessity," and the *feeling* of the impossibility of its opposite. But "Sufficient reason" is summoned into existence in order to account for the possibility of an assumption—an assumption, however, which *happens* to be true; for *our* knowledge *is* systematic, though it might have been otherwise.

Now the difference which Lotze finds between these two laws is important for two reasons. In the first place, it shows that he derives the ultimate principle of knowledge from a subjective source; and, in the second place, it shows that the transition from the categorical to the hypothetical judgment is not, as at first appears, a movement in the gradual process of discovering the ultimate conditions of thought.

That the ultimate starting point of Lotze is psychological scarcely needs proof. The *feeling* of the necessity of the law is not merely something which *accompanies* that necessity. In that sense there would be no occasion to deny Lotze's view. There is no doubt that appropriate feelings accompany every activity of the intelligence, or that every exercise of thought or will has its own emotional quality. But to Lotze this feeling of necessity is not merely a subjective suggestion of the value of a necessity already in existence, but it generates the necessity itself. In other words, if we ask Lotze why we should believe in the validity of the law of identity, he lays his hand upon his heart and answers, "I feel that it is true, and so do you." But if we reply that many men, women, and children, feel many other things to be true, and afterwards find that they have deceived themselves, and ask him why this feeling should be more trusted than others, he can give no answer. He might, indeed, point to its universality in the sense that everyone feels it; but, of course, that may be due to a contingency that has never *happened* to vary. Necessity can never be attained by that path. Nor has "immediate conviction" any right to be authoritative. In the progress of knowledge we are continually overturning our "immediate convictions." The very essence of all proof, whose function and aim is to create and justify conviction, is to supplant immediate by mediate conviction. The superiority of thought over sense lies in its relativity. But Lotze, by running the principle of knowledge back into immediate conviction, turns that superiority into a defect. He is unfaithful to the greatest lesson that Kant, whom he professes to follow, has taught to the modern world, namely, that *no truth has the right to convince except the whole truth.* Systematic knowledge is to him a contingent affair. Clinging to the associationism which vitiates his whole procedure, he desires some one fixed point of certainty to which he would attach all other knowledge; and he finds that fixed point, that principle of all objectivity, in the most subjective of all facts, namely in a particular feeling. He bases the pyramid of knowledge upon its apex, as if that process had not been proved by Kant and his predecessors to end in its ruin; and he is therefore loyal, not so much to the constructive as to the sceptical element in Kant's doctrine.

But he has concealed that scepticism under a show of a dialectical movement from coincidence to coherence. The transition from perception to conception, from conception to judgment, and from the categorical judgment to the hypothetical, seems to spring from an impulse inherent in thought, to make explicit the operation of a concrete, dominant universal in all particulars. We seem to be going back gradually upon the systematic conditions in virtue of which alone our knowledge is possible. The categorical judgment seems to push us on to the hypothetical, because the latter contains the condition of the possibility of the former. S is P seems to be possible only if both S and P fall under a condition, or, in other words, are parts or elements in a system. And that would involve that the law of identity is itself explained in the light of, and therefore derives its authority from, the law of sufficient reason. The unity and the differences which are both implicit in the law of identity, the universal and the particulars which are both bare, are made explicit in the second law, which, so far, brings to light a system of mutually related elements, and holds in its hand a unity, a universal, which is concrete. That system, as I shall show, and as Lotze himself in a manner shows, becomes still more evident in the disjunctive judgment. But by subordinating reason and consequent to identity, Lotze has robbed this process of all its meaning; and by regarding the authority of "the system of knowledge" as inferior to that of immediate conviction of a particular truth, he has stultified the deepest impulse of thought, namely, the impulse to mediation or coherence. On his principles, having found that the attempt to say that S *is* P really results in "asserting the sameness of everything with itself, and in placing two different things in the relation of mutual exclusion," we should cease to endeavour to mediate or relate. The end of thought, dominated by such a principle of identity, is not to say that S is P *if* S is x; nor even that S is S, and P is P; but to say S, or P, and to be unable to proceed from the one to the other. Instead of thinking, which is mediating or relating, we should point with the finger; and even the act of pointing to an object S or P would convey more meaning than we have a right to express on this theory.

Lotze is saved from this issue only by his inconsistency. But that the unconscious drift of his thought leads him to the verge of this absolute scepticism will become more evident when we come to consider the ultimate results of his doctrine, and in particular the manner in which he makes "thought" and all its process secondary to sensible and supersensible perception.

If this criticism of Lotze's procedure is just, comparatively little value can attach to his transition from the Conditional to the Disjunctive Judgment—a transition which in his hands is not at all clear. Partly on this account, and partly because I believe, as Mr. Bosanquet indicates, that the disjunctive judgment is not anterior to the more elementary forms of inference, I shall deal with it here very briefly.

It is evident that Lotze's intention in passing from the hypothetical to the disjunctive judgment is to complete the connection of particulars by universals. From his mode of representing matters it might seem that all that is done in the latter which was not done in the former is the substitution of the particulars within P, namely p^1 p^2 p^3, for P. But such substitution in itself marks no advance. The only difference between the hypothetical and disjunctive types he furnishes is that the latter is a hypothetical weakened by doubt. 'If S is M it is p^1 p^2 p^3' is not necessarily a true disjunctive. There is no more disjunction, to take a concrete example, in the statement, "If this animal is a mammal, it is either a horse, or a cow, or a dog, etc.," than in the statement, "If this animal is a mammal, it is a vertebrate." The essence of disjunction does not consist in the freedom to choose amongst several particular predicates, but in the *necessity* to choose some *one* of them to the exclusion of the others, that necessity springing from the subject in such a manner that the predicates must be one of a certain number *because* they constitute, and together exhaust, a system. We cannot say whether "If S is M it is p^1, p^2, or p^3," is a true disjunctive or not, unless we know that S acquires such a character through its relation to M as to articulate itself in these predicates. Without that knowledge the proposition simply expresses a hypothesis which is further weakened by doubt or ignorance. In the proposition, "A triangle is either equilateral, isosceles, or scalene," we have true disjunction; for our conception of a triangle (1) compels it to take one of these forms, and (2) to take one only, and (3) excludes all other alternatives as impossible. These alternatives, therefore, form a system of mutually related parts within the single conception of the triangle. And if we wish to show how the hypothetical judgment develops itself into a disjunctive, we must show how the idea of "condition" implies this conception of a system.[1] But the emergence of the conception of a system in the Disjunctive Judgment is by no means emphasized by Lotze as the vital matter in this transition. On the

[1] This question is admirably worked out in Dr. Bosanquet's *Logic*.

contrary, we might conclude from his exposition that the idea of system was already adequately expressed in the hypothetical judgment, which is by no means true. No doubt that idea is *involved* in the hypothetical; it is present even in the categorical. It is just this implication of a system in the most elementary form of judgment, and its fuller expression in the sequent forms as we ascend to the disjunctive which give unity to the logical act, and make thought one function. S is P *only* because a condition under which both fall is fulfilled; that is to say, only because they are elements in a universal, or parts in a system. This is brought out in the transition to the hypothetical. But it is imperfectly brought out. The hypothetical judgment, "If S is M it is P," expresses only the dependence of P upon S, and S upon P. That is to say, M is shown to be necessary to S, and S to P; but P does not seem to be necessary to S, nor S to M. The relation is not *shown* to be mutual, and, therefore, the system is not complete. Thought *seems*, in the hypothetical form, to be in pursuit of a universal which is necessarily always receding. For just as S could not be P unless it was M, so it cannot be M unless it is N, and it cannot be N unless it is O. And so on *ad infinitum*. The universal which is to enable us to combine the elements of experience always escapes us. We are obliged under this form of thought to explain everything in terms of something else, and consequently we can never completely explain anything. But although it is only a condition which is *expressed* in the hypothetical, a self-inclusive system is *implied*. For if M is verily the reason of S, then S is also the reason of M. Once we escape from the confusion of taking the rational nexus of reason and consequent as if it were a causal sequence in time, it will become evident that if either conception is a reason for the other it may also be derived from it. So that the hypothetical implies mutual or systematic relation. It is this implication which is made explicit in the disjunctive judgment, whose essence is that it expresses the conception of a universal which articulates itself in a number of elements that mutually exclude each other, and, taken together, exhaust or constitute the whole. From this point of view, the sequence of the forms of the judgment becomes intelligible; they take their place in the series according to the fulness with which they express the universal, which *from the first* is present in judgment as the condition of its possibility. But this conception of a self-articulating universal is necessarily foreign to a theory of thought which starts from the presupposition that the function of thought is to connect elements given as discrete. In other words, it necessitates a view of the nature of thought which is fundamentally different from Lotze's. Its highest law cannot be that of mere identity, but a system of related differences;

its principle cannot be an abstract and powerless, but must be a concrete universal that produces its own differences and holds them within itself; its starting point must be coherence and not coincidence; its task must be the articulation of a unity, not a combination of differences. The movement of Lotze's own thought forces him towards it, and exposes point by point the unsatisfactory character of its opposite. But instead of yielding up the associative view based upon bare identity as radically false, he endeavours to correct its errors by combining with it the systematic or idealistic view; and the result is that the latter hovers before him as an ideal which is both necessary and unattainable, and that while he is satisfied that the mechanical view of knowledge in which its parts are externally related is inadequate and even finally self-contradictory, ending both with universals that are empty and particulars that are disconnected, he is unable to rise to the organic view. And his doctrine culminates in condemning thought because it *is* thought, and in an endeavour to escape out of the sphere of relation into that of dogmatism, or of immediate perception and feeling, which he denominates "Faith."

CHAPTER V

LOTZE'S DOCTRINE OF INFERENCE AND THE SYSTEMATIC FORMS OF THOUGHT

LOTZE'S definition of inference is strictly analogous to his definition of judgment. As judgment "combines the matter of two ideas," so "The form of thought which combines two judgments so as to produce a third is, speaking generally, *inference*."[1] Thought is driven to the use of this form by the failure of the disjunctive judgment to determine the subject in such a manner that a definite predicate shall necessarily belong to it. That judgment left us a choice; and choice, unguided by any principle, is nothing better than chance. The task of further defining the subject, so as to bring to light a completely determining principle, is taken up in the first place by *Subsumptive Inference*, of which there are three forms; namely (1) the Aristotelian Syllogism, (2) Induction, (3)

[1] *Logic*, § 74.

Analogy. I propose to follow, as briefly as possible, Lotze's account of these forms.

The most perfect types of the Aristotelian Syllogism are, of course, to be found in the first figure, in which a particular case, expressed in the minor premiss is explicitly brought under the general rule expressed in the major. But that general rule may be understood in two ways, namely, as an Analytic or as a Synthetic Judgment. If we take it in the Analytic sense, that is to say, if we understand in saying M is P, that P falls into M as one of its marks without which M could not be conceived, then the universal rule is certainly valid. But in that case we cannot subordinate the minor to this rule without *presupposing* that it is an instance which falls under the rule. This will appear at once if we take a concrete instance. If "All bodies have weight," and if "air is a body," then certainly "air has weight." But we have assumed that air has weight in assuming that it is a body; and the general rule is not possible unless the truth of the special instance particularized in the minor premiss is assumed. Hence, the two premises, instead of enabling us to advance to a new conclusion from their own independent truth, are themselves valid only on the supposition of its truth.[1] If air has not weight, then air is not a body, or some bodies have not weight, that is to say, both the major and the minor presuppose the

[1] *Logic*, §§ 98, 99.

conclusion. Instead of an inference we have a *petitio principii*, "a double circle"; and this form of inference represents thought as tautologous.

If we take the general rule, or major premiss, in a Synthetic sense, we shall avoid this apparently vain repetition. Having combined M with something new, P, in the major, we are also able to combine S with it, seeing that S is M. In this case the conclusion, S is P, would be a further characterization of S, and we should have advanced by inference to a new truth. But, on the other hand, we have not as yet found any logical justification for such a synthetic major. In other words, it has not been shown how we *can* add a new mark P to the subject M; and, until that is seen, the validity of the major, and, therefore, of all the subsequent inference which depends upon it, remains doubtful. Thus the Aristotelian syllogism throws no light upon this problem, and the subsumption which it attempted proves to be impossible, or is at least quite unjustified. In the first case, there was no subsumption, in the sense of bringing anything new under the rule, or of proceeding to a third truth from two given truths: there was only repetition. In the second case there is subsumption, the conclusion is new, but it is not *proved*, because the truth of the major is not demonstrated. Taken analytically the syllogism is valid but tautological; taken synthetically it is progressive, but not demonstrably valid, and, therefore, not logical inference.

In both cases alike the principle of coherence fails to bind together new elements; for in the first case there is no advance, and in the second there is no necessary bond. Hence, either inference is not a synthetic movement of thought, or else syllogistic subsumption is no example of it. But Lotze does not permit us to doubt the first of these alternatives, or to reject "the really fruitful exercise of thought. There must be a method for finding minor premises which subordinate a given subject to a genus before it has been shown to possess fully all the marks of that genus."[1] That is to say, there must be a way of avoiding the futile tautology of the first form. But that is as much as to say that there must be a universal which has in itself a right to connect elements that are new; or, in other words, there must be a way of demonstrating the validity of the synthetic universal of the major premiss. One way suggests itself at once, namely, that of subjecting it to a condition from which it necessarily follows. But this method of justifying the universal would simply lead to an infinite regress: the discovery of the universal that carries necessity within itself is simply postponed, and the syllogism can neither justify itself nor derive its justification from anything else.

This endless regress might conceivably be arrested in two ways: (1) we might perceive immediately the synthetic universal required, that is to say, it

[1] *Logic*, § 100.

might be given us straightway as a fact; (2) we might be able to find within thought itself a principle which justifies us in regarding a synthesis as universal *before* we had actually observed within it the presence of all its particulars. The first alternative is set aside by Lotze. He is *here* not sure whether " the immediate perception of the universal truth of a synthetical judgment is possible," and he is clear that we should be " only very rarely in a position to rest the content of a universal major premiss upon this ground." In other words, we should be justified *only now and then* in resting our ultimate principle upon a purely dogmatic foundation! So he adopts the second alternative, and seeks to find a way of making the major synthetic *a priori, i.e.*, to find a law of thought which justifies us in asserting a universal of a content which we have not already included within it. Such a law seems to be operative in the second and third forms of subsumption: namely, in *Inductive* and *Analogical* inference.

"The problem of all inferential processes," he says, "is naturally this, from given data or premises to develop as much new truth as possible."[1] Now, experience presents us continually with premises which show that a number of different subjects have identical marks, and which show that a number of similar subjects have different marks. We might express such premises respectively by the

[1] *Logic*, § 101.

symbols *PM, SM, TM, VM,* and *MP, MS, MT, MV.* The problem in each case is to discover a law within these premises which will hold universally, and, therefore, in subjects and marks which lie beyond the limits of our observation. We solve this problem when we infer by *Induction* and *Analogy*. In the former case we extend our universal over new *subjects, LMN, WXZ;* in the latter case we extend our universal over new *marks*, and discover more about the subject *M*. The problem of logic is to justify these processes; and the justification of both, if it exists, is the same. For Lotze does not regard the distinction between induction and analogy as fundamental. "It is hardly worth while **to separate in such** applications of logic the **part played by induction** from the part played by **analogy; nor** is it worth while to find fault with **the loose** usage which confounds the two expressions."[1] The point of paramount interest is the transition **in either form** from given premises which can never be, *as given*, logically universal, to universals.

As Lotze took **the** step from the categorical to the hypothetical judgment by *supposing* a system, so in like manner he supposes a system here. In fact **the** transition which he has to make is essentially the same in the two cases: he has to pass from an identity which is tautological to an identity which **is concrete.** "When we observe the

[1] *Logic,* § 257.

same mark in different subjects, we are predisposed to think that the agreement is not a chance one, and that the different subjects have not, therefore, stumbled upon the same predicate each through a special circumstance of its own, but are all radically of one common essence, of which their possession of the same mark is a consequence."[1] That is to say, P, S, T, V, in the inductive premises PM, SM, TM, VM, are not really, or at least, not essentially different, else their possession of the same mark M would be contingent and unintelligible. Their possession of the same mark M must be the consequence of the presence in them of some identical element. In other words, "P, S, T, V will be different, but still co-ordinate as species under a higher concept Σ; it is not as different individuals, but only as species of the genus Σ, that they bear the common mark M as a necessary mark of that genus. Our conclusion, therefore, runs as follows, 'all Σ is M,' and in this conclusion Σ stands for the higher universal to which we subordinate the individual subjects, and for the true subject of the M which before appeared as a common attribute of those individuals."[2] The same result, *mutatis mutandis*, follows the analysis of the analogical premises MP, MS, MT, MV; we grasp the identical element in these different predicates, the element in virtue of which they all inhere in the same subject is, and we express that identical

[1] *Logic*, § 101. [2] *Ibid.*

element by the symbol Π. Our conclusion in this case is "All M is Π."

Now Lotze, as we have just seen, speaks as if P, S, T, V remained under Σ or Π respectively, as "co-ordinate species under a higher concept." That is, he speaks as if they retained their differences within the universal to which they are subordinated. But this is just the point at issue. We have advanced beyond the tautology of the Aristotelian form of subsumption and reached a concrete universal which is richer than that with which we started, only *if* the differences are retained, and *if* their retention is justified. But, on the other hand, how can that difference be said to be retained if we treat all the given elements simply as cases of Σ or Π, and assume that every new case must also be Σ or Π? What was required was to advance by inference to new instances. But if we know no more than that every new instance is simply a case of Σ or Π, that is, a mere repetition of that which was given as the only *relevant* factor in the premises, no advance has been made. We have omitted the differences in order to find coherence, and made the function of thought in induction and analogy simply tautologous. If the unobserved instances are identical with the old there has been no inference, and if they are not identical no inference is possible. Inference and analogy seem, therefore, to be open to the objection, "that if they are complete, their information is certain but not new; while so long as they are incomplete, it is new but not certain." If we know that all which can be connected with M is Σ or Π and must be Σ or Π, there is no fruitful exercise of thought, or increase of assured knowledge. And further, this was the very thing we were supposed *not* to know, for we wished to contemplate new cases. Hence this analysis has only served to show that they must *not* be new cases, but must fall within the same universal as that which was found in the given premises. If LMN, P, S, T, V, etc., are different we cannot subsume them under a universal, if they are not different there is no inference. We seem, therefore, to lapse once more into an identity which excludes differences and into differences which refuse to be combined; and thought, in both cases alike, fails to reveal the coherence of different elements within a universal, which is its permanent task.

Lotze is not unconscious of the pass into which he here brings thought; and he endeavours to obviate the difficulty in a very significant way. He finds the objection, which is urged in precisely the same way against all the three forms of subsumption, to be relevant, not against the logical process itself but against our application of it to the different materials of our experience. Owing to the complexity of the material with which we deal, and to our own ignorance, we often make mistakes in the application of these methods, but these errors do not diminish the value of the logical principle where the application is correct. "That principle asserts, that no rightly conceived content of thought consists of an unconnected heap of marks, which we may increase at pleasure by adding no matter what new elements."[1] "It does not lose its logical significance because the truth of the universal includes, or, if we prefer it, presupposes its truth in all particular instances; on the contrary the very meaning of the syllogistic principle is that the two are inseparable."[2] And the same truth stands in the case of induction and analogy. The subsumption of particulars under a universal, at which all these forms of inference aim, "is the logical ideal, to the form of which we ought to bring our knowledge"; and the only condition on which this ideal can be reached is that the universal which is found at the end should be presupposed at the beginning. This, it is evident, is equivalent to admitting that, since thought must end by systematizing experience, it must begin from the conception of a system. That is to say, the elements of experience which first presented themselves as merely coincident or associated externally, were *always* coherent, and never simply coincident. The work of thought is, therefore, once more, not to bring differences together but

[1] *Logic*, § 104. [2] *Ibid.*, § 102.

to articulate further the concrete universal which is its true starting point. I admit the truth of this: it is what I wish to urge; but it cannot serve as a defence for Lotze. I have no doubt that many of our errors, probably all of them, spring from the wrong application of correct logical principles. But that does not show that the logical processes which he describes are valid *as he describes them*. Nor have I any doubt that the ideal of knowledge is the subsumption of all particulars within a concrete universal; but that does not prove that the logical processes he has described are consistent with the attainment of that ideal. His own analysis seems to me to have proved the opposite. For, while the ideal at which thought aims,—as an actual activity manifesting itself in growing knowledge,—is rightly described as a systematic whole of knowledge, these processes have been shown to be inconsistent with any system. Subsumption, as Lotze describes it, ends in tautology: the universals, which are empty, are simply reiterated, and the differences remain outside and unconnected. But instead of concluding that there is no *such* subsumption, and endeavouring to re-interpret it so as to make it consistent with the ideal of thought, he allows it to remain, and tries to correct processes which are radically defective by adding to them other and different processes. He proceeds from *subsumption* to *substitution*.

What defect, or what unsolved problem, presses

Lotze onwards from subsumptive to substitutive inference? It is the imperfect specification of the universal: the same defect as that which attached to judgment even in its highest form. Indeed Lotze seems to have a passing suspicion — definitely shown to be true by Mr. Bosanquet — that this kind of subsumptive inference is a less advanced form of thought than disjunctive judgment. The true disjunctive, as we have seen, implied such a unity between S and P, as to make S determine itself necessarily in some one of a definite number of related elements falling within and constituting P. The syllogism was intended to bring out that specific element; but instead of doing so its ultimate conclusion is that S is P, *i.e.*, it connects universals with universals. But the aim of thought is to deal with *particulars* (or individuals) in a universal manner. The process whereby we conclude from the premises "Heat expands all bodies," and "Iron is a body," that "Heat expands Iron" is valid, of course, but it is barren. "What we want to know is how iron expands in distinction from lead,"—that it expanded somehow was already involved in the premises. "This, then, is what the new forms have to do; they have to make the individual felt as a species of the universal and so to enable us to argue from its distinctive difference to its distinctive predicate."[1] The problem is thus pre-

[1] *Logic*, § 106.

cisely the same as that which confronted Lotze in his endeavour to pass from the categorical to the hypothetical judgment; it is that of passing from bare identity to a self-articulating principle. And just as, in the former case, he introduced from without the conception of a system, so in this case he appeals from form to content. In both cases he makes use of the idea of the mutual determination of elements within a whole, instead of the idea of the otiose, side-by-side existence of general conceptions.

Now, the simplest form of a system in which the elements may be regarded as mutually determining is that which is constituted by the idea of a *quantity*. In other words, the step from the general conception S, M, or P, to the particulars which, taken together, constitute these, is more easily taken in the sphere of pure quantity than it is elsewhere. We can scarcely regard an organism as equivalent to the sum of its parts—to head *plus* body, *plus* limbs, *plus* internal organs; for, in this case, the nature of the relation of the parts to each other and to the whole has too much importance to be neglected. But we can without error substitute $20+35+15+30$, or the units which, taken together, constitute each of these, for the whole sum 100. Lotze, therefore, proposes to substitute for M its developed content; or, in other words, to supplant the indefinite, unanalyzed middle term of which alone subsumption could make use, by means of its definite, distinguished, and mutually determining elements. The advantage he gains from this substitution is that he is able to determine the influence which the introduction of any new relation will exert upon the data from which we start. As long as we remain in the region of universals this is impossible. "Nobody, for instance, will undertake to judge how the working of a machine will change under the influence of a force s, so long as he merely has the machine before him as a simple object of perception, M, a steam-engine in general: he must first get to know the inner structure, the connection of the parts, the position of a possible point of action for the force s, and the reaction of its initial effect upon the parts contiguous to that point. Accordingly, it is only by *substituting* for the condensed expression or concept M the developed sum of its constituent parts, with attention to their mutual determinations, that we can hope to follow the influence of s."[1]

Let us, then, examine the method and the results of this inference by Substitution. The result we desire to obtain is the connection of a specific subject with a specific predicate in the conclusion, instead of the connection of indefinite, general terms. Our data are M is P and S is M, as before. But we have seen already that S is M only if a condition is fulfilled. In order to come together they must

[1] *Logic*, § 109.

be mediated by each other. Some part of M must be identical with S. Hence our minor premiss really is $S = s.M$.

But M is equal to its developed content, that is, in Lotze's necessarily arbitrary symbolism, $M = a \pm bx \pm cx^2 \ldots$. Thus the minor premiss, S is M, takes, in the process of its interpretation, first the form $S = s.M$, and then $S = s(a \pm bx \pm cx^2 \ldots)$. The major premiss is M is P. From this we may conclude that $s.M = \sigma P$, the s being converted into σ because it receives a more definite and, so far, a new significance from its relation to the term P. Hence the argument as a whole assumes the following form: $S = s.M = s(a \pm bx \pm cx^2 \ldots) = \sigma P$, and, instead of the general conclusion $S = P$, we obtain the definite conclusion $S = \sigma P$, which was not attainable by the method of subsumption. I shall postpone for the present the examination of this process of inference, and follow Lotze's extension of it beyond this sphere of abstract quantity.

It is clear that the possibility of inference by substitution depends upon the possibility of analyzing a concept into elements which, when taken together, are equivalent to it. It is also clear that when these elements receive new significance from the manner of their combination, as, *e.g.*, in the organism, such immediate substitution of a sum of parts for the whole is impossible. "Thus the effect in use of our figure is confined to the region of Mathematics, and primarily to the relation of pure quantities."[1] Where differences of quality enter, the application of the method would seem to be impossible. But it is not to be forgotten that, as we have seen before, difficulties in applying the method are not to be regarded as flaws in the method itself. "If only it were practicable, the penal law itself would draw conclusions in our figure of syllogism, it would break up every crime by substitution into its several elements . . . . and deduce the kind and amount of punishment which the particular instance demands."[2] And it is also to be borne in mind that every object of thought whatsoever has its quantitative side; it has extent or degree of existence. And, therefore, this method is, in this respect, universally applicable. The value of the results which it will yield will vary with the different materials to which it is applied. The truth which it yields is primarily based upon and limited to the conception of pure quantity. But nothing is pure quantity. In other words, everything has its own character as well as its own degree of being; and quality is no less omnipresent than quantity. Hence the equational method of mathematical substitution is never entirely true, for there is no object whose parts have not their own character. Even inorganic matter is not a mere sum of undistinguished units, the relation of which to one another and to the whole have no significance. The universal of mere quantity is

[1] *Logic*, § 111. [2] *Ibid.*, § 112.

always abstract, and its abstractness detracts from the value of the results which a quantitative method can yield, in proportion as the unity which we consider is rich in content. Even in the sphere of Physics we cannot rely on pure quantities; for even although it *is* a science of measurement, it measures not pure quantities, but quantities of different objects, in terms of different units. In the sphere of biology, and still more of Psychology, or Ethics, or Philosophy, the use of substitution all but vanishes. Mind, The English Nation, The British Constitution will not be much better understood even if we did analyze them into the sum of their constituent elements, all of which admittedly have their quantitative side. Nevertheless, the method of analyzing the whole into its constituents remains the ideal of our knowledge even in dealing with these subjects, and our knowledge is defective in proportion to the degree in which *this* ideal remains unattained. "Even in those cases where the demands of these logical activities cannot be realized, they are still the ideals of our logical effort. For if they can be applied directly to none but quantitative relations, it is true on the other side that wherever we are quite unable to reduce the object of our investigation to those relations, our knowledge of it remains defective, and that no other logical form can help us to the answer which a mathematical treatment of the question, if it were practicable, would give us."[1]

[1] *Logic*, § 112.

By this, Lotze seems to mean that wherever the method of mathematics fails, certain and accurate knowledge ends; beyond its sphere we can only give *general* solutions, which are not capable of strict verification, because our whole is not strictly analyzable into constitutive parts.

The question of the possibility of extending the method of equivalence, or of measurement, being tantamount to the possibility of the extension of our knowledge of demonstrative truth, thus becomes a matter of the greatest interest. Natural Science proves that such an extension is possible, for it "has certainly succeeded in establishing links of connection, even between incommensurable phenomena or attributes, which allow us to infer from one to another."[1] The law of the Conservation or Transmutation of Energy within which physics works is itself an example of the possibility of establishing quantitative relations between phenomena which remain to the end qualitatively different. The same method is found practicable even with respect to the relations of physical, physiological, and even psychological facts to each other. "I may recall how physics has reduced the qualitative differences of our sensations of colour, tone, and heat to merely mathematical differences in commensurable motions of incommensurable elements."[2] It is the task of Logic to discover the laws in accordance with which these processes have been carried on.

[1] *Logic*, § 113.   [2] *Ibid.*

It is by the use of *inference by proportion*, which is an extension of inference by *pure* quantity. Proportion is, of course, the equivalence of ratios. It starts from a purely empirical basis. It is given us as a matter of fact by observation that as A changes into A^1, a changes into a^1, or B into B^1. The pitch of a note, for instance, changes with the number of vibrations per second, and although we cannot actually convert a note into vibrations, we can discover that there is a constant law which dominates their respective changes and makes them measurable. Provided we can institute a *ratio* between the changes on *each* side, we can institute a *proportion* between the changes on the *two* sides. In this respect we can measure incommensurables. "Two angles E and e are commensurable; so are two segments of a circle T and t; but an angle and a segment are incommensurable, and cannot be directly measured by any common standard; so, too, the difference of two angles which again represents an angle is incommensurable with the difference of two curves, which again forms a curve. Nevertheless, if it is once established that a certain length of curve t belongs to an angle e at the centre of a circle of a given diameter, and if we form the angle E by m times e, another corresponding curve T by n times t, then the pure numbers m and n are commensurable. . . . . For the circle, geometry tells us, that $m = n$. Given, therefore, the two units e and t, we only require to know a definite number E of e in order to arrive at the proper value of T by the proportion $E:e::T:t$. Expressed as a syllogism, then, the whole process would answer to the scheme,

$$E : e = T : t$$
$$E = F(e)$$
$$\therefore T = \frac{F(et)}{e}._{n\,1}$$

We must now examine the limitations of this method of inference by proportion. In the first place, as has been suggested, its basis is empirical; and it is important to note, what Lotze has not made sufficiently clear, that this empiricism extends not only to the terms themselves but to the ratios on each side of the equation. In the case quoted above, the ratios are expressible by the same pure number, that is, $m = n$. But in the case, say, of gravitation and distance the increase is inverse, and inverse to the *square* of the distance; so that m is not in that case equal to n. It is expressible by a number but not by the same number. In a word, the law of the changing units must be given to us by observation as well as the changes themselves; and in many cases the correspondence between these laws is not numerically expressible. Even where it is expressible the empirical element in the correspondence cannot be eliminated. That is to say, *inference by proportion* does not enable

[1] *Logic*, § 114.

us to ascend from coincidence to coherence. "Hitherto no attempt has succeeded in showing how the distance contrives to weaken the force." Nor do we know how changes in the number of vibrations per second alter the pitch of a note or the quality of a colour. Proportion does not enable us to do anything more than give a more accurate expression to a correspondence which is empirically given, and which remains empirical to the end. "It makes no attempt to fuse the two elements into an undiscoverable third, but leaves them both in their full difference, and merely points out that, in spite of their mutual impenetrability, they come as a fact under a common law by which they mutually determine one another."[1] That is to say, the incommensurable has not, strictly speaking, proved commensurable after all. The units have no common measure; the ratios no explanation. The qualitative difference remains an insurmountable bar to exact thought, and the measurement, useful as it has proved in science, floats upon a purely empirical medium, and has not revealed to us in any degree the principle which would account for the correspondence of the changes, and thereby convert their coincidence into coherence. The method culminates in making the existence of such a principle highly probable, without throwing the least light upon its character.

[1] *Logic*, § 115.

It is scarcely necessary to insist upon the fact that in a great portion of the material of our thought, the discovery of a unit capable of definite increase or decrease has so far proved impossible. And I would deny that science, physical, physiological, or psychological, has so far gained the point of departure for making sensations of colour or pitch commensurable with physical changes. We can only, so far at least, judge of their correspondence in a lax way, and instead of proportion we have to be content with general and indefinite comparison based upon no explicit standard. I am also inclined to say that the failure of proportion in such a sphere must be ultimate, because, in the case of these sensations, gradations of quantity pass immediately into differences of quality; but it is in part a matter of language whether, for instance, we call difference in the shades of blue, or, indeed, differences in *any* two sensations, however similar they may be, qualitative or quantitative. I refer to this because it suggests the law of a limit which proportion cannot pass beyond, and which Lotze acknowledges, though I am not sure that he is aware of its full significance, or of the extent of the sphere of its operation.

Proportion fails, therefore, wherever the unit within which the ratios would fall has any real significance. It is valid, like enumeration, only in the abstract sphere of quantity, even though it seems to bring together quantities of different things. Wherever the whole is more than a mere sum, wherever it acts as a determinant upon its elements, relating them to each other in a definite order, wherever in a word the whole is an individual, explanation by proportion becomes inadequate. Proportion, as distinguished from enumeration, does, indeed, *imply* that the unit with which it deals is an individual, *i.e.*, an object with unique characteristics; but it is not capable of doing any justice to that implied individuality beyond the mere admission of it. Lotze expresses this by saying that the proportion varies with "the nature of the subject in which the changes are united." "Heat expands all bodies, but the ratios of the degree of expansion to an equal increase of temperature are different on different bodies." The ratio of change is, in other words, conditional upon the nature of the thing in which the change takes place. Hence, the proportions we establish between ratios are only true if a certain condition, hitherto neglected, is observed. S changes as P changes only if both S and P have a certain character. That is to say $T:t::E:e$ only for a *specific* subject, S, *i.e.*, only if S is an M. And while it is true that only experience can give us that subject, logic has to show "how a concept M can be found at all, such that the proportions required between every two of its marks can be derived from it."[1]

This implies that proportion can only deal with

[1] *Logic*, § 116.

universals, and that it is, in this respect, analogous to the Categorical Judgment. Hence, just as S could not be P unconditionally or immediately, so S cannot vary as P varies, unless they both fall under some law which determines that their changes shall correspond. They are, in fact, instances of a rule which acts in both of them, and is dominant within their differences. We must, therefore, proceed to look for this rule, just as we had to find the *condition* in value of which the judgment S is P was possible. But to find such a rule in the changing objects is to lift some one element in them into a position of superiority as regards the other elements. And this is equivalent to abandoning the point of view of quantity; for its essential characteristic is that all its elements are homogeneous, and all its units are simple, isolated, equal in value, and incapable of determining each other except in the abstract way necessary for their summation. With the admission of differences of value, other than that which springs from difference in quantity, the method of mathematical reasoning, or of substitution based upon equation, is no longer available. We need another form of thought, which will admit the unequal values of the constituents in a concept, distinguish some of them as essential, and others as derivative and secondary, and also explain the principle in accordance with which such a distinction emerges.

That ordinary thought is able to employ such a

method is evident from the way in which objects are classified, even before science enters the field. Had thought been confined to the quantitative stage, things would be classified according to their size, or intensity of colour, or weight, or some other differences of qualities that appeal most immediately and aggressively to the sensuous consciousness. But objects are not classified into great and small, white and black, heavy and light, etc., but into organic and inorganic, rational and irrational beings, and so on. That is to say, the classifications are frequently based upon qualities that are not sensible, and to which quantitative measurement does not seem to apply. And yet we do not classify at random. On the contrary, in all such classifications, thought has been unconsciously guided by a method which has enabled it to light upon "authoritative" principles in objects, which distinguish between qualities that are essential and those which are not. In other words, ordinary thought seizes upon some elements in an object, and regards them as determining what does and what does not belong to it, while the excision of other qualities seems immaterial, and to leave the object as a whole practically unchanged. "In the beginnings of thought there was no logical rule for this selective guidance of attention." Nevertheless, "in the actual course of its development, thought was directed to those universal concepts which really contain the law for the complete formation of the individuals for which they are acquired."[1] And it is the task of logic to explain, and thereby to justify the process which thought has thus always employed in its classification of objects; the process, that is to say, by which it succeeds in fixing upon a certain quality M, and not another quality N, as really constitutive of certain objects. "These tendencies, which have hitherto unconsciously put us upon the right way, we have now to translate into logical activity; in other words, we have to become conscious of the reasons which justify us in setting up a certain universal M exclusively as the authoritative rule for the formation of a number of individuals, instead of some other N to which we might have been led by comparing the same individuals on a different principle."[2] Recognizing that a concept is not in reality any group of common qualities, but one in which some qualities are essential and others unessential, we have to show how this distinction is drawn and on what authority it rests.

The first step in this process is that of observing the same object under varying circumstances; or, failing this, that of comparing objects which are similar in some respects, and not in others. The result of these observations will be to show us that a nucleus of elements hang together, while others fall away; that the disappearance of some elements leaves the remainder, comparatively speaking, as

[1] *Logic*, § 122. [2] *Ibid.*, § 123.

they were, while the disappearance of others would either carry the remainder away with them, or else essentially modify them, and change the character of the object. By continuing this process of seeking the permanent amidst the variable, we "find ourselves on the way to classification" according to essential and constitutive marks. "The authoritative principle will appear to us to be in that inner circle of marks which, when we ascend through the next universal to higher and higher degrees of universality, remains together the longest, and unchanged in its general form; and the only way to conceive completely the nature of the particular is to think of this supreme formative principle as being specialized gradually, in the reverse order to the grades of universality, by new accretions which come within the influence of its reaction."[1]

The nature of this logical classification, and of the universal which it employs, will become more evident if we contrast it with "combinatory classification." The object of the latter kind of classification is not so much to explain the particulars as to arrange them methodically; and the classification rests, therefore, not upon any significant element in the objects classified, but on the subjective purpose which is to be reached. Words are arranged in a dictionary, for instance, in the order of the letters of the alphabet, and the principle of arrangement throws no light whatsoever

[1] *Logic*, § 124.

upon the inner content of the words. In other words, the principle is not constitutive of the contents of the class; and, therefore, it merely sums them, sets them side by side, and leaves them indifferent to each other. It is not a principle which systematizes; and, therefore, we are always liable to err by excess or defect, that is, to bring in objects into a class which do not really belong to it, or exclude others which do; for we have no criterion of completeness, and are reduced to the method of enumerating one part after another. The "mark" employed as a universal does not enter vitally into the objects of the class, nor in any way regulate them so as to make them internally coherent.

But Logical Classification, on the other hand, seizes upon a mark because it is deemed to be constitutive of the object. As constitutive it is the source of all the other marks, and "the law which determines their order." In a word, the universal in logical classification is converted from an otiose quality into a *condition*. Upon that mark, as condition, the existence and the whole character of the objects in the class are supposed to depend. And as all the other marks are present in virtue of the same condition, they form a system of elements which mutually determine one another through their relation to the dominant quality.

The object of thought which results from taking a mark as a determining condition differs in the most significant manner from the concept. The latter, which is a mere collection of "*notiones communes, i.e.*, of marks which are known to occur in the most different objects without exercising any recognizable influence upon the rest,"[1] can only give us an image of a motionless and changeless object; and the complete arrangement of such concepts or images in an ascending series would, as has been seen, only reflect a world whose order is fixed. But a thought which grasps an element as constitutive of others, and as dominating them, seems to become "living in our hands." In fact, instead of the concept, we have the *Idea (Idee)*, the "thought of the object," its "formative law."[2] That law seems to exercise "an operative force, whose unvarying and constant activity gives rise to a series of different forms." These different forms, in other words, as they issue from the same law, seem to be the manifestations of a principle that is able to articulate itself; and the order in which they are placed under its authority seems to imply the presence of an authoritative "*purpose*" throughout them all. The law, in fact, appears to be also an "End," toward which they all strive, from which they all derive their existence, and which is realized, more or less completely, in every member of the series.

But Lotze, in consistency with his resolution to maintain at all costs the distinction between logic

---

[1] *Logic*, § 128.   [2] *Ibid.*, § 129.

and ontology, or between thoughts and real objects, rejects these conceptions of "life," "operative force," and "purpose," as extra-logical. Thoughts, being thoughts, must remain static; but the thoughts *of* "life," "force," "purpose," though they will not themselves have any life, or purpose, or force, have their logical use. We must, therefore, run these operative entities into their logical equivalents. "End" must be explained as "coherence of species" dependent upon a single mark; and "active tendency" must be analyzed into equations between the parts of the conditioned and conditioning facts. This is the task which still lies before us. "We regard the idea for which we are looking, neither as the intention of a reflective consciousness striving for fulfilment nor as an active force which causes its results, but merely as the conceived or conceivable reason, the consequences of which, under certain conditions, are the same in thought as those which must follow in reality, under the like conditions, from an intelligent purpose, or a causative force."[1] The arrangement of ideas in the world of thought will be *similar* to that of facts and events in a world of reality which is dominated by the living power of an active and intelligent will; but it will not be the *same*.

Now a supreme idea which corresponds with the 'intelligent purpose' and 'active force' must also explain the manner in which the same universal comes to be realized, with different degrees of com-

[1] *Logic*, § 130.

pleteness, in different concepts; so that the concepts may "form an ascending or descending scale in which each one has its uninterchangeable place between certain others." It must, in other words, give a static representation of a world whose objects can be regarded as stages in the development of a single principle which realizes itself in all things, but in some things more completely than in others. But it is evident that a mere concept can yield no such view of the world. On the contrary, the universal or common element in a concept, or in a series of concepts subordinated to one supreme concept, is set in "hard antithesis" to the particulars which lie side by side within it. And, therefore, it cannot admit any difference of degrees, or be regarded as more fully present in some individuals than in others. The universal either includes every object equally, or else it entirely excludes them. Indeed, in the last resort, the antithesis between the universal on which such classification is based, and the objects which fall into the class, ultimately turns into direct and destructive antagonism. The contents must be completely absorbed in the universal, as the condition of their inclusion in such an abstract universal; while the universal, owing to its antagonism to its differences, destroys itself and becomes empty. In fact, as every element in the universal must simply sink into it, classification itself becomes impossible. "That living thought should not be satisfied" with such a universal is inevitable, for all thought is made impossible by direct antagonism between unity and difference. "Living thought" must "distinguish species which correspond or are adequate to their generic concept in various degrees." And Lotze might have concluded that *all* thought is living, or, in other words, that a *purely* artificial and external universal cannot be used as the basis even of combinatory classification.

But what is the logical process which enables us thus to distinguish various degrees in the species of a generic concept? How do we logically prove that the universal is more completely realized in some objects than in others. Lotze answers, that it is by reducing the differences between them into differences of quantity and then measuring them.[1] Every one of the simple and stable qualities which ordinary thought regards as belonging to objects has its own quantitative value: each object has a certain number of parts, each part has its own intensity, magnitude, or degree of existence. Each of these parts or elements is capable of increase or diminution; there may be more or less of each of them within an object. The differences of *quantity* in these elements is our clue to the differences in *quality* of the objects in which they are found; and from these differences of quantity in the same elements there arises difference of species within the same genus. In fact every change in the quantity of the elements that constitute an object

---

[1] See *Logic*, § 131.

modifies the character of the object itself. For if we change the quantity of an element in the whole, we change its relation to and modify its effect upon other elements. The whole system is changed, because the parts are vitally inter-related. If that change of quantity is great, the character of the object as a whole may be so changed as to tend to make it pass beyond the limits of the genus and demand a place under another — under the genus N, instead of under M.[1] We may, for instance, shorten one axis of an ellipse, in proportion to the other, to such an extent that the ellipse tends to pass into a straight line. And this consideration enables us to distinguish the species which is the truest type, or the most perfect realization, of a genus. It is that which is furthest from passing into any other genus; and it is furthest from passing into another genus if "the *total amount*" of *all* its divergencies from other genera is greatest *when taken together*. That is to say, each of the characteristic elements in a perfect species exists in the greatest quantity consistent with the greatest quantity of the others. "The highest perfection of a species depends upon the equilibrium of its marks": it is the TYPE to which the other species approximate. Hence we conclude, that differences of species depend upon quantitative differences and lend themselves to mathematical calculation.

[1] See *Logic*, § 131.

But in the course of our experience we learn that there are some kinds of objects, or some genera, in which the equilibrium of marks cannot apparently be maintained. These objects seem to contain an element that constantly tends to disturb the equilibrium, an impulse to intensify some one mark at the expense of the others. We are familiar with such objects in the region of biology. In this region the determining consideration which we constitute into the principle of classification and arrangement is not that of the quantitative equilibrium of a sum of marks, but some single element which imposes its own law on others, constantly changing their relative quantities and therefore their mutual interaction, pushing some into the background as insignificant and bringing others to the fore-front. That determining element seems to be *in process*, and to have a "*destination*." It is hardly necessary to indicate that Lotze will not admit "process" of this kind, or "destination" into his static logic; nevertheless logic has to do with the intelligible principle, or condition of its possibility.

It is evident that such a "destination" is explicable only if we cease to regard each genus as complete in itself, or as the source of the law which it imposes upon its contents so as to limit the quantitative variation of the marks of its species. The most perfect species, from this new point of view, will not be that which most perfectly maintains the equilibrium of its marks, but the one which most shares the *tendency to change* which is the law of the genus, and most completely embodies its impulse towards a certain destination. Hence the formation of the species under M does not ultimately "depend upon anything in the generic type M itself, such as could be discovered by merely examining its own constituent marks; on the contrary, the formation of this genus M is not rightly explained until we compare it with another genus N into which it passes, and with a third L from which it came by a similar transition, and these again with those which went before and came after them."[1] We cannot otherwise catch the direction of the progress, nor understand the highest genus Z, of which L, M, N are species.

How are we to represent logically this relation of the genera? In the same way as we represented that of species within a single genus. We must in a word reduce the differences between the genera L, M, N, which fall under and move towards the ultimate genus Z, into differences in quantity; and regard that genus as highest which has within it the largest amount of the Z, which is to a varying extent present in them all. "Only in this way of measurement can we have any 'logical security' that every species has a place in the series of cognate species, the place answering

[1] *Logic*, § 134.

to the degree of essence which it expressed."[1] But by following this method we may arrange species and genera into series and organize the whole world of thought. The manner of that organization is *serial*, that is, "the members are not merely placed side by side, but follow each other in a definite order, leading from the province comprehended or dominated by one species into that of another; this order begins with those members which answer least to the logical destination of the whole system, and ends with those which express in the most complete and pregnant way the fulfilment of that destination."[2] It is not our present purpose to dwell upon the fact that Lotze considers that there may be several such series. "The form of natural classification in general is that of *a web or system* of series; even the culminating point of the system need not be a strict unity, for the most perfect attainment of the logical destination is compatible with a variety of precisely equivalent forms."[3]

But even if we were to succeed in classifying our objects of thought in this manner—arranging them, that is, according to the degree in which an Ideal is realized in them—there is still something left over unexplained. Classification, whether from the point of view of an *Ideal* which is progressive, or from that of a Type which is static, can only arrange its materials in an order which

[1] See *Logic*, § 135.   [2] *Logic*, § 136.   [3] *Ibid*.

is fixed. The ascending series is as motionless as the species and genera which simply lay side by side. The movement, the transition from species to species, "the process of becoming remains a mystery which classification cannot explain." The fact that genera fall into classes, serial or other, and have a relation to one another within the whole, is as little explained by classification as is the relation of S and P in the categorical judgment. The condition which *determines* their relation has not been discovered. We may say that one concept emanates from another; but a theory of emanation is not an explanation of a process: it is only the assertion of it. To explain, we must grasp that which emanates and discover the method of its process. We must, in a word, as in the case of the categorical judgment, discover the *condition* on which alone the relations of different concepts within a whole is possible.

Now, a little consideration will show that the *condition* is ultimately the same as that which was discovered in the analysis of proportion. For in this case, as in the former, the elements within the whole have different and changing values, and therefore react differently upon each other. It is plain that they would not be able to act upon each other at all, except for the presence of the same universal in them all; and it is plain that they would not be able to act in different ways were it not that each of them has its own law as well. To comprehend this process we must, therefore, keep before our eyes both the universal and the particular laws; just as we had in the case of "proportion" to maintain within our grasp both the general law of the change and the specific "subject" in which the change took place. So far we have paid attention to the comprehensive universals and neglected the interaction of the elements within the genera as wholes. But it is not the wholes as wholes which interact, or which condition each other. The wholes are in fact nothing but "condensed expressions for a definite union of separable elements, which act and react upon each other according to constant and universal laws, and give rise in one combination to one set of results, in another to another."[1]

From this it follows that the effective agency which places the genera in order and organizes the contents of our knowledge by reference to an ideal will not be found simply in that ideal, but *also* in the individuals which fall under it. Our principle of explanation must not be the bare ideal, but the ideal which has already articulated itself in its content. That is to say, the ultimate starting point of explanation is a *System*.

But, to start from the conception of a *System* is to start from a *hypothesis*, or, in other words, it is to make unverified knowledge the basis of demonstrative knowledge. Such a process may

[1] *Logic*, § 144.

seem both impossible and absurd: impossible because we cannot start from a system unless our knowledge is already complete; absurd, because one should say that an uncertain, or unverified, premiss can never yield certain knowledge. Nevertheless it is undeniable that modern science employs this method and employs it successfully. It always starts with "the conception of a law which fixes the particular result of a particular condition universally." Its method as a whole rests upon the assumption "that everything exists, and exists only, when the complete sum of conditions is given, from which it follows necessarily by universal laws."[1] Science does not decide what a fact is, nor, indeed, whether it is a fact or an illusion, until there is found a place for it within an interrelated system based upon a hypothetical principle.

Now, it seems to Lotze, that to explain each fact by its relation to other facts in a system and to the principle which is embodied more or less completely in every phenomenon, is to explain things as *mechanically necessary*. Nothing, on this view, is regarded as deriving its existence or its law of behaviour from itself; but all things act in subordination to laws which are external and derive their function and meaning from *relations*. Or if we still maintain that each thing has in some way its own law and its

[1] *Logic*, § 145.

own unique form of existence, without which it could have no value or activity and the system itself would become empty, we must also recognize that its law must be a subordinate and derivative one, and therefore that each particular object is only an instance or example of something higher which dominates it. Such a system of *mechanical necessity* is, according to Lotze, set up by natural science in its attempt at "*Explanation*." It is hardly necessary to point out that "explanation" of this kind—although it is much more satisfactory than the mere otiose classification of ancient thought, and although it is "almost the only form in which the scientific activity of our time exhibits itself"—is unsatisfactory. It does not meet the demands even of our cognitive consciousness; for the ideal which inspires it, namely the conception of a system, is fundamentally unrealizable. The system must be a hypothesis as long as we have not already found a place within it for every phenomenon, and the hypothetic character of the idea of system, which serves as the foundation of our knowledge, makes the superstructure as a whole insecure.

But quite apart from these objections that arise from the fact that the theoretical demands which we must make are not adequately met, there are others springing from another side of our nature. Even if a complete system of the kind we have described were realizable in thought, the needs of the human spirit would not be satisfied. On the contrary, we find that the very conception of such a completed system awakens unremitting opposition to itself. This opposition arises from the aesthetic side of our nature. From the aesthetic point of view we demand that an object should be in itself whole and complete; it must exhibit its own law, be the source of its own contents, and itself determine the relations between them. And this is precisely what the "explanatory" method of science, which refers each object to others and to a whole system, and reduces everything into an *instance* of a universal or an example of a law, renders impossible. The opposition between what science offers and what we must aesthetically demand thus seems to be final and irreconcilable.

But the opposition to scientific explanation which is offered by the aesthetic spirit is not directed against the "*order*" which "explanation" establishes, but against the founding of that order upon an ever-receding condition, or upon an eternal "if." This "if" allows the possibility to remain that everything may be really different from what it appears to be. And it is this final uncertainty against which our spirits are in revolt. We must, therefore, endeavour to find something which shall convert this "if" into a fact, or apodeictic certainty. Such a *"fact"* would give us, instead of *thoughts* in necessary relation, a *reality* which is its own law, "a being which, not in consequence of a still higher law but because it is what it is, is the ground both of the universal laws to which it will always conform, and of the series of individual realities which will subsequently appear to us to submit to these laws."[1] Such a reality the third form of thought, which we distinguish from both the "*explanatory*" or the *mechanical* and the *classificatory*, aspires to give, and Lotze calls it the "*Speculative form.*" We have an example of it in Hegel's attempt "to derive the world from a single principle," "to look on and see how the development followed from the inherent impulse of the Idea," to attain "to a vision of the universe springing out of the unity of an idea, which develops itself and creates the conditions of its own progress."[2] The characteristics of this form of thought are, that "it must have only *one* major premiss for all its conclusions, and this premiss must express the movement of the world as a whole; its minor premises must not be given to it from elsewhere, but it must produce them from itself in the form of necessary and exhaustive varieties of its meaning, and thus must evolve in an infinite series of conclusions the developed reality which it had conceived as a principle capable of development, in the major premiss."[3] This form, in a word, attempts to represent the world as an organic whole; and the impulse to employ this method

[1] *Logic*, § 148.   [2] *Ibid.*, § 150.   [3] *Ibid.*, § 149.

makes itself particularly evident at the times when the mechanical mode of explanation has done violence to our aesthetic and moral beliefs. So that the speculative form of thought, as an attempt to satisfy the demands of the whole spirit both cognitive and otherwise, would seem to have the highest value. In fact "it is the last in the series of forms of thought; it leaves no elements remaining in unconnected juxtaposition, but exhibits everything in that coherence which had been all along the aim of thought."[1]

The ideal of completely organized knowledge which it sets before us is, indeed, not capable of being realized. But that does not deprive it of its binding force. It only indicates that in order to reach that ideal we need other powers than those of mere thought. In other words, this form of thought "points beyond the province of logic," which can only deal with mere "forms." It reveals the incompleteness of mere thought, when taken by itself; for it demands that the supreme principle should be real and active, and capable of articulating itself into a systematic world of real objects. But thought cannot yield any such *real* principle. It deals with *forms*, and these forms must borrow from elsewhere the material which can fill them and give them meaning and value. Thought at its highest and best is, in its isolation, empty; and its highest form, namely, the "Speculative,"

[1] *Logic*, § 151.

so far from satisfying the theoretical and practical demands of our nature, only serves to show that in order to account for our experience we must take into consideration other powers of our nature, and strive to explain the world in the light, not of an aspect but of the complex totality of our intelligent existence.

Before I endeavour to estimate the value of Lotze's doctrine, I believe it will be useful if I recount, as briefly as possible, the main transitions which he makes as he follows thought upwards from judgment to its highest and ultimate, or speculative form.

Thought was left at the close of the last chapter at the stage of the Disjunctive Judgment. The processes of Judgment had revealed the need of a principle of coherence or copula, and that principle had in the Disjunctive Judgment determined the subject in such a manner that some one of a particular class of predicates was seen to belong to it necessarily. It failed to make the discrete data of experience coherent only because it did not succeed in deciding *which* of the members of the class constituting the predicate necessarily belonged to the subject. It left us an option, although it confined that option to the members of a class.

Inference was brought in to remove this option. Inferential thought attempted to perform this task in the first place by making use of *Subsumption*. Subsumption took three forms. The first, or the syllogistic, failed to carry us beyond the stage of the disjunctive judgment, for the syllogism allowed the predicate of the conclusion to remain indefinite; that is to say, the universal did not bring the *particular* data of experience into coherence. The syllogism also assumed what it proved, and was tautological. So that this form of inference missed the very essence of the thinking process, which is synthetical, bringing fresh material under a universal. This last error seemed to be capable of being corrected by the remaining forms of Subsumption, namely, Induction and Analogy. These apparently admit the synthetic advance; they enable us to extend our universals to new cases and justify us in applying principles in an *a priori*, and therefore in a universal, manner. But these forms also proved on examination to be either invalid or tautological. In so far as the processes were synthetic they appeared to be invalid; in so far as they were valid they were tautological. In fact, we were not able to bring under the universal anything but universals, and these universals had to be treated as identities.

Now it is certainly necessary in the course of thought to advance to universals, for we cannot combine in thought mere particulars; but it is also necessary to bring these universals back so as to find them within the particulars.[1] It is this last step that Subsumption fails to take. It leaves us

[1] See *Logic*, § 105.

in the region of mere universals. Lotze has, therefore, to have recourse to *Substitution*.

Substitution, that is, the displacement of an indefinite whole by the definite parts or elements which constitute it, is seen in its simplest and earliest form in mathematical equation, in which, instead of a whole inadequately grasped, we may use the sum of its units. This kind of inference, therefore, seems to give us what was required. It enables us to articulate the universal, and get valid, definite results. But, on examination, it is seen to have the defect that, while it is applicable to every phenomenon it completely explains nothing whatsoever. The mathematical method is true of everything in so far as everything *has* quantity, it is true of nothing in so far as nothing *is mere* quantity. In a word, it is abstract, and in order to be practically valid in its application to objects this abstractness must be remedied. We must be able to equate or to measure something other than *pure* quantities. This is done by the *equating of ratios*, or by proportion.

Inference by *Proportion*, as modern science amply shows, enables us to measure things which are qualitatively different, or intrinsically incommensurable. But Proportion has an empirical basis, and its empiricism cannot be cleansed out without lapsing back into the consideration of abstract quantity. Its advance in practical usefulness is obtained at the expense of its logical validity.

Ratios are taken instead of pure quantities, only because the different units between which the ratios exist are not reducible to each other—the units of sensation, *e.g.*, into units of physical motion. Hence it only *suggests* the presence of a law which determines that the changes shall be correspondent; but it neither proves its existence nor explains its nature. And, further, it neglects that element in each subject which gives to its changes a specific ratio: it cannot explain, for instance, why the ratio of the expansion of iron and lead to the same temperature should be different. Hence it leaves out an element necessary to the knowledge of any real concrete fact of experience; it stops, that is, at the universal—that S varies as P varies—without showing the condition which brings the correspondence into being in any particular case. Nay, the existence of any such condition is not consistent with the principle on which mathematical inference rests; for the idea of a condition implies that a certain element in an object, or series of objects, has superior value to the rest and a power to dominate them, while mathematical inference starts from the supposition that all the units, or elements, are homogeneous and are indifferent to each other. If we follow up the consideration of this condition that lies in each specific subject we are led on from Mathematical or Substitutive inference to Classification.

Classification makes a certain mark or element

in the individual subject its first consideration, regarding it as dominant over all the other qualities which it possesses, or, in other words, converting it into a *Condition* of the other marks. And it arranges the world of objects in one of two ways: *first*, in accordance with the conception of a *Type*; second, by reference to the conception of a Regulative *Ideal*. The first arrangement gives us a fixed system of species which, while falling under the same genus, maintain their own specific character, the difference in the character of the species being due to the different *amounts*, measurable by quantitative methods, of the sum of their characteristic qualities. But the defect of this form of thought is that, like the Conceptual view of the world, it leaves the real world of motion, and change, and variable interaction entirely unexplained.

But Classification by reference to an Ideal is able to deal with change; and it represents each object, each species, and genus as in *process* of realizing within itself, more or less perfectly, a highest principle. So that the explanation of each phenomenon is found to lie in the place which it occupies in reference to other phenomena, and to the central principle which manifests itself in different degrees in all of them. It is explanation by reference to a *System*.

At first sight *Systematic Explanation* seems to be all that can be demanded by thought, and we might consider that at last thought had succeeded in making experience inwardly coherent. But examination leads once more to disappointment. For, in the first place, the explanation is *Hypothetical*. We must assume the whole in order to account for the part, and we cannot know the whole because we do not know the parts. In the second place, it is *Mechanical*, for everything finds its explanation only in something else. That is to say, the explanatory principle is never discovered, and this form of thought is of necessity incomplete. For the necessity it traces everywhere is traced to no *origin*; nothing is a law to itself, and everything is *necessary* on account of something else. We require, therefore, some reality which is at once a *ratio essendi* and a *ratio cognoscendi* both for itself and for all other things.

Such a reality is furnished by the *Speculative* form of thought. This form of thought is the highest and the last. It promises to satisfy the demands of the intellect, which the hypothetical method of science failed to meet, and also the demands of our aesthetic and moral nature, which the scientific form of thought when taken as ultimate positively violated. This form, then, yields a supreme principle which differentiates itself in all that is and in all that comes to be; and it brings coherence into all the manifold data of experience.

But it achieves this task only *if* any form of thought can yield such a real, active, self-articulating principle. And as thought is a faculty of pure forms, and logic the science that reveals the laws of formal activities, it cannot yield such a reality. Hence thought culminates in pointing to the need of other intelligent functions, if the world in all its rich content is to be explicable by man.

I shall proceed to the examination of the theory thus advanced by Lotze in the next chapter.

CHAPTER VI

EXAMINATION OF LOTZE'S ASCENT FROM SUBSUMPTIVE TO SYSTEMATIC INFERENCE

I HAVE ventured to say that Lotze's philosophy owes its suggestiveness not so much to any new solutions that it offers as to its being consistently occupied with a single significant problem. The account which he gives of the various forms of thought bears this character. The demand which he makes upon thought at the very outset—that it should represent experience as inwardly coherent—is pressed upon each of its forms as they successively emerge. In dealing with his view of the earlier forms of our intellectual life, whose activity he regards as preliminary to those of thought proper, I indicated an ambiguity in his statement of the task which thought had to perform. Lotze did not make it clear whether thought was required to *produce from itself*, or merely *to find in its materials* those grounds of coherence, or "accessory notions," in virtue of which human knowledge is a systematic whole, and not a mere collection of elements externally connected, according to the contingent circumstances of the psychical experience of different individuals. He has not brought this question of the receptive or constructive nature of thought to a definite issue; otherwise he would have been obliged to abandon the intermediate position, which he consistently endeavoured to maintain, between the Scepticism which condemns knowledge and the Idealism which "deifies" it. For this question constitutes what one may call the main watershed in modern philosophic theory, dividing its streams in directions that diverge to meet no more. Lotze's attempt to combine both of these views, by representing thought as partly receptive and partly constructive, seems to be identical with that of Kant, and to make him so consistently Kantian as to render it unnecessary that he should "go back to Kant." But we must draw this important distinction between these two philosophers, namely, that Kant represents *the process* of transition from one view to the other, and that the conflict of these elements in his doctrine comes *mainly* from the fact that he did not reconstruct his first presuppositions in the light of his last results. The war of tendencies in Kant's doctrine is characteristic of all great writers who, in the course of their own thought, bring about the transition from an old to a new view of the world. But Lotze, on the other hand, permanently attached himself to the point of equipoise, which Kant had reached at the close of his first Critique, and presented the conflict as a fixed battle in which the combatants are immovably interlocked. He would bring peace by compromise; or rather, seeing that compromise is impossible, by yielding all to each in turn.

It is this alternation which constitutes the characteristic feature of Lotze's doctrine. We found evidence of it in his account of the processes of intelligence which are preliminary to the operation of thought proper. Experience was first presented to us as so void of all intrinsic coherence that it was impossible to raise the first and the most fundamental of all questions for a thinking being, namely, that of the truth or the falsity of his experiences. All was *given*, and the "given" as such is neither true nor false. Moreover, the "given" was a discrete and disconnected manifold; or, what comes to the same thing, the connections that were present were purely external, and contingent upon the psychical experiences of the individual. The connection, therefore, was not between the phenomena themselves, but was imposed upon them from without; that is to say, feelings and other subjective states, in some inexplicable manner, connected objective things, though only contingently. Hence the principles of inward coherence, or grounds of connection, which were objective, had to be produced by thought out of itself. Thought, which was purely receptive as to its content, was purely creative as to its forms. No sooner, however, is this view enunciated than difficulties begin to emerge. For why should "the grounds," or universals, which thought brings out of itself, have objective validity, any more than the chance combinations of a purely associative intelligence? How can universals which thought produces, bind contents which are given to it as disconnected? Such a view would attribute to thought both too little and too much. If its universals are really to bind, that is to say, if they are to make the phenomena of experience inwardly coherent, then they must have been present in the phenomena and constitutive of them from the first. Hence thought would from one point of view make all, and from another point of view make nothing. It would make "all" because the phenomena of experience could not exist except as elements in a whole; it would make *nothing*, because, the whole being there to begin with, there was nothing to make. Thought would find *itself* in all its materials on this view. Reflection would add nothing to that which is; it would not be called upon to *produce* even the universals. But if reflection is discovery and not creation, it is because what it reflects is already thought. The real *is* the rational, and reflection is *its* consciousness of itself. This conclusion, however, is uncompromisingly idealistic, and if it does not "deify abstract truth," as Lotze thought, it at least insists that the real is the ideal. Hence Lotze compromises. Conscious of the fact that the abstract universals of thought cannot be applied to an entirely foreign material so as to make it coherent; that it does not go out, to use his phrase, to meet the manifold which flows in, with a series of empty forms in its hand; and that, if it did, the forms could never be applied to the data; and conscious, on the other hand, that to find these forms present in the material from the first, as concrete and constitutive universals, would involve the interpretation of the world in terms of thought, he strikes a middle path. He cannot do without *any* inward universals, for pure Associationism is Scepticism; and he cannot attribute these universals to thought, for that would imply Idealism: so he attributes them to Sense. He makes them correspond to, incite one by one, the universals of thought. So that he is able to retain his view that thought is formal, and its universals abstract in the sense of not producing their content, and yet he is able to regard experience as coherent. The questions that still remain unanswered are, How can sense produce universals? How, if sense, or intuition, or immediate perception does give these universals, the sense-universals are related to the universals of thought? Are they the same? Then why not attribute all to sense or all to thought? Are they different? By what means then is that difference mediated? Lotze does not even ask these questions. And, in consequence, a convenient ambiguity enfolds the whole matter. Thought remains formal and its universals abstract, and yet, through the interposition of the psychical mechanism and preliminary processes of intelligence, it is able to perform the task of making experience inwardly coherent, just as if its universals were concrete and constructive. He makes sense perform the processes of thought, or rather, he sinks reflection in perception. He *presupposes* that the universals of thought are abstract, and that those of sense are concrete. Thought must *produce* the universals from itself, because idealism is not true; and it must *find* them in sense, because associationism is false.

The same attempt to strike a middle path between a formal and a constitutive view of thought characterizes his treatment of Judgment. We have seen that Judgment makes its appearance in order to "express a relation between the matters of two ideas." But it is not made clear whether the relation it expresses already exists and has only to be made explicit, or whether, the matters of the two ideas, are given without connection. The question recurs, Does thought produce, or does it find, the universal? Is the universal in itself bare and empty and to be applied to a "given" material, or is it concrete and constitutive of that content, in the sense that the particulars cannot exist except in their coherence? Lotze, once more, does not confront the issue; but he proceeds, as far as possible, upon the assumption that thought is formal, and that it does not originally comprehend and penetrate its content; and when he can go no further on that hypothesis he starts from the idea of a system. He does not see that both views cannot be true, but tries to subordinate the latter to the former. In support of this view of his attitude, I have only to refer to his transition from the Categorical to the Hypothetical Judgment. He assumes that the universal of thought is a unity which is inconsistent with differences, and asserts that S cannot be P so long as the law of identity holds; and he makes the subject of the Categorical Judgment qualify the predicate, and its predicate qualify the subject in such a manner that this Judgment is made purely tautological. Then he proceeds to correct this result by first assuming, and then seeking to prove, that knowledge is systematic, and that its universals are, therefore, concrete and formative. And he brings in the law of sufficient reason, and even strives to make it an extension of a law of pure identity, ignoring the fact that he had assumed as his starting point, and amended the Categorical Judgment on the supposition, that what the Judgment *means* is pure identity, and that nothing but pure identity is consistent with the supreme law of thought. Lotze had not learnt the value of the negative in Logic, or, what is the same thing, that affirmation is definition.

Judgment can be understood in two ways, and the ideal which is gradually realized in its successive forms is capable of two expressions. First, we may regard it as an attempt on the part of thought to combine ideas which are at first independent, so that it must produce its own universal, which, therefore, has in itself no content, and must be applied *ab extra* to the unconnected data. Secondly, we may regard Judgment as the process whereby a *single idea*, or an indefinite universal, which, on this view, is the datum of thought, articulates itself in a subject and predicate. That is to say, "the Judgment is a process of explicating the copula," and exhibiting its concreteness in the difference of the subject and predicate. On both views the ideal of knowledge is the exhibition, in all the contents of experience, of the primary law of thought; and the primary law in both cases is the law of identity. But the law of identity on the first view is a law of pure unity which excludes differences, and its realization would empty knowledge of all contents; while, on the second view, the law of identity is simply the most abstract, and therefore the most imperfect, expression of a unity which includes differences. That unity is taken up and expressed more fully in the law of sufficient reason, and is again taken up in the law of systematic disjunction, where both the unity and the differences are made explicit and emphasized in their necessary relation. On this latter view the ideal of knowledge, and, therefore, the fundamental law of thought, is the conception of an all-inclusive totality which is systematic, that is to say, whose universal is completely concrete. Lotze's whole doctrine is based upon the first view of thought and its laws, but its verisimilitude is made possible only by making use of the second.

The same attempt to unite an abstract and formal view of the processes and laws of thought with a concrete view of knowledge is manifested in his view of *Inference*. For Inference can, like the Judgment, be understood in two ways. It may be regarded, with Lotze, as a process of "combining two judgments for the production of a third and valid judgment which is not merely the sum of the two first," or, in other words, as a process of "bringing two concepts into connection" by the help of a medium, in such a manner that they "can meet in the conclusion."[1] Upon this view the demand which is once more made upon thought is that it should combine what is given as disconnected. In the second place, Inference may be regarded as the process whereby the apparently *immediate* connection of two concepts is shown to have been really *mediate*. That is to say, on this view inference neither makes a universal which

[1] See *Logic*, § 83.

combines, nor applies it to foreign data; but, beginning with a universal which is partially differentiated in judgment it makes that universal more explicit and concrete by showing that it is a necessary system of interrelated differences. On this view, if I may so express it, thought *starts* with a system, and its task is to explicate it in two ways at once: it has to express the universal more fully by bringing out the differences in it, and it must throw new light upon the differences by showing that they are necessarily related under the universal. The data must be shown to include the conclusion, as the conclusion must be shown to imply the data; that is, the wholeness and unity of the system must be vindicated. "You can no more have data or premises without conclusion than conclusion without data or premises."[1] But if the data or premises in order to be data must contain the conclusion, we do not begin with two propositions in order to produce a third, any more than in Judgment we begin with two ideas and then connect them by means of a copula. The process of Judgment is one by which thought forms distinctions within a single indefinite idea, and the process of Inference simply carries the movement of systematization, or articulation, one step further. Dr. Bosanquet calls inference "*mediate* judgment." That is to say, inference seizes upon a single datum already known to be a unity of differences, and "it drags into con-

---

[1] Bosanquet's *Logic*, Vol. II., p. 7.

sciousness the operation of the active universal as a pervading unity of content." It is not judgment with reason "annexed," but judgment with the reason already there made explicit. That is to say, when we infer, we show that ideas are necessarily connected; and there is only one way of showing that they are necessarily connected, namely, by showing that the differences can exist at all only *in virtue* of the universal, and the universal only in and through the differences.

These two views of Inference bring with them radically different conceptions of the goal of knowledge. The perfect example of inference, or of perfectly reasoned knowledge, would, on the first view, be found in the Aristotelian Syllogism as explained by formal logicians. These writers quantify and qualify the subject and predicate, because they *assume* that in judging we endeavour to express the identity of concepts; and in consequence the syllogism is found simply to say the same thing three times over. Each of the premises, as Lotze was well aware, presupposes the conclusion; for M is *identified* with P, and S with M; and therefore S and P are also directly and completely identified; hence the syllogism is purely tautological, and thought makes no synthetic movement but simply repeats itself. But, on the second view, the perfect example of inference, or of reasoned knowledge, would be found in what Lotze calls the "Speculative form of Thought," in which, as we have seen, the "Universe" is represented as "springing out of the unity of an idea which develops itself and creates the conditions of its progress," a universe rich with an endlessly varied content.

Now Lotze, in strict analogy with his manner of dealing with Conception and Judgment, starts by assuming the first view, follows it until it leads him into the deadlock of pure identity, and then avails himself of the second view without rejecting the former as false. The only difference in his method of procedure arises from the fact that the self-contradiction of formal or tautologous thought reveals itself sooner in inference than in its other forms. The Categorical Judgment conceals the unity between the concepts expressed in the subject and predicate, and Conception conceals the differences within the unity. Both *appear*, though for different reasons, to fall below system. But the very statement of the premises of an inference betrays the systematic nature of thought. For we cannot begin with any two propositions, but with two propositions given as related through a middle term : both the universal and its contents are in this manner explicit from the beginning. But immediately the syllogism is subjected to examination by Lotze and the formal logicians, it is deprived of its systematic or synthetic character; and, as we have seen, it turns out to be invalid if it advances to anything new in the conclusion, and to be tautological if it does *not* advance to anything new.

This is sufficiently well known, and I need not dwell upon it. What I wish to show is, that it turns out to be either tautological or invalid, only because it is assumed that thought is formal; or that, because it brings connections *to* its materials, it cannot connect them except at the cost of reducing them into complete identity with itself. In fact, if we quantify and qualify the subject and the predicate in both premises, the syllogism will show itself to be expressible by one circle three times repeated; and even the repetition is illegitimate.

Now Lotze admits this conclusion, and insists nevertheless that thought in inference must be progressive. But instead of rejecting the view of thought as formal, which makes it impossible that it should be progressive, instead, that is to say, of rejecting this interpretation of the syllogism, he endeavours to remedy its defects by *adding* to it two other forms of subsumption, namely, Induction and Analogy. In these forms of inference the demand for a movement to a new and broader conclusion is explicit; or, to express the fact more accurately, the universal, which is presupposed in certain cases or instances, has to show itself inclusive of *other* instances or cases, which are not at first recognized as contained in it. I need not add much to what I have already said on this matter. Lotze's treatment of Induction and Analogy is such that these inferences also show themselves to have the same radical defects as the Aristotelian form of Subsumption; that is to say, the universal can subsume nothing except that which is completely identified with it, and the argument is either tautologous or false. We have to reduce S, P, T, V, into Σ or Π; that is, we have to eliminate their differences in order to conceive them as having the same subject or predicate, M. And further, even if we did this, we do not justify the conclusion under Σ or Π of the new cases LMN, or WXY; and the inclusion of apparently new instances is the sole purpose of induction and analogy. In a word, both the given instances and the new instances can be brought into relation with the common term only by insisting solely on their sameness.

That no other method was really available to Lotze might be shown by considering his way of taking the premises of Syllogistic Subsumption as *either* analytic *or* synthetic.[1] It seems to me to be self-evident that if the premises are taken as analytic *merely*, the inference must be tautological; if taken as synthetic *merely*, it must be invalid. Analysis rejects the differences, and synthesis neglects the unity—unless we take them as correlative aspects of one activity necessarily implying each other. But Lotze, always unconscious of the significance of the negative, did not recognize their mutual implication. That is to say, the judgment could not present itself to him as both analytic and synthetic — analytic *because* it is synthetic, and

[1] See *Logic*, § 99.

synthetic *because* it is analytic—for he did not recognize that every definition of an object is both affirmation and negation.[1] Had he admitted this, he would have found himself in the dialectical movement whereby the universal advances in concreteness through distinction, which is the core of the idealistic view of thought.

There is thus, on Lotze's view, no genuine advance in the movement from the first to the second and third forms of subsumption. The only difference between them is that the same defect is exposed from different sides. In syllogistic inference we proceed from a universal with the view of finding what was in it, or in ordinary language, we proceed from the whole to the parts; in induction we start from the parts with the view of finding their universal or necessary connection. Both attempts fail for the same reason: the universal in the first case is taken as abstract, and the data in the second are treated as if they were mere particulars. And the remedy in both cases is the same, namely, that of regarding both the universal and the difference as present from the first, and viewing inference as a process whereby the relation between them is shown to be necessary. On this view we start neither from a bare universal nor from pure particulars, but from both in their relation. The

---

[1] He admits that intuition gives us truths which are at once synthetic and analytic, but intuitional apprehension is not to him logical, or thinking apprehension. (See *Logic*, § 361.)

relation between them is, however, indefinite and uncertain; and the inferential process consists in re-explaining the general law and its contents in such a manner as to make their mutual implication explicit. That this is the genuine process is manifest if we bear in mind that the major from which syllogistic inference starts is taken as having a specific content which only needs to be explicated, and that the facts or events from which induction and analogy start are not *any* facts or events, but those which we *surmise* to be "instances" of the law we desire to establish. Inference consists in the first case in the explication of the general law, and in the second case in an examination of the "instances," with a view of discovering the law which explains them. In the first case the surmised differences in the universal, in the second case the surmised law in the particulars are converted into a certainty, by showing their necessary mutual implication. There is no transition *from* a universal *to* particulars in the first case, nor *from* particulars *to* a universal in the second. Nor does inference ever proceed to that which is new; for, as we have seen, the data must contain the conclusion. But it does not follow that inference is tautological repetition; on the contrary, the discovery of the necessity of their connection throws a new light both on the unity and on the differences. The symbol of inference is not mechanical connection but organic growth. It is the evolution of the contents of a single, though not a simple, idea; and evolution neither admits of anything new nor simply repeats itself. This view of inference, however, would not only radically modify Lotze's theory of subsumption, but overthrow his theory of the fundamental function of thought. That function would be shown to consist not in connecting the discrete, but in differentiating a unity.

I have already shown that Lotze was aware of the fact that his interpretation of subsumptive inference was inconsistent with the 'living' movement of thought in synthesizing experience.[1] He is practically compelled to admit that the aim of inference is to exhibit a universal as persisting in and permeating differences.[2] But instead of drawing the apparently inevitable conclusion that either the subsumptive inference, as he has described it, is not inference at all, or that his description of it is erroneous—seeing that it led to tautology, he allows it to remain. And he endeavours to adjust matters by bringing in still another form of reasoning, namely, reasoning by *Substitution*. By doing so he is able, without rejecting his view of thought as formal and as combinatory of material supplied

---

[1] See *Logic*, §§ 102, 104.
[2] In converting the surmised law into a known law, multiplication of instances is of the highest value, not however on account of their multitude, but because each new instance brings in a new difference, which is nevertheless compatible with the universal. The universal, that is to say, becomes more concrete, and therefore more cogent.

to it from without, to escape the tautology, and to exhibit thought as progressing towards a concrete, or systematic representation of the world. Henceforth, therefore, he employs as his datum a concrete universal, that is, a universal which contains explicit differences within it, and he represents inference as the process of exhibiting the necessity of the mutual implication of the whole and the parts. But while doing so, and while compelled to do so in order to make any advance, he still considers that the thought whose evolution he is following is formal, and he continually lapses to the tautological view. It is the contradiction which springs from the attempt of Lotze to follow both of these tendencies—the tendency towards tautology which is imposed upon him by his original theory of thought, and the tendency towards systematic wholeness which the undeniably concrete character of knowledge forces upon him—that I wish to make clear in what remains of this chapter.

In making the transition from Subsumption, as he conceived it, to Substitution, Lotze is unconsciously moving into a new mode of thought inconsistent with the first. He is, as suggested, employing a concrete universal and watching the process of its evolution into differences, instead of an abstract universal with which he vainly endeavoured to combine data given as different. The importance of the transition is concealed from him for more than one reason. The main one is, of course, that he was never led by any difficulties to reconsider his first assumption that the function of thought is that of *combining* data borrowed from elsewhere. But the immediate reason is that in substitutive inference the universal is the least concrete, the nearest to the abstract universal of tautological subsumption, which thought employs. The boundaries march, and Lotze does not recognize that he has passed into a new territory. And the third reason is that his analysis of substitutive reasoning is, for him, unusually defective.

That the new universal is concrete, although its concreteness is of the lowest degree, is evident from the fact that it expresses the identity of a whole with the total number of its distinct and separate parts. Subsumption, on Lotze's view, stopped short at universals. The only conclusion which it yielded was that S is P, or rather that SP is SP; for we had completely to identify M and P in the major, and S and M in the minor, and therefore S and P in the conclusion. The conclusion might therefore be expressed in the form of $x=x$. But Substitution yields the conclusion that $x=a+b+c$; the elements which constitute x are given as separate. The universal, or the quantitative identity *of the two sides* of the equation, is thus manifestly an identity which consists with their difference. There is definite advance from tautology, now that the whole is not merely reiterated but interpreted into a number of elements existing side by side in a sum.

But Lotze was not aware of the significance of the step he had taken in passing from subsumption, as he explains it, to substitution. He was not conscious that he was employing a concrete or self-differentiating, instead of an abstract and tautological universal. This is evident from the fact that he called this kind of inference *Substitutive*. For Substitution is not inference at all. It is, rather, the result of a process of inference. The mathematician will not substitute $a+b+c$ for x unless he has already ascertained that they are equivalent; and the process of inference lies in the discovery of that equivalence, after which the act of substitution may follow as a matter of course. That process of inference is miscalled 'Substitution' by Lotze, and left entirely unexplained. Had he even endeavoured to explain it, it is probable that he would have discovered the genuine movement of thought in drawing necessary conclusions; for nowhere is the movement of inferential thought more simply exposed, or its inferential validity more manifest. And it manifestly consists in the substitution of a definite, and analyzed, and systematic, for a more indefinite universal; the latter, during the process, passing into the former. We begin with a whole that contains parts, or a universal conceived as concrete; we end with a number of parts which, taken together, constitute the same whole; and we pass from the one to the other by analyzing the sum into a number of homogeneous units, or, what is the same thing, by enumerating the units under the guidance of the conception of the required sum. What I wish to make quite clear is, that we are dealing with the same universal during the whole process and simply making it more explicit. We *prove*, or infer, that $37 = 16 + 5 + 3 + 13$ by setting out the parts one by one and enumerating them; or, in other words, by analyzing it, so as to make its contents distinct. I speak with diffidence, but I should say that all mathematical reasoning exhibits, in the most complicated of its processes, precisely the same movement. And, I should say further, that all reasoning whatsoever consists in the same kind of movement of the self-differentiation of a concrete but indefinite unity or universal, into a unity which is more concrete because its contents are more clearly set forth in their mutual relation.

The distinction between the mathematical and other reasoning processes does not spring from any difference in the essential movement of inferential thought. In fact, thought has only one way of proving a truth, namely, that of showing that it is already contained in the premises. And it shows that it was already in the premises by a more exhaustive investigation of them. The proof will wear a deductive or an inductive appearance according as the immediate purpose of the investigator throws the emphasis upon the discovery of the parts in the whole, or upon the discovery of the law which is implicit in the parts. That is to say, the movement of thought may *appear* to be either analytic or synthetic, but as a matter of fact it is always both. The analysis of the unity is not only the discovery of the parts, but the explanation and reconstruction of the law of the whole; and the synthesis of the parts under a necessary law is not only an exposition of the law, but a reconstruction of the parts. So far, then, all reasoning is the same. Different proofs spring entirely from the different things proved.

But, on the other hand, it is evident that the process by which we discover the equivalence of mathematical quantities is different from that which we employ in inferring the effects of a physical cause, or the results of a political action. Physics brings in considerations of the direction of a force, the point of its application, and many other matters which make the problem much more complex than that of simple addition and subtraction. And so do each of the other sciences. And we are not entitled to transfer the method which yields true results in regard to the joint action of physical forces to any other sphere,— *e.g.*, the moral sphere,—and apply it at once to the combined action of the motives of an intelligent being. Mathematical reasoning, so far from being the type of all possible reasoning, is capable of being employed in a valid manner only within the abstract region shut in by the definition of its subject. It moves safely only within the region marked out by its clear hypothesis. Indeed, the question of the possibility of regarding any specific method of reasoning as the type or norm is raised. May it not be the case that every object of investigation demands its own method; or, in other words, that while all reasoning is the explication of a universal into a mutually related system of contents, each universal, or unity, demands a specific mode of treatment?

This question is brought before us by Lotze under the form of the possibility of extending the sphere of application of Mathematical Substitution. Recognizing that the equational method is immediately applicable only to abstract quantities which are not real objects, but a single aspect of them, and recognizing that the object of thought is to combine into a coherent whole the complex facts of experience, Lotze is pressed on to the consideration of *Ratio* and *Proportion*. These conceptions are introduced by Lotze in order to enable us to connect, by necessary laws, data which are not reducible to homogeneous units of quantity; in order to "measure the incommensurable," as he expresses it. But, as was seen, no such result issued from their employment. I need not recapitulate the reasons which led us to conclude that what was incommensurable at the beginning remained incommensurable to the end, namely, the different *qualitative* characteristics which necessitated the employment of ratio and proportion, instead of the comparatively simple method of addition and subtraction. In this respect there was no advance made by making use of them; for what was calculable was the pure quantities, while the different units from which the calculation of proportions started were neither reduced into each other nor into instances of anything higher. Strictly speaking, therefore, the method of Substitution was not extended. And yet, on the other hand, it is undeniable that the employment of the conceptions of ratio and proportion has led to the greatest triumphs of the most completely inferential and predictive of all the natural sciences, namely, Physics. Physics, in fact, is a science of measurement, and it measures by establishing proportion between changes in objects qualitatively different. How then are we to account for this inferential power which physics has shown? It is evident that even *its* measurements are absolutely confined to the quantitative side of the objects which it investigates. The *qualitative* difference between one form of energy and another is not touched by its mathematical calculations. These remain empirical data to the end, and one form of energy is not resolved into another when a law of proportion between their changes is established. That bodies generally expand under increase of temperature is a fact of observation which mathematical substitution, by ratio or otherwise, cannot explain. And, as Lotze shows, no general law of expansion can be applied indifferently to any body: each metal exhibits its own specific ratio of change of magnitude to change of temperature. Observation and experiment must come in at every step; for it is these, and not the quantitative laws, which reveal the specific individuality, so to speak, from which the varying ratios spring. Comparison of quantities suggest *a* law of concomitant change, but the nature of that which makes the changes concomitant is not brought to light. Physics, in a word, employs observation and experiment as well as mathematical processes; and, just as observation without the latter would simply lead to a natural history of the facts and a mere collection of disconnected particulars, so the latter, by itself, would give nothing but empty quantitative relations that would throw no light upon the law of the changes of objects. The extension of substitutive inference is impossible. It may, of course, be applied to all objects, provided we can grasp the quantitative side, which all objects whatsoever must have, and fix upon a definite and constant unit; but this is not an extension of the method *beyond quantity*, as might be gathered from Lotze's expression.

Are we to consider, then, that where science makes use of the conceptions of ratio and proportion it is making use of two methods, the one for computing and the other for observing facts? If so, in what relation do they stand to each other? Can physical investigation be fitly described as mathematical substitution *plus* empiricism? Or, on the other hand, does its observation of data, its experimentation, its preparation of its material for mathematical calculation, also involve processes of inference which are *not* mathematical?

These questions, I believe, bring the fundamental difficulty of Lotze's position into clear view, and enable us at once to discuss the value and validity of his whole movement from Substitution to Proportional inference, and thence to Classification, Explanation, and the Speculative form of thought. Lotze recognizes the difficulty. He admits explicitly "that the group of mathematical forms of inference ends here,—with the emphatic recognition of the fact that the point which does not admit of being dealt with mathematically is the disparateness of marks"; and he also admits that this "is precisely the point which we cannot avoid considering." That is to say, mathematical reasoning stops short at quantitative equation; but we are forced onward by the demand which thought makes that experience shall be systematic, and shall include in its system the qualitative differences of objects. We must pass from equation to definition; we must consider the combination of different qualities and different objects, as well as their quantitative differences. So that the question is unavoidable, whether, when we thus pass to the consideration of qualities, we leave all inference behind, or make use of another method of reasoning which yields universal laws of connections between the qualities of real objects; in other words, whether the "definition" we must employ involves inference, or is merely descriptive; whether, in defining, we do more than set side by side the qualitative differences which observation yields to our empirical observation.

I find Lotze's answer to be hesitating. He is once more drawn in two directions by the theory of the formal nature of thought from which he starts, and by the demand which experience makes that its systematic necessity shall be revealed by thought. In obedience to the tendency which springs from his theory of thought, he is impelled to give over to other powers than those of logical thought all that refuses to yield itself to mathematical computation; in obedience to the second, he is led to recognize elements of necessity and universality in the processes of Classification, and Scientific Explanation, and Speculation, although these processes do not appear to rest upon Computation.

The phenomena which in presenting themselves force this problem upon Lotze, we may arrange as follows:—*First*—the qualitative differences which give rise to the employment of ratio and proportion; the units which refuse to be expressed in terms of each other. *Second*—the differences *in value* or significance of the qualities of objects, leading us to regard some of these as essential, and as exercising a dominant function over others, and enabling us to raise them into principles of classification according to type. *Third*—the apparent transition of one genus into another, leading us to regard some special genus, or some special principle embodied in it, as the source of a law which dominates all other genera, and to arrange objects in an ascending order, according to the degree in which this highest principle is realized in them. For, in all these cases, as Lotze sees, there is evidence of the operation of regulative laws which make our experience systematic. Classification, as he shows, was no matter of mere empiricism even before science entered the field. Ordinary thought was in some way led to employ principles of classification that were to some degree explanatory of objects, and apparently constitutive of them. And it is still more obvious that systematizing thought which, to say the least, does not appear to be purely mathematical in its character, has been operative in the building up of our scientific and philosophic theories. Since thought has achieved these results, logic cannot avoid the problem of revealing the nature of the processes which thought has employed.

How, therefore, does thought, by means of the conceptions of ratio and proportion, establish laws of correspondence between the changes of objects, between whose qualities there remains a permanent and insoluble difference. What is there found in Lotze's view beside mathematical computation? Observation of data! "The ultimate discoverable laws of phenomena will always be found to involve determinate relations between disparate elements which we can only accept as facts, and utilize in the form of proportion, without being able to show the reason why the two elements must be proportional." "From one disparate thing to another our thought has no means of transition; all our explanation of the connection of things goes no further back than to laws which admit of being expressed in the form of proportion; and these laws make no attempt to fuse the two elements into an undiscoverable third, but leave them both in their full difference."[1] The stream of inference, which is merely computative, and the observation of facts flow side by side without mingling, so far as Lotze shows us anything to the contrary; and the processes of necessary connection according to law, seem to belong purely to the former, while the latter is presented as purely empirical.

If we turn in the next place to the classification of objects according to essential qualities, and ask how it has been brought about, we receive practically

[1] *Logic*, § 115.

the same answer. The mere fact that thought has been guided in such a manner as to be able to distinguish between the essential, dominant, constitutive qualities of objects, and those which are, comparatively speaking, contingent and without significance is undeniable. But when Lotze comes to enquire *how* this has been done, he practically says, in the first place, that logic cannot answer. Logic issues a prohibition, gives a "general direction not to choose as bases of division *notiones communes, i.e.*, marks which are known to occur in the most different objects, without exercising any recognizable influence upon the rest of their nature." But "the positive direction answering to this prohibition, viz., how to find the decisive basis of division, *logic leaves entirely* to be given by special knowledge of the matter in question." The errors of merely combinatory and meaningless classification are "avoided in practice by concomitant reflection and an estimate of the different values of the marks, based upon knowledge of the facts or a right feeling, often merely upon an instinctive taste."[1] Classification, in a word, is based upon the knowledge of the facts—a view which no one, I should say, would care to deny—and that knowledge of the facts is *not guided* by rational or logical principles of thought, a view which is most doubtful. Indeed, a little further on, we find Lotze himself resile from handing over this most important function

[1] *Logic*, § 128.

of classification to "right feeling" or "instinctive taste," or to any other such contingent, or, at least, unanalyzed process. In the case of Classification according to an *Ideal*, which leads on step by step "to the systematic organization of the whole world of thought," computation or mathematical inference once more comes in, and takes at least a remnant of the truth from the hands of mere contingency. The distinction between the various degrees in which species correspond to their generic concepts, is found to have its quantitative side. All objects, all elements, have "intensity," "number of parts," and "specific relations"; and these can furnish a foothold for equational reasoning. "The possibility of making this distinction depends primarily upon quantitative measurements to which the several marks and their relations are possibly or necessarily accessible."[1] If, in a scheme of development such as the biological kingdom, we wish to account for the way in which some animals are placed lower in the scale than others, we can count and measure. And similarly in the case of Classification according to *type*, and the distinction between natural and forced classification. "An instructed taste will partially obviate" the evils of the unnatural classification, and besides "taste," we can avail ourselves of computation. This method will show us how, by increase or decrease of qualities, an object tends to pass from one class to another;

[1] *Logic*, § 131.

and it enables us to fix upon that species as the most perfect example of the type whose essential marks are, at their greatest quantities, in equilibrium. "We always regard as the typical and most expressive examples of each genus those species in which all the marks are at the highest value which the combination prescribed by the genus allows."[1] And the highest value is, as he has explained, the highest quantitative value. This side, namely, the quantitative, lends itself once more to logical exposition; that is to say, it consists of inferential processes of thought. "This point of view belongs entirely to logic, and is independent of the views which we may form on other and material grounds as to the value, meaning, and function of anything which has the law of its existence in a generic concept."[2] But what shall we say of all that remains over, and is, on Lotze's own showing, not reducible into merely quantitative differences? No doubt the knowledge of material grounds of value, meaning, and function is requisite for classification; but is that knowledge, because it is material, not guided by rational and necessary principles of thought which are susceptible of logical justification? Apparently not, on the view of Lotze. All that refuses to yield itself to calculation has to be handed over to "instructed taste," "instinctive taste," "right feeling," "concomitant reflection," and such other intuitive processes resting on material knowledge

[1] *Logic*, § 133. [2] *Ibid.*, § 132.

as fall beyond the sphere of the logician, although logic deals with all conceiving, judging, and reasoning, with all the processes which build up experience into systematic knowledge. Conceptions of purpose, end, destination, the active self-differentiation of a supreme principle, force themselves upon Lotze. By employing these conceptions, modern science and philosophy have achieved the most momentous results, and carried knowledge beyond the classificatory methods of ancient times. But we look in vain to Lotze to find the logical justification of these processes. If we ask "how Classification by development reaches its required conclusion, the certainty, namely, that it has really found that supreme law or logical destination which governs the particular object or the universe at large," he replies: "To this we can only answer, that by way of mere logic it is quite impossible to arrive at such a certainty." "The whole realm of the real and the thinkable must be regarded as a system of series in which concept follows concept in a determinate direction; but the discovery of the direction itself, and of the supreme directing principle, it leaves to positive knowledge to *know as best it can*."[1] Once more, I would emphasize the fact that no one can well deny that for all these purposes "positive knowledge" is necessary; but is this all that logic can say of "positive knowledge," namely, that it must know these things *as best it*

[1] *Logic*, § 138.

can? Does inference stop where we fail to count and measure? Is it not possible to give any rational justification for classing together the ox and the horse and the rhinoceros, rather than the ox and the oak and the east wind, except such as issues from the addition and subtraction of homogeneous units of quantity? And is there no other logically justifiable reason for regarding man as higher in the scale of creation than the tiger and the cat or the snake, except that the equations which would set forth the quantities of their different elements would be different? Lotze's answer is explicit. "The form of proportion indicates a limit to knowledge," and proportion, as explained by Lotze, is adding and subtracting *plus* empiricism.

Lotze's analysis of the process of inference has the high merit of placing the problem of logical or necessary thinking in a clear light. He helps to make the choice between a formal and material view of its processes inevitable. For either Science and Philosophy must be content to forego their pretension to any definitely assured knowledge that passes beyond the limits of mathematical computation, or else we must regard the systematic character of the results they have attained as due to processes of inference which are not capable of being characterized as mathematical. In other words, there is no strictly verifiable knowledge except mathematics, or else thought is not merely mathematical and subsumptive. In its dealing with qualitative differences, with considerations that spring from the conception of the significance of elements, their real relations, their interaction, destination, purpose and end, in a word, with all that leads mind to find in the world something which demands more than that its objects should be counted and measured, we must either regard thought as being led by principles not capable of being justified as inferential; or else we must consider that Lotze's view of the logical processes is utterly inadequate. We have to condemn either Lotze's view of thought as formal, or all knowledge as uncertain, and perhaps invalid, except that which is based upon the abstract conception of quantity. The choice will be the less hesitating if we examine once more from another point of view his exposition of Mathematical Inference.

It is evident from what has just been said that Lotze's attempt to advance from Substitutive Inference to Classification, Explanatory Theory and the Dialectical Ideal of Thought has failed. For the only inferential element in these processes, that is to say, the only element which could be logically justified as the source of necessarily valid relations, was the Mathematical. What remained over was that which material knowledge gains "as best it can." We are no doubt driven to employ these forms by the impulse towards complete systematization which characterizes thought. And Lotze is at some pains to show that the ideals after which these forms of thought strive are in themselves valid—the defect lying solely in our imperfect application of them, or, in the last case, in some weakness that attaches to human thought as such.[1] But, on the other hand, "if the validity of these ideals is not at all impaired by the fact that human knowledge is not able to apply them to every given instance," how does it come that logic is able to give no better justification of them than that they are realizable only on the quantitative side —the side which misses entirely all that we can mean by the nature of objects, their interaction, and their functions? For these have been explicitly given up to material knowledge, which proceeds as best it can. "A demonstrative method, or a method which involves no logical jumps, a sure logical receipt for arriving at a true universal law of a series of events, does not exist."[2] "The discovery of an universal law is always a guess on the part of the imagination, made possible by a knowledge of facts."[3] Lotze's resolute exclusion from the sphere of logic of material considerations narrows the operations of thought which it can justify to mathematical reasoning.

But if we exclude material considerations we cannot justify even the mathematical processes. Not those of ratio and proportion; for these, as we have abundantly seen, must derive the units which they employ from empirical observation of the facts of

---

[1] See *Logic*, § 151. [2] *Logic*, § 269. [3] *Ibid.*

experience. What then of purely Mathematical Substitution? That Lotze has given no logical justification of this process we have already seen. The obviously undeniable equivalence of a mathematical sum and the total number of its homogeneous units led Lotze to regard the *act* of substituting as logical, and to overlook the fact that the process of enumerating the units, or of analyzing the sum, was the inferential process which demanded logical justification. But no logical justification of it is possible on Lotze's view of thought, on the view, namely, that qualitative differences act as an absolute bar to inference. For even although a quantitative sum is the unit of thought which has the least concrete character, or in which individuality is at its lowest point, it is not without *any* character or individuality. Even in this extreme of abstraction thought has not succeeded in rejecting all content. Even in a quantitative sum, as Kant has pointed out, the synthetic element must not count for nothing; or, in other words, there is a genuine process of transition through difference to unity in concluding that $7 + 5 = 12$, as all who have watched the first attempts of a child will readily acknowledge. After all, $7 + 5 = 12$, is a different statement from $7 + 5 = 7 + 5$, or $12 = 12$, although analysis would show that in this latter statement also there is evidence of the operation of a thought that recognizes unity *only* in difference. Nor is the universal entirely inoperative: on the contrary, while leaving its parts comparatively free, so that we can say that $12 = 7 + 5$, or $5 + 7$, or $3 + 2 + 4 + 3$, and so on, it still directs that its parts shall be explicable as definite and homogeneous units; 100 or 1000 is not the sum of *any* quantities; a unit is not *any* thing, although it may be the quantitative aspect of any concrete object. But the idea of a universal that is operative in its contents, giving them their character, or of a universal that maintains itself in and by means of difference is manifestly not admissible to a logician who makes bare identity the ideal of thought. It is as impossible for purely formal thought to make the transition from $7 + 5$ to 12, as from S to P. We require the condition on which the categorical statement of their equivalence rests; and that condition cannot be given, as our analysis of Subsumptive Inference showed. For Subsumption, on Lotze's principles, either lapsed into tautology, or else had to be pronounced invalid. Thus, step by step, the apparent advance towards forms of thought more adequate to combine the concrete data of experience proves illusory. The higher processes of philosophical systematization, Scientific Explanation and Classification, have no logical justification except that which issues from mathematical reasoning by ratio and proportion. But reasoning by ratio and proportion, if we eliminate the empirical or material element, sinks into pure Computation, or Substitution; Substitution, in turn, lapses into Subsumption; Subsumption is either tautological or invalid. Thus thought can combine no differences, and that was its only function. The exclusion of the matter and the attempt to treat thought as purely formal has led to its extinction.

What Lotze has done in his ascent from Subsumption to Dialectical Thought is really to expose the inadequacy and invalidity of his view of the function of thought. Formal reasoning, as long as its formality is manifest, fails to move at all. As long as S and P have no definite meaning we cannot bring them together by means of premises; nothing can mediate between them, and we have to conclude that S is not P, and Σ is not M, or M II, unless by means of accessory notions, which as formal they cannot yield, we reduce them to identity. In Substitution the movement of genuine reasoning began; but it is due to the fact that our data have meaning, or material content. It is because we recognize that the sum is a sum of definite units whose character is known, that we proceed to explicate its contents by analyzing it into these units. In that analysis we are progressively showing the construction of the sum and the systematic nature of the datum from which inference sets forth, and inference consists simply in following the movement of this datum from an implicit system to a system whose parts are articulated.

When we ascend to reasoning by ratio and proportion, we begin to deal with objects whose whole nature refuses to yield itself to merely quantitative expression; and what Mr. Bosanquet calls "the very travail of the mind" begins, namely, "the enquiry into actual and material conditions or connections." And the purely mathematical element in this enquiry, just in so far as it fails to grasp the actual nature of the objects, ceases to have value as inference. For, in truth, mathematical proofs come in *ab extra* in order to verify, by accessory and contingent considerations, inferences that have been already made; and *because* they come in *ab extra*, and do not issue from anything deeper than the quantitative aspect of the objects, the demonstration they yield is incomplete. As Lotze himself has shown, all that proportion between changes in different subjects establishes is the existence of a constant relation, or rather, a strong *presumption* that there is a common law which binds them. That is to say, failing actually to discover in what way one form of energy,—say mechanical energy, passes into another form,—say the energy of heat, and knowing only that energy disappears in one form and that it reappears in another, the physicist concludes, after he has convinced himself by the exclusion of all other possible sources of energy in the second case, that the same energy has persisted through the change of form. The inference is in no wise *based* upon mathematical considerations, but upon the material premises; and into these premises the investigator throws all the wealth of his previously acquired knowledge of nature. And the more discriminative his knowledge, or the more systematic, or the greater the degree in which he is able to focus the light of the whole world upon the problem in hand, the greater his success in developing the indefinite system which is in the datum, into an explicit system of necessarily relative elements. It is consideration of the material that enables him to predict, and to extend his universal law over cases not yet observed; and, just in so far as the material, or data from which he starts, is already recognized as connected by real relations to his conception of the physical world as an orderly totality, or, in other words, just in so far as his world enters into his datum, the progress of his inference is valid. Mathematical calculation is not, even in physical matters, of the essence of the inferential process. For instance, even in the case where the astronomer infers the existence of a planet in a certain quarter of the heavens from the disturbances observed in the path of another body, calculation is only an instrument, although a most powerful one, in the hands of the astronomical system which is presupposed, and apart from which it would be powerless. The inference really springs from the complex, material considerations of objects acting upon each other by gravitation with a force varying according to distance; and these are verified, not by mathematics, but by the constancy with which they hold in every fresh application. The inference is guaranteed by the cogency of the whole system which is employed in making it, that is to say, by all the relevant *material* considerations which the astronomer is able to adduce. The aberrations in the path of the planet force him to choose between his whole astronomical system, and the truth of the aberrations he has observed. The exception threatens the whole body of his science, while his reduction of the exception into a new example of the general law corroborates the hypothesis on which the whole science rested. The cogency of the mathematical element in the argument, as contrasted with that which springs from material considerations, is only due to its comparative simplicity. We can analyze a mathematical datum into its contents in such a way as to shut out doubt, because the identity of the sum and the whole series of its parts are plain; but to throw all the emphasis of proof upon quantitative equality is to regard science as tending towards an abstract construction of the universe, and to ignore the fact that its triumphs are marked by its articulation of nature into a more and more concrete system.

As we leave the sphere of Physics, which is able to make so powerful a *corroborative* use of quantitative measurement, to those spheres in which life and intelligence complicate our problem, such measurement not only becomes less available but less valid. The validity of mathematical reasoning as applied to the physical universe is complete only where we deal with the abstraction of quantity, and it becomes more and more untrustworthy in its results the more concrete the material on which it is employed. To count all men as one, and no man as more than one, was a valuable ideal for an age where the equality of man had ceased to be an effective principle in social and political matters; but to raise the consideration of mathematical equality into a dominant principle which should override all other considerations, would render the conception of social or political organization impossible; and any inferences based upon such a hypothesis would be falsified by every private and public action. To make valid inferences regarding a state or community we must know it, and towards such knowledge the computation of the units that compose it would go but a very little way. Differences in qualities, so far from prescribing the limit of inference, are its very essence. They bar all progress in reasoning only if we *presuppose* that the aim of reasoning is to find pure identity, and that thought is formal. It is true that differences in quality present us with a problem; but they present us with a problem only because they present us also with an indefinite unity which demands articulation. It is scarcely too much to say that the main steps which science takes in its interpretation of nature are due to exceptions, that is, to differences which begin with challenging the ordering law. By further knowledge of these the law is modified and re-interpreted through the modification, the light of the exception being reflected into the system. And yet, on the other hand, the exception itself would not have the requisite power to compel reconstruction if it had not systematic knowledge behind it. In other words, the bare particular is as impotent for inference and as valueless for reason as the bare universal. But no qualities of objects are mere differences: their resistance to a law derives all its power from their affinity to it. In a word, they must be relevant to the system which they threaten. Hence every effective exception is a new aspect of the unity, and all genuine differences bind; just as every universal is effective and combines by necessary law only in the degree in which it reveals itself as concrete.

Inference, therefore, is progress from system to system; and it would arrive at necessity only when all the manifold data of experience reveal themselves as manifestations of a single principle which lives in the deepest differences. Up to that point, which we can never reach, scientific systems, including mathematics itself, will remain hypothetical, and the truths they contain will rest upon unverified assumptions. But as that point is approached, every material datum whose nature is exposed by analysis, and every general law whose synthetic power is shown in its extended application, more or less corroborate previously acquired knowledge, and bring it nearer to the ideal. The true history of thought, and the true science of its laws and operations, will follow step by step the evolution of its material into a systematic world of necessarily related objects.

But such a view of thought is impossible to a theory which has staked its destiny on the presupposition of its formal nature, and whose only result is, on the one side, to make any inferential movement of thought unintelligible, and, on the other, to hand over the whole world of science and philosophy to the empiricism which systematizes "as best it can." That Lotze's view of thought renders all its processes nugatory, and that it leads him to attribute all the processes that are effective in the growth of knowledge to sense, perception, and faith, and thereby to consequences whose sceptical nature is concealed only by their dogmatism, will become more evident as we discuss the general considerations which follow Lotze's analysis of the thinking processes of conception judgment, and reasoning.

CHAPTER VII

THE SUBJECTIVE WORLD OF IDEAS AND THE SUBJECTIVE PROCESSES OF THOUGHT

LOTZE ends both the first and the third book of his Logic with a sympathetic reference to Idealism. In the former he admits that in the Speculative form of thought, "if we could give that form to the whole material of thought, our mind would find all its demands satisfied;"[1] and in the latter he says, "I will at least close with the avowal that I hold that much reviled ideal of speculative intuition to be the supreme and not wholly unattainable goal of science."[2] His quarrel is not with the idealistic view of the ideal of knowledge, but with the doctrine that the ideal is attainable by thought. He does not so much desire to establish another view of the world, as to prove that the truth is attainable by other means than those of the discursive understanding with which he identifies thought.

[1] *Logic*, § 151.   [2] *Ibid.*, § 365.

We have seen what extreme difficulties meet him in the attempt to confine thought to the formal activity of combining externally given contents: how formal thought, at each step of advancing knowledge, showed itself more and more inadequate to the demands that were made upon it; how the apparent transitions from one form to another, from Conception to Judgment, from Judgment to Reasoning—nay, from each of the subsidiary forms of these latter to the higher one—proved to be unintelligible, the higher being only *apparently* higher than the preceding form; we have seen, in other words, how thought lapses back, in Lotze's hands, into mere tautology, each of the forms of reasoning, judgment, and conception failing in turn to break its fall. But none of these difficulties roused Lotze to reconsider his fundamental presupposition that thought is a formal, combining function. On the contrary, while the method of his procedure allowed a certain doubt to remain as to whether thought might not after all be constructive and systematic; while thought seemed in conceiving to *find* its laws in its materials, in judging to *find* the contents of experience to be systematically and inwardly combined by a law of sufficient reason, we are explicitly told at the end of the process that "the universal laws are produced by thought from itself alone." That is to say, it does not reveal these laws within, but externally superimposes them upon, the contents of experience. And the result is, of course, that these universals, being the products of thought, are artificial and subjective, and not to be taken as objective and constitutive of the facts which they serve to explain. Here Lotze definitely asserts that it is this confusion between the necessary forms of thought and objective principles of unity which constitutes the fundamental error of Idealism. Pushed himself to the very verge of Idealism by the facts, which he acknowledges in no stinted fashion, that knowledge grows in concreteness, and that its ideal would be the recognition of a single self-articulating principle, he is drawn back from the precipice by the presupposition that thought must be formal, and that its laws must be only principles of arrangement without any content of their own. Not that he wishes to deny that such an objective principle exists, nor even that it is possible for us to know it, at least in part; but what he insists upon is that we cannot know it by means of thought. Thought, which is a faculty of pure forms, can yield no material knowledge; and Hegel had no right to convert a merely logical conception, although it is necessary for us in arranging the material of knowledge, into an objective principle of reality. The ideal system ought to be for thought, but what "ought to be" for thought must not be changed into the actual existence of direct experience.[1]

[1] See *Logic*, § 151.

From this it follows that the question of the value of the whole philosophic endeavour of Lotze is concentrated into this single problem: Is thought formal? In the last chapter I tried to show that if it is, it is tautological, and entirely incapable of performing the only function attributed to it by Lotze, namely, that of combining the data of experience. All its universals proved empty and powerless; they could not combine what was given as different, nor convert the contingent coincidences of experience into a necessarily coherent system. But there are reasons which Lotze adduces in favour of his invincible conviction that thought is a faculty of pure forms, and in no sense constitutive, that still remain to be examined. These reasons are given by Lotze, and with uncommon dialectical power, in the Third Book of his *Logic*.

Side by side with the statement that the speculative or idealistic form would satisfy all the demands of thought, Lotze places another, namely, that "the condition under which human thought is placed may be altogether inadequate to achieve the speculative ideal in more than a few instances, perhaps even in one."[1] By that condition he means the eccentric position, "somewhere in the extreme ramifications of reality," to which we have already alluded, and which prevents human thought from immediately grasping its material and "penetrating it with its presence." Thought, in order to obtain

[1] *Logic*, § 151.

a systematic view of the world, and avoid a presentation of it which is out of focus, must approach its task in a mediate fashion by means of relations, producing these relations out of itself. These relations are not part of the reality, nor a part of the explanation of reality, but *means* towards explanation—paths to the mountain top, scaffolding to the building, as the reader will remember. Hence, Lotze's task of justifying this view is tantamount to the task of proving that the products of thought are artificial, and that its process concerns *it* alone, without any participation in them by the experience and reality which they are employed to explain. He has to prove that thoughts are not things, and that the principles of our thought do not "penetrate things with their presence."

It might be considered obvious at once that thoughts are not things. Common sense, no less than philosophy, revolts against the immediate identification of the world with the representation of it made by thought. Nor is there any doubt that Idealism, if it is to be regarded as an endeavour to evaporate the real world into empty and unsubstantial products of the activity of our intelligence, has either an inveterate prejudice or an invincible truth arrayed against it. It seems too evident to need demonstration that the world of ideas is not the world of things. I would go so far as to state unconditionally that it does not matter whether such ideas are adequate or inadequate, true or false, held by man or by some superior intelligence, they are in no case the things which they represent. It is inconsistent with the possibility of knowledge that it should *be* the reality which it represents; knowledge is incompatible alike with sinking the real in the ideal, and the ideal in the real. Absolute scepticism, the paralysis of all intelligence, follows alike the complete and indistinguishable identification, and the complete separation of the real and the ideal. And it is most important that we should keep *both* of these collateral truths steadily before our minds. The philosophy of Hegel and the philosophy of Lotze may be regarded as deriving one of their fundamental distinctions from the fact that they ward against the same scepticism upon different sides. Hegel, as against his predecessors, opposes mainly the tendency so to separate the real and the ideal as to obscure or annul the principle which reveals itself in both of them; Lotze directs his main attack against what he conceived to be their immediate identification by Hegel. And it is this which, in my opinion, makes him so valuable as an expounder of Idealism, and helps us to know more clearly than Hegel's immediate successors what he meant by the principle of thought which he identified with the principle of all reality.[1]

[1] It is no part of my present endeavour to expound or defend Hegel's view, or to endeavour to show that Hegel's thought was not thoughts as Lotze believed, and that in pronouncing the

The first part of the task of Lotze consists then in proving that the real and the ideal are not identical; the second, in proving that while not identical they are still not separate. In performing the first part of his task he endeavours to show (1) that ideas are not things, and (2) that they are not even like to, or images of, things; in performing his second he tries to show that ideas are valid of things, and that their validity while real does not *exist* as an additional element over and above the objects and connections concerning which we have valid knowledge.

I do not think it is necessary to say much of Lotze's attempt to prove the first of these points.¹ It seems to come to him as an immediate conviction, superior to the need of proof, that things do not pass into thoughts. Indeed, the opposite view, that we know not ideas but things seems to him to be entirely meaningless. It is a "fallacy" to think "that the conception of a knowledge which apprehends things not as they are known but as they are, means anything intelligible at all."² But, while the very immediacy of the conviction that the only objects on which thought can be engaged are ideas, or that thought is inevitably confined

---

principle of reality to be spiritual, he did not regard it as the product of any intelligence in the sense of an idea, or a world of ideas.

¹ See above, chap. ii.
² *Logic*, § 311. See also §§ 312, 313, and so on.

within the circle of its own ideal contents, stands in the way of direct proof, he finds it indirectly proved by scepticism, which he subjects to a most interesting analysis.[1] Scepticism, he thinks, derives all its vitality from its attempt to travel beyond the boundaries of the sphere of ideas, so as to compare knowledge as a whole with some presumed reality that exists beyond its boundary. It does this in two ways, by conceiving and then refuting a world of real objects which is either (1) identical with, or (2) similar to the world of ideas. But once it is seen that no such world of real objects is predicable without contradiction, scepticism loses its only foothold. In other words, its condemnation of ideas for not being identical with, or images of, things, falls to the ground as soon as it is recognized that it is no part of the function of ideas either to be or to image things, and that we have no possible means of apprehending the things beyond knowledge by reference to which we may condemn it. The criterion of knowledge is not an "assumed external world of the Real which comes in here between our ideas as the standard by which their truth is to be measured; the standard is always the conception of which we cannot get rid, of what such a world must be if it does exist, is always, that is to say, a thought in our minds."[2] The criterion of thought is its own content, or that which is of the same nature as its

[1] See *Logic*, Book III., chap. i.   [2] *Logic*, § 306.

present content. We condemn knowledge by our conception of fuller knowledge, not by that which is not, and cannot possibly be, knowledge. "A scepticism which indulges the apprehension that everything may be in reality quite different from what it necessarily appears, sets out with a self-contradiction, because it silently takes for granted the possibility of an apprehension which does not apprehend things but is itself things, and then goes on to question whether this impossible perfection is allotted to our intelligence."[1] And it is evident that the same contradiction is involved in asserting the *similarity* of ideas and things. Here, also, what is defined as beyond knowledge is taken to be known. And besides, the slightest examination of the ideas of "imaging" and "copying," which are so freely used in this connection, will show that they are mere metaphors, entirely inapplicable to the matter in hand. The mind is not a mirror, ideas are not pictures; even if the mind were a mirror, and if the external world reflected itself upon the mirror, the presence of the picture and the recognition of it as present are entirely different things. "The apprehending consciousness is no resisting surface, curved or plain, smooth or rough, nor would it gain anything by reflecting rays no matter in what direction; it is in itself and its own co-ordinating unity, which is not a space and not a surface, but an activity,

[1] *Logic*, § 309.

that it has to combine the separate ideas excited in it into the perception of a spatial arrangement, which perception again is not itself an order in space, but only the idea of that order."[1] In a word, the crude idea of similarity is sufficiently refuted by the equally crude distinction between spaceless objects of thought and a spatial world of real objects. There is no need to follow this further. As against the scepticism which comes from the immediate identification of things and thoughts, or their mediate identification through the conception of their similarity, Lotze guards by confining mind entirely to its own contents, and repudiating altogether a world of objects beyond the confines of knowledge. Truth "belongs to the world of our ideas in itself, without regard to its agreement with an assumed reality of things outside its borders."[2]

But it may well seem that in his attempt to destroy the basis of scepticism, that is to say, in insisting that mind is absolutely confined to ideas —"that this varied world of ideas within us, it matters not where they may have come from, forms the sole material directly given to us, from which alone our knowledge can start,"[3]—Lotze has conceded all that the sceptic could desire. That is to say, the sceptic does not deny that we know, or have, ideas; what he denies is, that that knowledge, since it is neither identical with nor

[1] *Logic*, § 327.   [2] *Ibid.*, § 313.   [3] *Ibid.*, § 306.

similar to its objects, is true. By cutting away the ground from the sceptic, Lotze seems to have also cut it away from himself. If the sceptic cannot prove that knowledge is false, it might appear that Lotze cannot prove that it is true; in fact, unless we can compare ideas with the realities which they mean, both truth and error would seem to be equally impossible. There is no knowledge because there are no knowable objects except ideas. Lotze, in endeavouring to avoid sinking thoughts in things, may seem to have fallen into the equally grave error of abolishing things in favour of thoughts.

But Lotze does not admit this. He draws a distinction instead. For it is one thing to assert that we cannot know real objects by means of thought; it is quite another to say that we cannot find by other means that they exist. And again, it is one thing to say that ideas cannot *be* their objects, or that ideas cannot be *images of* their objects, but it is another to say that they cannot be *valid* of objects. Although, as we have seen, "it is not a necessity of thought that thought itself should be possible,"[1] it is still conceivable that there may be some other necessity why thought should be, and why its contents should reveal the true nature of the world of facts. We cannot prove that things are from the idea of them, or pass from necessity in thought to necessity in fact, or actuality; neverthe-

[1] *Logic*, § 346.

less it may be possible to start from the actuality of some fact, and proceed therefrom to the validity of knowledge. In any case, Lotze will not willingly permit any doubt to remain as to the complete subjectivity of all knowledge, human and other; for "this is no prejudicial lot of the human spirit, but must recur in every being which stands in relation to anything beyond it."[1] Nor will he admit that the subjectivity of knowledge implies that it is untrustworthy. On the contrary "This universal subjectivity, belonging to all knowledge, can settle nothing as to its truth or untruth." Whether our knowledge does or does not correspond to the presumed outer world of real objects, we cannot by means of thought say. We cannot compare our knowledge to any such objects, seeing that we know only ideas, and we cannot pass judgment upon our knowledge without thereby employing principles whose validity is being questioned. Thought may construct its system of ideas, making it all compact of invariable connections, and conclusions following necessarily from data; so that thought, starting from any datum and going in any direction by "the most roundabout tracks," would still be led to the certain discovery of the result it requires. Nevertheless the whole system would hang in the air. All that thought can determine by its laws is that a thing *if* it exists must be identical with itself, and that *if*

[1] *Metaphysics*, § 94.

a certain condition exists, certain consequences will follow; that is to say, the whole system of thought connections is based upon a hypothesis which thought itself cannot verify. "To no single constituent b of the ideal world can thought ascribe, over and above the eternal validity which within that world belongs to it, a necessity of realization in the order of events in time."[1] One matter of fact, one "pin-point rock" of reality might serve to actualize the whole system of necessarily related thoughts. "If only this reality belongs as a matter of fact to a second such element a, with which b stands in necessary connection, it can then pass over to b also."[2] But thought can furnish no such point. There is a great gulf fixed between the world of ideas and that of reality, so that no unsubstantial thought, no shade that wanders in that realm, which is valid without existing, can take upon itself the body of actuality, and be.

But in this extremity Lotze finds help in another quarter. Where thought fails, perception, or experience, or intuition, on the one side, and feeling on the other, succeeds. While all our knowledge is hypothetical as respects thought, "it strikes in at a particular point in a reality which it finds, as a matter of fact, given to it, in order to deduce from this real premiss, as themselves *real*, the consequences which attached to the thought premiss as necessary."[3] This "matter of fact," this "real pre-

[1] *Logic*, § 348. [2] *Ibid.* [3] *Ibid.*

miss," must not be confused with anything that thought may, in its own right, endeavour to represent as incontrovertible and necessary, although "within the world of ideas itself there are fixed points, primary certainties, starting from which we may be enabled to bring the rest of the shifting multitude of our ideas into something like orderly connection."[1] In all our knowledge "we start from some truth which operates upon the mixture of our thoughts, which is submitted to the test like a fermenting matter, assimilating that which is akin to it, and rejecting that which is alien."[2] But even these fixed points and primary certainties are only ideas, and the fermentation will only issue in a consistent system of mere thoughts. The things, the realities to which they refer, are still beyond reach. Indeed, thought being a process of mediation, always comprehending one fact only by reference to another, can, strictly speaking, yield no fixed point, or primary certainty, or matter of fact. And yet, "on the possibility of an immediate knowledge of *some* universal truth all certain belief depends."[3] Whence, then, can we derive this immediate knowledge? The answer which Lotze gives is analogous to that which we have already discussed in connection with the relation of thought and its preliminary processes. When he contemplates the mediate and formal character of thought, he is driven to seek for the fixed certainties in

[1] *Logic*, § 209.   [2] *Ibid.*, § 322.   [3] *Ibid.*, § 356.

"experience," in the sense of direct perception. "Facts of perception," he says, "we acknowledge without question; our misgivings begin with the interpretations of those facts by discursive thought, more especially when we consider the protracted and intricate webs of ideas which thought spins in abstraction from the facts of sense, yet always with the expectation of reaching a final result which perception will confirm."[1] From this point of view he examines the sure truths which are yielded by Mathematics and by Natural Science, and finds that they are all dependent upon direct perception. In the end everything "is given *to* thought and nothing *by* thought." It depends entirely upon "the grace of facts." "Neither the idea of quantity as such, nor the more defined conception of its capability of being summed, nor finally any one arithmetical proposition, ever enters into our consciousness without being occasioned, and the occasion can always be traced in the last resort to an external stimulus."[2] It is not "the bare logical principle of identity," nor, indeed, any other logical principle or law of thought, "but the perception of quantity, . . . which at once guarantees the truth of arithmetical reasoning, and is the source of its fruitfulness."[3] As he himself admits, he has to "invoke the aid of Perceptions to supply both subject, predicate, and copula of the judgment in which we express the *a priori* principles, from

[1] *Logic*, § 334. [2] *Ibid.*, § 353. [3] *Ibid.*

which we proceed to extend knowledge and discover the laws of nature." He is obliged by his view of thought, as dependent for each of its activities upon external stimuli, to find everything in experience. And the difference between him and the empiricists, whom he criticises, amounts simply to this, "that to him, principles presented as truths are valid always, whereas, in the view of empirical philosophy, each particular apprehension of them must in consistency be regarded as a psychical fact and nothing more, as to which there is no certainty whether it will recur in a similar case or not."[1]

When, however, he turns to the examination of experience, he finds that, apart from thought, it can yield nothing whatsoever. "Without the assumption of the unconditional validity of some absolutely certain principles not drawn from experience, the very deliverances of experience itself could be no one more probable than another."[2] Perception, in the ordinary sense of the term, is penetrated through and through by thought. We require thought, as he shows, even to recognize that a thing is identical with itself. In fact, the criticism of empiricism on the one hand, and of a pure *a priori* procedure of thought on the other, have both so told upon Lotze that he is able to attribute certain knowledge to neither of them. Thought can yield only universals, which are not facts; pure perception can

[1] See *Logic*, § 355. [2] *Logic*, § 356.

yield only particulars, if the term is applicable, or bare stimuli, and not knowledge.

In this difficulty he has recourse to "*Intuition*," which has both the immediacy of direct experience and the universality and necessity of thought. What, then, is "Intuition"? Lotze answers that it is a form of knowing in which there is "no sort of procedure consisting of the connecting of various single acts, whereas there is one in the case of thought." Intuition is therefore indescribable, its parts or elements cannot be set side by side. "The attitude of Intuition towards its content is that of passive receptivity, and its work is done so completely at a single stroke, that no steps or stages in it can be distinguished or could be described. This must not be misunderstood."[1] There may be, and indeed, there must be, steps which lead up to this intuitive knowledge. "When geometrical intuition teaches us that two straight lines intersecting each other can only have one point common to both, there does undoubtedly take place, regarding the act as a psychical event, a certain succession of ideas. We might explain how we first think each of the two straight lines in itself, then place them each in the same plane, make them from a parallel position converge, follow each to the point of section and then beyond it; . . . but this is not the geometrical intuition itself; so far we have only brought all the different points which go to

[1] *Logic*, § 357.

make up the relation in question, and now intuition pronounces on these points of relation, *as by a single instantaneous revelation.*[1] Analysis of the act of intuition itself is impossible. It is "absolutely immediate apprehension." It grasps the many in one at a single stroke; it is a synthesis without process; it sees the unity in difference, and escapes at once the bare universality of thought and the pure particularity of sense, yielding truths which are self-evident, shining in their own pure light. We cannot prove its deliverances to be *logically* necessary, it is true; for logical necessity can only come through discursive processes, which should lay out the elements in the intuitive truth one by one, making them dependent on each other. But, on the other hand, they have an *aesthetic* necessity, and will "accordingly find the touchstone of their validity no longer in the unthinkableness, but in the plain absurdity of their contradictories."[2] Once they are recognized, these truths are *immediately felt* to be true. "Each one is its own evidence, and stands in no need of support from others." The characteristic of the self-evident truths given by intuition is that "by their clearness and strength they force themselves upon consciousness, and at once claim recognition without constraining it by any process of proof."[3] And "clearness and strength" are ultimately "their sole credentials." No doubt it may be urged that false knowledge

[1] *Logic,* § 357. [2] *Ibid.,* § 364. [3] *Ibid.,* § 356.

often appears to be self-evident. "That state of repose and peaceful equilibrium of the mind, in which the self-evidence of knowledge, regarded as a psychical fact, consists in the last resort, may also be produced by conjunctions of ideas of by no means universal validity."[1] But there are logical rules, says Lotze, "through which we seek to free ourselves from these illusions." And in any case the false application of a test does not destroy its worth, and there can be no other ultimate test of truth, except that it constrains belief. He who denies the self-evident cannot be convinced of anything, and gives himself up to disputation for disputation's sake. Here, therefore, in the immediate deliverances of intuition, we have the fixed points and ultimate certainties on which all the world of thought ultimately depends, and from which it derives its validity. Intuition gives what thought could never itself reach, and converts the hypothetical knowledge of a possible world into the immediate and direct experience of reality.

What then is the value of this attempt to meet the sceptical denial of a world of objects corresponding to the world of ideas to which, as Lotze never doubts, the thought of man is inevitably confined? To answer this question it will be sufficient if we examine Lotze's ultimate resource, namely, intuition. For although there are many expressions which would lead us to regard him as appealing to

[1] *Logic*, § 356.

sensuous perception for deliverance from the subjectivity of ideas, he is, on the other hand, convinced that mere empirical perception cannot yield either certain or general truths, and sometimes, that it is not possible without thought. We should, by examining his view of thought and of perception, be condemned once more to watch the futile process of first referring all things to sense, and then all things to thought, in the vain attempt to bring together what are presupposed to be mutually exclusive. We have shown already that if sense is a pure manifold and thought is purely formal, their combined activity in the production of knowledge is not conceivable. And it is not necessary to insist further that Lotze, so far from questioning the validity of his presupposition as to the discreteness of the material and the formal character of the laws of thought, makes it his main endeavour to account for knowledge upon these premises, in opposition to the Hegelian view that thought is a constitutive and concrete reality.[1]

There remains for us, therefore, to examine briefly the intuitive form of knowing, which, on Lotze's view, yields self-evident truths. Now, there is no doubt that a self-evident truth must be taken as valid, or that it constrains belief and shuts out all possible doubt. But, as Lotze admits, there is a difficulty in recognizing what truths *are* self-evident, and what truths or illusions have only a spurious

[1] See chap. iii.

self-evidence. Errors have often seemed to be self-evident, as, *e.g.*, that the sun moves round the earth, and they have had the "strength and clearness" to constrain belief. That is to say, they have had all the marks of "aesthetic necessity," and their denial has seemed not only contradictory but "absurd." Lotze, therefore, proposes to subject the presumed self-evident truths, that is to say, truths which constrain conviction by their clearness and strength, to a logical test. The object of that test, as Lotze shows us,[1] is to separate the contingent and alien elements in the truth from the essential and necessary. But that is as much as to say that the self-evident truth is self-evident because it is recognized as a system of elements which are through and through rationally coherent; or, in other words, it is to make "the sole credential" of self-evidence consist in the complete revelation by reflective consideration of all the elements which are necessarily related in the system. The necessity of the truth would thus spring, not from its immediacy, but from the fact that thought had *completed its mediating process* by revealing the object as a totality of mutually related parts. And no truth would be necessary, or self-evident, except that which is ideally complete, that is to say, except the whole truth. We are, no doubt, often so convinced by many truths, short of the unattainable whole of truth, as to call them self-evident: that

[1] See *Logic*, § 356.

two straight lines cannot intersect more than once, is an example of such self-evident truth. But it remains self-evident only as long as we are content, as the mathematician is, to isolate the sphere of pure quantity and to treat it as a *whole*, by assuming a certain view of space. If, instead of Euclidean space, we conceived a spherical space, all straight lines would, I suppose, intersect twice. Genuine self-evidence belongs to no partial truth. Nothing can be regarded as necessary except the whole, or, in other words, the actual. The partial truths which we regard as self-evident are so only because we treat them for our purposes as if they were complete systems, or concrete wholes, as in the case of a geometrical construction; and even there the self-evidence is not immediate, but *completed mediacy*.

But Lotze's "credentials" of self-evidence, namely, "the strength and clearness which constrains belief," rest on the confusion between the aesthetic *result* of the recognition of truth and that recognition itself. There is no doubt that a self-evident truth brings conviction, or constrains belief, nor that systematic coherence when it is recognized produces a satisfaction which is well-named "aesthetic." We find that satisfaction in the contemplation of a work of art, which impresses us with its harmonious totality, or in the apprehension of a completed mathematical proof, or in the conception, so far as it is possible to us, of a universe as the manifestation of a single principle and the witness to one presence. The absence of such completeness on the part of the objects of our thought is, on the other hand, when once detected a source of dissatisfaction, which spurs us on to further effort after knowledge. Nevertheless, this does not justify us in regarding either the fact that belief is constrained, or the fact of being convinced, or the feeling that accompanies the conviction and the clear vision, as if it constituted the self-evidence, or were itself a test of truth. To have the consciousness of being convinced, which is followed by aesthetic satisfaction, is a very different matter from recognizing that the conviction is true. We are convinced immediately whenever any thought *appears* to be valid, but the thought cannot be assumed to be immediately valid because we are convinced. Yet Lotze seems to be employing the subjective feeling that follows conviction as if it were itself a valid ground for that conviction: a process which is equivalent to asserting that every conviction must be true simply because we are convinced. This is to make that feeling or belief the source both of itself and of the completeness and self-evidence of the object which generates it.

But, apart from this confusion of an immediate or subjective fact with clear objective knowledge, intuition, as described by Lotze, cannot give the sure standing ground for knowledge, or otherwise relate mere ideas to objects. Intuition, taken as the negation of all process, and as an attitude of pure recipiency, could guarantee no truth nor yield any. No doubt the mere setting out of the elements of a truth one by one *without* combining them cannot yield a self-evident truth; but neither can the mere act of grasping them together without the comprehension of each of them. Lotze has seized the last stage in the apprehension of an object, and isolated it from the antecedent process which alone makes it possible, and called it Intuition. And there is no doubt that the intuition of poets, or men of science, baffles all analytic attempts to set forth its stages one by one. Nevertheless the intuition never takes place through *ignorance* of the elements which are grasped together, and apart from any process. We do not step at once from the elements to the whole, as Lotze implies, but each element has all along been treated as an element in the whole. In a word, the universal which is self-evident at the completion of the process was active throughout the whole movement of thought, from the first indefinite apprehension of an uncertain something, to the clear view of the object as a systematic totality carrying within it its own explanation and evidence.

But, in the next place, even intuitive truth is only truth, and truth, we are told, is never reality. Intuition cannot, after all, take us outside the sphere of ideas, or show that there are any objects corresponding to thoughts. Even if we admit that there are some truths which may be regarded as ultimate principles, which form "fixed points of certainty" that give security to the rest of our ideas and rational coherence to our experience, still, that they are themselves true *of facts* cannot be proved on Lotze's theory. They, too, fall entirely within the subjective sphere of mere ideas, as Lotze is constrained to admit. "As regards the ultimate principles which we follow in this criticism of our thoughts, it is quite true that we are left with nothing but the confidence of Reason in itself, or the certainty of belief in the general truth that there is a meaning in the world, and that the nature of that reality which includes us in itself has given our spirit only such necessities of thought as harmonize with it."[1]

Thus Lotze appeals from reason to faith, or from cognition to the conviction of the goodness of God. If "thought can never settle the question whether it alone exists, or whether there is a world of existence outside it to which it enters into relation," and if no logical argument can carry the sceptic from the idea of a thing to the actuality of it—there is another class of arguments which we can use. These arguments "pass from the incontestable *value* of an object of thought to the belief in its reality."[2] And value, as has already been seen, is given in feeling and not by thought; so that thought cannot controvert its

[1] *Metaphysics*, § 94.   [2] *Logic*, § 348.

deliverances. The beliefs in "a supreme good, in a life beyond the earth, in eternal blessedness, rest upon an extremely broad, though an unanalyzed foundation of perception. Such beliefs start from the fact of this actual world as it is given us in experience, in which we find certain intolerable contradictions threatening us if we refuse to acknowledge that these ways in which the structure of the world extends beyond our perception are real complements of that which we perceive. . . . Starting from the reality of a as given in experience, they connect with it the reality of b which is not so given, but which appears to follow from a as a necessity of thought."[1] In this passage we seem to have a reminiscence of the Kantian theory of the three ideas of reason which at once transcend experience and give the only ground of its possibility. And as knowledge for Kant implied these supreme ideas, so experience for Lotze demands these objects which have "incontestable value." Thought postulates these objects, and they lie beyond its confines, inasmuch as by its processes of mediation it can never reach completeness, or, in other words, attain to an object whose value lies in itself alone. That is to say, thought shows that if any knowledge is to be valid, these supreme objects must be. But in Lotze's view there is—on the ground of thought—no *absolute* necessity that thought should have valid results, nor even

[1] *Logic*, § 348.

that it should be. And consequently thought cannot go beyond demanding these objects; it cannot show that its demand must be satisfied. Hence it cannot guarantee that these objects exist; for what is itself contingent cannot supply grounds for the necessity of anything. In a word, thought can only 'point out the empty place which these objects could occupy,' with the advantage of converting its postulates into actual facts. "We have, therefore, the right to say that all our conclusions concerning the real world rest upon the immediate confidence or the faith which we repose in the universal validity of a certain postulate of thought which oversteps the limits of the special world of thought."[1] Thought postulates the Good; feeling *gives* it. For feeling is the source of our consciousness of value; and the value of objects is their essence and reality. To feeling we must therefore turn for those real objects, by depending from which our thoughts shall have objective reference and be true of actual facts.

Thus feeling once more appears as the pivot on which Lotze's doctrine of knowledge ultimately turns. It alone pronounces upon the worth of objects, and therefore witnesses to the existence of the Good, for which, and by which alone, even truth exists. It is only the Good which has in itself the complete right to be, and its reality cannot be denied without that inward and intolerable

[1] *Logic*, § 349.

self-stultification to which Lotze gives the name of "absurdity." The Good is therefore the *fact* which gives meaning and validity to our thoughts, and carries us beyond the sphere of mere ideas, which in themselves would be empty and vain.

Now, I am not concerned at present to discuss the question whether the Good and the Real may thus be taken as identical, or whether Metaphysics is ultimately based upon Ethics. What we have to determine is whether the Good or the Real manifests itself to feeling and *not* to thought; or, in other words, whether feeling, and feeling alone, is the appraising faculty which pronounces upon the worth of objects. In chap. v., Book II. of the *Mikrokosmus*, Lotze asserts that 'to become aware of the value of objects in terms of pleasure and pain belongs to feeling, in the same way as to become aware of changes in the self, which arise through its varying relations to objects, belongs to knowledge.' Indeed, herein lies the essential superiority of feeling over thought. For, while thought can apprehend only varying relations in the self and in the objects—only the outer order of their mutual and changing connections, feeling grasps their reality, their inner worth, their unique and constitutive individuality.[1] Feeling appreciates this

---

[1] In his *Metaphysics*, Lotze tries to prove that *für-sich-seyn*, or self-feeling is the core and essence of all real objects. For an object to exist and to be aware of itself in feeling, or to be in direct emotional relation to itself, are the same thing. Nothing

constitutive worth of objects something after the manner in which the "Moral Sense" alone, according to the English Moralists, pronounced upon the goodness or badness of actions. We cannot derive the deliverances of feeling from any other source, nor dispute their authority. Feeling, through the pains and pleasures attached to every activity, guides us to our good: and it guides us unerringly. For these pains and pleasures are, in some unknown way, made to arise in us when the conditions of life respectively disagree or harmonize with our welfare; and so far as they lead us, they are to be absolutely trusted. No doubt "pleasure may arise from the sweet taste of a poison, and the antidote is bitter"; but even in this case "the feeling is in the right, for in the former case there is momentary harmony between the impression and the energy of the nerve, and in the latter an antagonistic disturbance of the prevailing state. Experience does not retract these judgments; it merely gives a warning not to rely on them exclusively, and teaches us to judge of the total value of an impression only when we have struck the balance of the total sum of its consequences, and of the helps or hindrances attached to them." The testimony of feeling *seems* false in such a case only because it is illegitimately extended

is, except that which feels itself. By feeling itself an object shuts itself within itself, and has an individuality of its own. And yet by feeling it participates of the nature of the whole, which is also feeling: for God is Love.

as if it applied to the welfare of the whole body, instead of to that particular nerve which is irritated. In short, if these different feelings did not arise from our activities—and in ways which we can neither regulate nor anticipate—we could have no conception of the conditions of life which contribute to our welfare, that is to say, we could not know the good, nor in what to seek it. Strictly speaking, indeed, we should, on Lotze's view, know nothing whatsoever without feelings; for, without them, as already shown, knowledge could neither be inspired nor tested. Objects would have neither interest nor worth. We should be passive and inert spectators, simply recognizing what is, indifferent alike to growth and decay, action and inaction, development and degradation; for all would be without purpose, and therefore without significance.

In order to avoid raising psychological questions which could not be thoroughly discussed here, it may be admitted that feeling, whatever its ultimate relation to thought may be, gives us the consciousness of pleasure and pain. We cannot attribute this function to any other power without confusion of terms. It may be admitted also that, on the whole, pleasure may contain an indication of the harmony between the self and its environment, which is the condition of our development, and, consequently, of the value of objects for us. But the question which Lotze has raised is, whether feeling makes these indications apart from and without the co-operating activity of thought, so as to be the only source of our knowledge of the good. Can a pleasant state of consciousness be at once identified with the judgment that an object has positive value, and pain with the judgment that the object has negative worth? Is every being that is pleased *ipso facto* conscious of objects, of the relation between objects and the self, and of the value of that relation; or, on the other hand, is there a transition involved in passing from the feeling of being pained or pleased to the knowledge of the existence and of the nature of objects?

It seems to me that Lotze's error is exposed by merely asking these questions. If, as he himself has said, there may be beings who feel and do not know, then such beings could be pained and pleased without in the least *recognizing* that either pain or pleasure has worth, and without recognizing that that worth resides in objects, or even that objects exist at all. They would live entirely within the world of their own sensations, oblivious to all else. To be in a certain state of consciousness, and to know by reflection upon that state that it exists, that it is due to objects, and that these objects have any character whatsoever, are surely very different matters. The former is an immediate fact which means nothing, but is a mere occurrence in consciousness; the latter are the result of the interpreting activity of thought, and quite beyond the power of feeling to produce—unless we endow it with the functions of thought in addition to its own. Lotze has obliterated, in the case of feeling, the distinction that exists between all the facts of consciousness and those of self-consciousness, or even between sensitive existence, experience, and the interpretative intelligence. From the fact that reflective thought cannot produce its data, and that its whole operation consists in making clear that which already exists, he has concluded that in this sphere thought does not even interpret; and he has attributed to immediate feeling the process of interpretation as well as the data. Now, it seems to me that Lotze has precisely the same reason for attributing all knowledge except that of pleasures and pains exclusively to sensation, as he has to attribute the knowledge of these latter to feeling. That is to say, on his theory, sensations of colours, sounds, smells, and so on, occupy the same position as feelings of pains and pleasures; for they are means to knowledge of objects, or qualities in objects, which his formal thought could not achieve. Hence, if Lotze has a right to pass from feelings of being pleased or pained to judgments of the value of objects, and to attribute these judgments not to thought but to feeling, he has the same right to pass immediately from sensations of colour, sound, etc., to judgments regarding their qualities. Indeed, one of the main criticisms we endeavoured to enforce was, that Lotze, so long as he bore in mind his conception of the purely formal character of thought, had to attribute to sense all the activities of thought, so that thought could only repeat, one by one, the processes which had already been performed on the lower level. But in the case of sensation, thought, according to Lotze, *did* repeat the processes; and it had to repeat them on condition of escaping extinction, and of having no function whatsoever. Had Lotze, however, passed at once from sensation to judgments of sense, and been consistent to that view, as he has passed from feelings of pleasure and pain to judgments of worth, thought would have been expunged, and Lotze's Sensationalism would have been explicit and complete.

We may perhaps make Lotze's position clearer if we put it in another way. We have seen above[1] how Lotze asks, with a certain consciousness of triumph, whether "love and hate" are concepts, whether "the living nerve of righteousness," "good and evil," "blue and sweet" are given in thoughts. The answer is obvious. They certainly are not, if thought, as Lotze believes, is a purely discursive and formal faculty, exercised upon data received from sense as an external source. But we might ask in turn whether love and hate, and righteousness, and right and wrong, and blue and sweet, can be given *without* thought. The answer is equally obvious. Sense, by itself, gives as little as thought does by itself. The whole problem lies in

[1] See chap. ii.

the nature of the relation between these two factors. No one now can well deny the need of either, and the difficulty which we have to meet is how to conceive of both so as to enable them to co-operate and produce the concrete fact of knowledge, in which form and content interpenetrate. Lotze tries to bring them together *after* defining them as practically exclusive and independent; Hegel and his followers would find a unity beneath their differences, and regard that unity as best characterized by the term Thought or Spirit. That is to say, they deny that thought is formal, and that sense is pure discreteness; for they find both in the result, and would find both in its conditions. Lotze himself could really deny neither of the factors. Every possible object, even the datum of sense, necessarily has its ideal side or relation to thought, for it is a fact *of* consciousness; and, on the other hand, every object is presented *to* thought. But he was satisfied with expounding these aspects in their isolation, now attributing all to sense, now all to thought, as if the fact were now merely real and now merely ideal. But in the case of the feelings of pleasure and pain, the hesitation between the two inconsistent views disappears; the ideal side of pains and pleasures, without which even they could not be, or be for consciousness, which is the same thing, is at once attributed to feeling. He has not analyzed feeling, as sensations had been analyzed during the progress of modern philosophical thought, nor laid bare the presence of thought in its data, and their absolute emptiness and unintelligibility apart from thought. Had he done so, it seems to me that the presence of the relating activities of the intelligence would have been as manifest in the judgment of worth as in all other judgments. It would have been clearly seen that a process of inference is involved in the transition from feelings of pleasure and pain to the recognition of the self in which they exist, of the objects which incite them, and of the worth which, in relation to the self, resides in those objects. Inference, it is true, arrives at nothing except what is given in the data; but, on the other hand, it reveals what *was* given in the data. Hence we must interpret the data in the light of that which is shown to be in them, and not the conclusion in the light of the undeveloped premises. We find the truest expression of the reality, not at the beginning but at the end of the process, where the presence and activity of thought is undeniable. Feelings yield no objects, any more than sensations do. Feelings *have* value no doubt, just as colours and sounds have their qualities; nevertheless "value" can no more be felt than quality or quantity, a "footlong" or a "yard's distance" can be felt. Taken by themselves, if, indeed, we could take them by themselves as Lotze endeavours to do, pleasures and pains are transitory phenomena like sensations, standing in the same need, on Lotze's theory, of being "objectified," and "posited," and "reified," by the activity of thought. Feelings apart from thought are as blind as sensations apart from thought. But Lotze has not thoroughly realized the inward mutual implication of the content and forms of our experience. In other words, he has not clearly and consistently recognized that the ideal and the real, the subjective and objective, are inseparable, *and that as either may be taken as the adjective of the other*, neither can be by itself considered as either substantial or adjectival. Consequently, neither the phantom of a feeling or sensation that is not for thought, that is to say, of a reality that is not ideal, nor the complementary phantom of an ideal construction that is pure general law without any specific content, entirely disappears from his theory. In dealing with the data of sense, he alternates between Sensationalism and Idealism, and in dealing with feelings he confuses them, attributing to feeling the functions of thought besides its own, —as if these *same* functions could be valid when performed by feeling, while invalid when performed by thought—and even calling feeling in one place "Reason appreciative of worth."

The Judgment of Value then cannot be attributed to feeling. Feeling gives pleasures and pains, and nothing more. It gives us neither objects, nor the self, nor the worth of objects in relation to the self. Hence we do not *feel* the Good, even if we were to admit that the Good is the hedonistic

Good, which alone can spring from feelings of pleasure and pain. It is probable that many beings feel much pain, and enjoy many pleasant sensations, who have no conception of objects, for whom the distinction of the self and the not-self does not exist, and who have no idea of their worth; it is certain that if we eliminate the cognitive processes from our own thought and live entirely under the guidance of feeling, the supreme ideal of our practical life, and the ultimate goal of knowledge, could not present itself to our consciousness. Feeling is as little capable of giving us the reality which shall give content to our otherwise pale and empty world of ideas as Intuition or Perception; and Lotze's last attempt to escape from the sphere of subjectivity entirely fails, for he has no other weapon to turn aside the Scepticism which assumes, as Lotze himself does, that we know only ideas. Scepticism denies that any objects knowable to us correspond to these subjective ideas. Lotze asserts the contrary, but fails to make good his assertion. To meet scepticism we need other methods than those which alternate between sense and thought, and confuse between feeling and reason.

Before I endeavour to indicate the source of Lotze's difficulty, and the direction in which its solution may be sought, I must follow his exposition of his final reasons for regarding thought as formal and subjective, the reasons which, I have no doubt, seemed to Lotze to have most cogency, and which at first sight, at least, may appear to be the most difficult to meet. I refer to his proofs of the subjectivity of the *processes* of thought, as distinguished from its laws and its products which we have already discussed. With these our task of exposition will end.

In defining the scope of the present inquiry I anticipated its main result by the assertion that Lotze, in his exposition of the processes of thought, *while denying the presence and activity of the principle of reality in man's thinking, attributes value and validity to its results.*[1]

This denial which was *implicit* in his treatment of the forms of thought, namely, Conception, Judgment, and Reasoning, and in his view of the objects of thought as a world of mere ideas, is made explicit in chapter iv., Book III. of his *Logic*. He there takes up these thinking processes one by one, with the special object of showing that reality takes no part whatsoever in them. "Thought," he says, "as an activity or movement of the soul, follows laws of the soul's own nature; will these laws which it necessarily follows in the connection of its ideas, lead to the same result as that which the real chain of events brings round? Will the outcome of the process of thought, when at the close of it we turn once more to the facts, be found in agreement with the actual results which the course of

[1] See above, p. 81.

nature has produced? And if on the whole we consider it improbable that thought and being, which it is natural for us to regard as made for one another, should be entirely divorced, are we also to suppose that every single step taken by thought answers to some aspect of that which actually takes place in the development of the things thought about?"[1] Starting from the presupposition which is manifestly true, that thought in its processes follows its own laws, and from the presupposition which we shall question, that the laws of thought are not also the laws of things, he has to show that the results of thinking are true of real events and facts and he has to explain how thought comes to have this validity. In obedience to its own special laws, thought goes its own way, creating relations which it does not find, and which correspond to nothing which actually exists; and yet, by means of these relations, it ultimately places man at a point of view from which he attains objective truth, or a view of reality as it is. The steps of the process are purely subjective, they are merely the means whereby we discursively move from idea to idea towards the centre "from the extreme ramifications of reality," or towards the mountain top, whence the wide prospect of real existence may reveal itself. They are, as we have already seen, artificial means which we employ to nullify the distortion and limitation of view

[1] *Logic*, § 334.

which arise from the eccentric position which we, as distinguished from other possible intelligent beings, are originally condemned to occupy.

Lotze begins his proof of the pure subjectivity of the processes of thought with the exposition of the elementary activity of instituting Comparison between objects. "To whatever act of thought we direct our attention, we never find that it consists in the mere presence of two ideas a and b in the same Consciousness, but always in what we call a Relation of one idea to the other. After this relation has been established it can in its turn be conceived as a third idea C." That is to say, in every act of thought we find two facts and one connection; and Lotze wishes to prove that the two facts are given to thought, and that the relation is made by thought, and, as made by thought, has no reality which corresponds to it. "The idea of the identity of a and a, which is the result of comparing them, consists neither in the fact of their coexistence, nor in their fusion; it is a new and essentially single act of the soul, in which the soul holds the two ideas side by side, and passes from one to another."[1] That is to say, the act of comparison leaves the objects exactly where they were, and the relation which is formed between them is a mental product due to a mental act and superimposed upon the facts. If we compare a and b, red and yellow, we begin from "objects

[1] *Logic*, § 335.

directly given in perception." "The ideas of identity or difference, the connection *C*, we obtained as the result of the act of relation introduced by the mind." And those ideas of relation are absolutely necessary to the final comprehension of *a* and *b*; for we cannot think the terms except in their relation, nor the relation apart from the terms. Nevertheless the movement from *a* to *a* whereby we discover their identity, or from *a* to *b* whereby we discover their difference—"the movement backwards and forwards between them through which we discovered their relation to each other is *merely a psychical process*."[1] The things did not pass into each other, *a* did not *become a*, nor did *a* separate itself from *b* when we identified or distinguished them. The act is purely subjective and so also is the product of it, namely, the connection between the facts. Without this act, indeed, "our result could neither be obtained in the first instance nor repeated afterwards in memory, but it has nevertheless to be abstracted from the real significance of the act of thought to which it ministered, as a scaffolding is withdrawn when the building is completed."[2] That is to say, although *we* cannot know without these relations, yet thought makes these relations purely out of itself; although we needs must make use of these relations to understand facts, we must not conclude that they are themselves facts, or hypostasize them into objective

---

[1] *Logic*, § 336. [2] *Ibid.*

entities. There is nothing even *like* them in the real world. "How can the propositions '*a* is the same as *a*,' and '*a* is different from *b*,' express an objective relation, which, as objective, would subsist independently of our thought, and which thought could only discover or recognize? . . . What are we to make of a self-existent distinction *between a* and *b*? What objective relation can correspond to this 'between'?"[1] Betweenness, if the reader will pardon the term, is not a quality of *a* nor a quality of *b*. "Difference being neither the predicate of *a* taken by itself nor of *b* taken by itself, of what is it the predicate?"[2] The relations between them are manifestly the product of our thought springing into existence with our mental act, and they have a merely mental reality, that is to say, they are *valid*, but they have not existence; they enable us to know things, but they are not qualities of things. We cannot convert mental operations and mental products into real qualities of objects; if we did so we should fall into all the difficulties disclosed by ancient philosophy, and be obliged to regard objects as being in themselves both greater and smaller, and so on, and to build the mental scaffolding into the objective edifice.

But if the case stands thus, must we not conclude that the results of our thinking are invalid? If we can only know by inventing these relations, and if these relations are not qualities of any

[1] *Logic*, § 338.   [2] *Ibid.*

objects, how can our knowledge be true? Are we not forced to the conclusion, first, that thinking is a self-deluding process because it establishes unreal relations between things; and second, that real things are, as a matter of fact, quite unrelated, independent, isolated, particular? Lotze answers to the first question that "such is the constitution of our soul, and such do we assume that of every other soul which inwardly resembles ours, that whenever and by whomsoever they may be thought, they must also produce for thought the same relation, a relation which has its being only in thought and by means of thought. This relation, therefore, is independent of the individual thinking subject, and independent of the several phases of his thought."[1] We all think so, and must all think so, and therefore all is right. The universality of the process makes it unimpeachable. Our thoughts possess objective validity through these processes and products, and that is all which can possibly be demanded. The second question presents a graver difficulty. Lotze meets it by distinguishing between the relations of ideas to each other in consequence of which they can be valid, and the relation of things to each other in virtue of which they exist. The relation of ideas to ideas is a relation *between* them, the relation between object and object is a relation *in* them. The thought-relation *between* a and b "at once separates and

[1] *Logic*, § 338.

brings them together, and is nothing more than the recollection of an act of thought performable only by the unity of our consciousness."[1] Thought, and thought only, has passed to and fro between them, and the relation is the mind's consciousness of its own transition. But a real relation cannot be merely *between* objects; in the sphere of reality *both* severance and unity are not together possible. On the contrary, the idea of a relation *between* real objects both implies and prohibits the existence of an interval that separates them; which is direct self-contradiction. Hence we must regard that in the sphere of reality the relation is constitutive of each of the objects, and that each exists in and by its connection to the other; for otherwise they could not really interact upon each other.[2] Hence the relation *between* objects which thought finds, is, in the last resource, only an inadequate expression of the actual relation *within* real objects. The real relation is something more than the

---

[1] *Logic.* § 338.

[2] Lotze proceeds in his Metaphysics to show from this that only the One exists, that is to say, he makes the Unity of objects constitutive of their differences, and denies the entire independence of things. But, on the other hand, inasmuch as relations without related points, a One that is not also a Many, would be empty and meaningless, he gives to each object, to each atom, this power of relating itself to others, and builds up a kind of Monadism. And as this relation is a relation of each thing to itself, or a feeling, or a *für-sich-seyn*, feeling or *für-sich-seyn* constitutes every object.

thought-relation. In the case of "realities, things, beings, which we do not create by thought, but recognize as objects outside thought, the name relation expresses *less* than we have to suppose as really obtaining between the related things."[1]

An important consequence follows from this last conception, that the real relation between things "takes logical shape in the weakened form of a relation" *between* ideas. It enables Lotze at the same time to deny the actual reality of the products of thought, and to deny to thought the power of creating these relations purely out of itself. Passing on from the abstract relations of mere identity and mere difference, Lotze proceeds to examine the attempt which thought makes to represent identity *in* difference. This attempt is exemplified in its simplest form in conceptions; for conceptions are unities, or universals, which contain and connect different elements. Now, a general conception, Lotze shows, manifestly corresponds to no actual object, nor does the process of forming it correspond to any actual movement in the object. "It is commonly admitted as a self-evident truth, that the class to which a real object belongs is not itself real; this individual horse we see, horse in general is nowhere to be found."[2] Nor does the horse itself pass through a process analogous to that by which our minds form the conceptions; that is to say, it is not first "animal

[1] *Logic*, § 338.   [2] *Ibid.*, § 339.

in general, then vertebrate in general, mammal in itself, one-toed animal in general, horse in itself, black horse in general." The least examination makes it amply evident that the universals of thought are not true of any real objects, and that the process of forming them is simply and purely a psychical process. And yet thought must, in obedience to its own laws, perform these actions and produce these results. Does the difference between a universal of thought and a really perceived object, and the apparent independence of the thinking process of all reality, justify us, then, in absolutely severing them? By no means, answers Lotze. The perceived fact both inspires and guides the process, although it does not participate in its sequent stages, nor reveal its own nature in the results. "We could not so much as bring red and blue under the general name of colour, did not that common element exist in them, to our consciousness of which we testify in framing the name; we could form no class notions of plants and animals if the marks of individual plants and animals, and the modes in which those marks are conjoined, did not really possess such points of comparison as allow us to arrange them under general marks and forms, and thus, by setting these in the place of the merely individual, to construct the thought-form of the class, however impossible it may be to picture it to the mind."[1] Thought has, after all, to

[1] *Logic*, § 339.

find what it makes. The process of forming conception is *not* purely subjective, neither are the relations which it establishes. "Thus in the fact that we are *able* to think a universal, there is undoubtedly contained a truth of real and objective validity; the contents of the world of ideas, which thought does not create but finds, do not fall into mere individual and atomic elements, each one admitting of no comparison with the other; but, on the contrary, resemblances, affinities, and relations exist between them, in such wise that thought, as it constructs its universals, and subordinates and co-ordinates its particulars under them, comes through these purely formal and subjective operations, to coincide with the nature of that objective world."[1] We must not forget, however, that these existent relations which are given to us only *correspond* to the thought relations which we make; the real relations only serve to incite thought to an activity which produces mental relations. Both kinds of relations are real, but with a different kind of reality, as we have seen. "This Reality, which we desire to recognize in the general notions which are created by our thought, is a reality which is wholly dissimilar to Existence, and which can only consist in what we have called Validity, or in being *predicable of* the Existent."[2]

This complete dissimilarity between them, which nevertheless admits of that correspondence which

[1] *Logic*, § 339.   [2] *Ibid.*, § 341.

we can only call Validity, may be made still more evident by the following considerations. In the first place, the gradual process whereby a concept becomes a more adequate expression of the actual fact which it strives to represent, without ever attaining complete success, is totally unlike the growth of the object itself. Concepts gather concreteness by the external accretion or superaddition of other concepts; one independent set of qualities is superimposed upon another set as we proceed from the general concept towards the individual. But "there is no moment in the life of a plant in which it is merely plant in general, or conifer in itself, awaiting some subsequent influences answering to the subsequent logical determinations in our thought to settle the question what particular tree it is to grow up into." The concept may be made concrete in any manner we please. We may proceed from the general conception animal to any more particular conception of a special class of animals that happens to interest us, adding any qualities of animals that suit our purpose. But the growth of the living and real object is definitely conditioned from the beginning. *It* cannot develop into anything. In the next place, just as the constitution of the logical notion is arbitrary, so is the relation of logical notions to each other. Classification, by which we subordinate one notion to another, "has no real significance in relation to the actual structure and development of things themselves." We may classify the same things in many ways. And "different classifications of the same objects conflict owing to imperfect knowledge and observation, and thus introduce various and diverse ladders of universals between the highest universals and the objects. The logical right of thought is incontestable to start from any point of view it pleases," and to proceed in any direction. And even if thought were to hit upon the highest and best conception under which, as logical consequences, all other conceptions would find their true place, "this Logical structure, valuable as it would be for knowledge, would represent no real structure corresponding to it in the object itself."[1] Lotze therefore concludes as follows. "All the processes which we go through in the framing of conceptions, in classification, in our logical constructions, are subjective movements of our thought, and not processes which take place in things; but, at the same time, the nature of these things, of the given thinkable contents, is so constituted that thought, by surrendering itself to the logical laws of these movements of its own, finds itself at the end of its journey, if pursued in obedience to these laws, coinciding with the actual course of the things themselves."[2] The paths of thought and reality diverge; the paths of thought are many and not one, it may start from any point and proceed

---

[1] See *Logic*, § 342. [2] *Ibid.*

from one member in the system to another in any way it pleases; provided always, and only, that it follows its own laws, it will arrive in the end at an objective result valid of real objects.

Lotze subjects the forms of Judgment and Inference to a similar examination, and arrives at similar conclusions. We need not follow his exposition any further than is necessary to indicate the special difficulties which we have to meet if we are still to maintain that the products of thought are, after all, not merely subjective, nor attained without the participation of reality in the thinking process.

The Categorical Judgment is represented by Lotze as consisting of subject and predicate, given first in their isolation and then connected by a copula. For instance, in the judgment, "A triangle is a threesided figure whose angles taken together are equal to two right angles," we have first the idea of the subject, a triangle, then an idea of a figure whose angles are together equal to two right angles, and then a copula "*is*" expressing their identity. But it is evident that a triangle does not first exist, and then exist in a particular way. The process of passing from the conception of a triangle to its characteristics is a purely mental one, and the triangle itself takes no part whatsoever in it. In the next place, the Copula in the judgment has always one character, but the real relations between actual objects are many and various. "In the uniform Copula 'is' of the judgment, all objective distinctions in the connection between S and P are obliterated. They may be related as whole and part, as a thing to its transient states, or as cause to effect; in the form of the judgment they appear solely as subject and predicate, two terms which denote merely the relative positions which the ideas of them assume in the subjective movement of our thought."[1]

The pure subjectivity of the Hypothetical Judgment, both as a product and as a process, is still more evident. In the first place, a genuine or fully expressed hypothetical judgment always admits of simple conversion. The judgment, "If B is true then F is true," means that B and F both fall under some general notion M, which necessarily combines them in such a manner that each follows from the other. If B contains the whole reason for F, and for F only and not also for F^1 or F^2, then F contains in the same manner the reason of B. "We know the consequent from the antecedent, and the antecedent from the consequent." They are interchangeable, for they have the same significance; and thought may make either of them its starting point, and proceed with complete security to the other. But real antecedents and consequents, or causes and effects, are manifestly not thus related. The actual order of events is not thus reversible. Hence, in the process of forming these judgments thought moves free of reality in an ideal region

[1] *Logic*, § 343.

of its own; the facts and events do not follow its movements to and fro; and the relation which thought establishes, being thus reversible, is quite unlike anything that obtains between the objective facts. In the next place, the relation between the thoughts is quite general and vague: "F is in a general sense conditioned by B; but this, a mere abstract relation, is something less than anything that we obtain in reality between B and F as things or events."[1] In their case the determining conditions have a particular character leading to specific determinations, which are not expressible in the vague universals of thought.

"Finally, *Disjunctive Judgments* do not even purport to express any reality at all; the process of wavering undecided between several mutually exclusive predicates can answer to no process in the real world."[2] There are no real facts which are *either* this or that, any more than there are hypothetical facts, suspended between existence and non-existence, like the hypothetical ideas which judgment employs in saying that "*if A is, B is.*"

"A brief consideration of the various forms of *Syllogism* leads to similar results." The parts of the Syllogism have a fixed order of priority; we must proceed from the major premiss through the minor to the conclusion. But this process belies the truth, if it is taken to be anything more than psychical. The equality of the angles of an

[1] *Logic*, § 343. [2] *Ibid.*

equilateral triangle does not come to be, as a matter of fact, later in time than the equality of the sides, when we prove the former from the latter. And in a similar way, those principles from which we proceed in thought to explain the order of the world, did not really exist before the world, although we derive the idea of the latter from the idea of the former: "the reality of the world cannot be derived from something which is unreal, and which is yet essential and possessed of a regulative power."[1] The principles that determine our thoughts, even if they are valid, do not determine the actual sequences of facts, nor can we "subordinate the existent" to them without a fallacious process of hypostasization, and without confusing the evolution of meaning with the evolution of facts.

And as to *Induction*, "no one fails to see that the synthesis of particular facts in a general, not merely a universal, proposition is not the real ground of the validity of the general proposition, but only of our apprehension of that validity."[2] No one would maintain that the order of the planetary system came to be when it was discovered by Copernicus, or that the earth became stratified in a particular manner when the science of Geology came into existence.

"Still more convincingly does the variety of forms, which a Proof may assume, witness to the

[1] *Logic*, § 344.   [2] *Ibid.*

merely subjective significance of the several inferences of which it is made up. How many different proofs, direct and indirect, progressive and retrogressive, all equally inadequate, may be given for one and the same proposition? How many even in the form of direct progressive argument alone?"[1]

"Lastly, in regard to the final operations of thought, with the account of which the doctrine of pure Logic concluded," that is to say, in regard to *Classification, Explanatory Theory*, and the *Dialectical Ideal of Thought*, we found that there, too, " the proper essence of the thing does not make its way into our thought; it can only apprehend under these Forms, but the Forms do not create it, and do not fully express it."[2] Process and product are subjective only, and reality neither takes part in the former nor corresponds to the latter.

What, then, in the last resort, are we to conclude concerning the activity and the results of thinking? First, answers Lotze, that " the logical act of thinking . . . is purely and simply an inner movement of our own minds, which is made necessary to us by reason of the constitution of our nature and of our place in the world"; and that it can claim only Subjective Significance. Thought as an activity is, according to his view, our way of moving from the extreme ramifications towards the centre, or of clambering to the hill-top, whence the view of the real world is to be obtained. Being unable to

[1] *Logic*, § 344.   [2] *Ibid.*

know at once and intuitively, we must use these indirect methods of relating phenomena, or rather ideas, to one another, and explaining one by means of another, in endless regression. But the *result* of the activity, " the Thought itself, on the other hand, in which the process of thinking issues, the prospect obtained, has Objective Validity." And it has objective validity because all real thinking leads to the same result; the object which in the end presents itself to the individual "also presents itself as the self-identical object to the consciousness of others."[1] How then *can* a process which is purely subjective, as we have just been told, lead to a result which is objective? Lotze answers that it is not, after all, purely subjective; there must be *some* relation between the thought and the things on which it is engaged. "Yet, after all, some such relation there must be, if the Logical Thought in which they issue is to possess an Objective Validity which does not belong to the thinking act which issues in it." They "cannot stand altogether out of connection." What that relation or connection is Lotze does not explain. He only indicates in a figure that thought, with all its manifold and arbitrary processes of inference, which start from any point and proceed in any direction, must always begin from points in the same "geographical territory, the remaining part of which is what constitutes the landscape which

[1] See *Logic*, § 345.

is commanded from the summit."[1] He implies, what has been elaborated more fully since his time, that all the processes of thought start from perceptions, in which we "come into contact with reality." Or, as he has striven to show elsewhere, the activities of thought are each stimulated by an appropriate incentive issuing from the region of real facts. Finally, we are reminded once more that the Thoughts which we arrive at by means of these processes, although they are valid, are only valid; although they are objective, they are not objects; although they are real, they are not the real things which they indicate. "It is out of the question that this kind of Reality"—*i.e.*, the reality of "things and events in so far as they exist and occur in an actual world of their own beyond thought"—"should move and have its being in the forms of the Concept, of the Judgment, or of the Syllogism, which our thought assumes in its own subjective efforts towards the knowledge of that reality."[2] The objectivity of our thoughts consists merely in the fixity and invariability of their significance; but significance is not what is signified. "The nature of reality is not given in thought, and thought is not able to find it."

The importance of the issues thus finally raised by Lotze justifies a careful scrutiny of the arguments we have endeavoured to set forth, and I shall proceed to examine them in the next chapter.

[1] *Logic*, § 345. [2] *Ibid.*

CHAPTER VIII

THE PRINCIPLE OF REALITY IN THOUGHT AND ITS PROCESSES

IN the last chapter I endeavoured to set forth the arguments advanced by Lotze to prove that the contents and the processes of thought are subjective. His theory, as was seen, rests upon two main assumptions, which must now be examined. These are, *first*, that "it is the varied world of ideas within us which forms the sole material from which alone our knowledge can start"; and, *second*, "that the act of thinking is purely and simply an inner movement of our minds." Convinced of the complete and inevitable subjectivity of the data and products of thought, Lotze sought to find a foothold in the objective world by means of other powers of the intellect and heart. Thought being a mediating faculty was incapable of direct contact with reality, and could only move from one subjective idea to another; but "perception," "experience," "intuition," or "feeling" seemed to him to be capable of immediately grasping reality and of apprehending not only the relations of objects to one another, but their unity, individuality, and essence. They stand in need of thought, not because thought can add anything to what they present, but because thought can render it more definite, clear, and articulate; thought stands in need of them, because without them it would have no content whatsoever, no objects to connect, and no starting point whence to move.

I tried to show that these immediate forms of knowledge could not thus supply thought with its necessary data unless they were armed with all the powers of thought as well as with those which are peculiar to themselves. Lotze himself was virtually forced to admit this. He was obliged to regard sense as yielding universals of its own, and to make the sensuous consciousness the exact counterpart of the reflective; he represented perception and intuition as capable of yielding immediate knowledge of universal principles, as well as of objects in space and time; and he endowed feeling with a power to form judgments and to apprehend the inner worth, or reality of objects, as well as to be the consciousness of the state of being pleased or pained. But Lotze's theory, both of thought and of these other forms of our intelligent life, was such as to demand their rigid separation. The mediate processes of thought and immediate apprehension, knowledge of real things and knowledge of mere ideas, of individual facts and of connecting relations, are so sharply contrasted by him that it is entirely unintelligible how they can be attributed to the same mental functions, whether we call these feeling, or experience, or perception, or thought. And, on the other hand, they cannot be shared between different functions. For, on Lotze's own showing, if perception, experience, feeling, and intuition exclude thought and its mediate processes, they can yield no intelligible data whatsoever; and even if they did, that is, if they did supply thought with prepared material, thought could either not receive it at all, or else, in the very act of receiving it, would convert it into what is mediate and purely subjective. And, on the other hand, if these forms of intellectual apprehension do not exclude thought, then we must regard them as both immediate and mediate, as yielding both mere ideas and realities. But feeling and the immediate forms do not furnish us with knowledge of reality. Each of the outlets which Lotze offers us as means to escape from the subjectivity and mediacy of thoughts, ends in a blind alley; "the varied world of ideas within us is the sole material from which knowledge starts," and it is the sole result of knowledge. We have, as he finally admits, to fall back in the last resort upon faith. But the only faith which remains to us must be such as to contradict the conclusions to which the theory points, and itself incapable of all rational justification. For although Lotze was undeniably right in insisting that the contents of thought are subjective, because they can be given only *by* thought; yet if they are subjective *only*, thought can give no real knowledge: truth loses that objective reference to reality which is its essence, and faith becomes belief in the impossible.

We now turn from the data and products of thought to its processes. Here also Lotze advances a half-truth. That thought in thinking follows its own laws is undeniable: it is a truism. That in doing so it does not *also* follow the laws of the nature of things is a matter on which Lotze's arguments are not convincing. Indeed, as we have already partly seen,[1] Lotze himself had in a manner to retract his confident assertion of "the pure and simple" subjectivity of these processes. He was obliged to find appropriate "stimuli" for every one of the elementary activities of thought; and in dealing with the higher forms he was obliged to have recourse to material knowledge,—of the *condition* in the Categorical Judgment, of the *principle of distribution* in the Disjunctive, of *quantity* in Substitutive inference, of *empirical data* in Ratio and Proportion, of the *inner qualities of objects* in Classification and of *a supreme principle of reality* in Scientific and Ideal Explanation. Without this

[1] See chaps. iii. and vi.

guidance of facts, left entirely to itself, thought could not operate at all, far less operate in such a manner as to arrive at results which are true of the actual nature of things and course of events. In order to make the subjective activities lead to objective truth, he is obliged to admit that, after all, the processes of thought "cannot stand altogether out of connection with reality." But he does not explain that connection, nor is it explicable on his theory. He confidently asserts that if we move along "the spider-webs" of thought-relations from the "extreme ramifications" towards reality, or if we clamber in any direction and from any starting point to the hilltop, provided we proceed in accordance with the laws of thought, we shall obtain the objective view of the world of real being. But he offers no justification of his confidence, and does not explain the possibility of knowing the objective fact by subjective means. He falls back upon Faith and metaphor—faith, not directly in reason itself, but in the Reality which has given us reason, and would not give us a reason that is deceptive. And his faith, whether in the validity of knowledge or in the reliability of reason, is no doubt well founded; only, in that case his theory is wrong. For that which faith believes to be united Lotze's doctrine separates; and if the deliverance of faith that the subjective idea contains a reference to objective reality is valid, then the diremption of ideality and reality cannot be justified. Lotze thus has recourse to a faith which, instead of anticipating proof, like a hypothesis in science, and instead of pointing the way to reasoned knowledge and extending the clearly known along its own lines to a not yet clearly known, contradicts the results to which his own doctrine inevitably leads. What we must conclude on Lotze's theory is that thought is so *made* that it cannot meet with reality in knowledge; what we are to believe is that they nevertheless do come together. He therefore puts faith to an illegitimate use, and calls it to convince when conviction is impossible, except on condition of reconstituting the theory which demands it. It need hardly be added that the difficulty which shows the need of faith arises, on Lotze's view, from a presumed imperfection or incompleteness in the human mind, and not from any defect in the doctrine which he advances.

Lotze suggests in the *Mikrokosmus*[1] "that thought and being seem to be so connected as that they both follow the same supreme laws, which laws are, as regards existence, laws of the being and becoming of all things and events, and, as regards thought, laws of a truth which must be taken account of in every connection of ideas." But this is only a casual and tentative admission, made in the presence of the Scepticism which follows from their complete separation. He will not definitely assert any ontological relation between the two

[1] See Book VIII., chap. i.

elements of knowledge, nor admit the ultimate identity of the nature of thought and reality. That would have been Idealism. He rather gives these laws a double aspect; "as regards existence" they are one thing, and "as regards thought" they are another. He gives no hint of the relation of these aspects; but, in truth, introduces the dualism of thought and reality into these supreme laws themselves. Whenever Lotze endeavours to *explain*, or to show the possibility of the correspondence between thought and reality, or between the products of reflection and the objects of experience, he constructs the latter on the model of the results which have been achieved only by means of the former. The only difference is that sense is more concrete, and also less definite, or that thought is at once more abstract and more systematic, its relations being explicit. For it is quite evident that in order to account for the rich variety of the world of apparent knowledge there must be attributed either to the data or to the activities of thought, or to both of them, an adequate complexity. Both sense and thought cannot be *bare*. Mere stimulus plus pure form, even if they could be brought together so as to interact, could not produce varied knowledge. And inasmuch as the formality of thought and the mere universality of its relations must at all costs be maintained, the whole emphasis of Lotze's theory falls upon the data which are supplied to it, and upon the processes of perception, intuition, or feeling which are preliminary to it. Thought is all but redundant and supererogatory.

Now it is evident that Lotze's emphasis upon the variety and wealth of the given content, and upon the formal emptiness of thought, implies the subordination of mind to a foreign material in the way of Sensationalism. But the term "stimulus" proves valuable in this extremity. For a stimulus to knowledge is not knowledge, nor can sensible elements with all their variety do more than excite thought into activity. Thus we are left once more with mere sense-incitements on the one side, and the bare universals of thought on the other. In order to mediate between this pure manifold and the universal forms, Lotze interposes a psychical mechanism, or experience, or intuition, which seems to perform the same function on his theory as the imagination did on Kant's. But Lotze does not explain how any mediation is possible between these extremes of pure difference and pure unity; nor does he analyze the mediating activities in this connection. He rather conceals from himself the need of analysis by representing the psychical mechanism as unconscious, and perception, intuition, and feeling as immediate. Such a dogmatic process, however, is manifestly of no philosophical value. It only removes the problem from the sphere of thought and its data, to the sphere of these unconscious and immediate processes. But these are necessarily inexplicable, seeing that all explanation is mediation. And besides, even if these processes could be explained, the relation which they establish between sense stimuli and thought forms could only be mechanical. Indeed, the mechanical adaptation of the one to the other would itself be impossible. For even mechanism implies a unity *within* the differences, although the unity implied is more abstract than it is in an organic existence. But Lotze's antithesis of thought and stimulus is so hard and strict as to make any unity inconceivable; nothing can reconcile a pure manifold of sense with his purely self-identical thought. So that, in the last resort, Lotze does not solve the problem of the relation of thought and reality, nor reveal a way of escape from the subjectivity of a knowledge of mere ideas to a knowledge of objective truth.

In one passage Lotze casually suggests another view, according to which the reality on which thought is exercised is related to the truth which thought reaches, in the way of a self-developing identity. "The whole series of inter-subordinate universals are," he says, "contained not *actu* but *potentiâ* in the essence of the thing itself."[1] Here the organic view seems to be substituted for the mechanical or external view of the relation of thought and reality. But it is mentioned only once, so far as I have been able to ascertain, and

---

[1] *Logic*, § 342.

it is mentioned with a "perhaps." Above all, it runs contrary to the whole trend of Lotze's effort; for it involves that thought in its operations finds only *itself*, and that the reality on which thought is engaged receives its fullest expression and attains its highest form in thought as a spiritual activity.

We must conclude, therefore, that if there is a way of showing, either that the subjective activities can reach objective results, or that, "if we follow the laws of discursive thought and construct the intricate web of ideas in abstraction from reality, the final result will correspond to the actual course of events," Lotze has not revealed it to us. His theory, starting from the subjectivity of the contents and the subjectivity of the processes of thought, leaves us enclosed within a world of pure ideas without showing how any reality can be known at all, to say nothing of being known to correspond to the sphere of ideas. His treatment both of the results and the processes of thinking ends with a Scepticism which is concealed by contradictions and tempered by a faith that cannot convince.[1]

[1] The doctrine repeatedly advanced by Lotze that our ideas can be regarded as objectively valid and that the process of thought leads to objective results merely because every one, on account of the constitution of the human soul, must arrive at the same results, does not seem to me to be worthy of serious discussion. Error would not cease to be error though all should commit it. It would, probably, not be recognized

Now, Lotze's failure to account for the knowledge of reality is, on his premises, inevitable. Objective knowledge cannot be elicited from subjective data by means of subjective processes. Lotze seems to me to have the merit of making it plain—by an indirect method—that the only way to reach reality at the end of the process of thought is to take our departure from it, and that the only way in which the activities of thought can produce results which are true of reality, or indeed any results at all, is by the co-operation of reality in their production. Man's mind and the real world must work together if man is to know; and, on the other hand, if the world is to reveal itself to man's thought it must have ontological affinity to his thinking powers. To demonstrate this a theory of mind and a theory of reality fundamentally different from Lotze's is required; one which, instead of seeking a way of connecting given inner states which are merely subjective with given outer data which are objective, starts from a unity which reveals itself *in* the distinction of the ideal and real, and reveals itself more and more completely as the knowledge of man grows. All I can attempt here is to meet some of the main arguments by which Lotze sought to show that the world does not help man

as error. That all men do, and that all men must, think in a subjective manner upon subjective data does not bring us any nearer objectivity than if only one person thought in this way.

to think, or that reality does not participate in the thinking process.

Lotze bases these arguments on the contrast between what is presented to thought and what is effected by thought, and on the contrast between the respective modes of activity of thought and reality. Now, it is evident that this contrast can be instituted only if both of the terms compared are presented in knowledge; both of them, in other words, must fall within the sphere of experience. Hence the contrast is not between the world of thought and the real world, in the sense of a world out of all relation to our intelligence, of which Lotze sometimes permits himself to speak; but between facts as given in thought and facts as sensuously perceived, or as "given in experience." But the first doubt that arises is whether the phenomena of our mental life are thus distinguishable, *i.e.*, whether some of them can be attributed to sensation or perception only, and some to conception, or judgment, or inference only. I need not dwell upon this recurring difficulty. No doubt the sensuous and the intelligible elements respectively predominate in the different phenomena of our mental life, and the ordinary logical distinction between perception and conception is both useful and valid. But it cannot be made absolute; the perceptive element cannot be eliminated from conception, nor the conceptual from perception. There is no intelligible datum which is either purely particular or purely universal, which is either unrelated stimulus or bare form. Lotze himself does not deny the Kantian dictum that perception without conception is blind, and conception without perception, empty. Nevertheless his contrast between the facts given to thought and the products effected by thought loses all its meaning unless they are thus isolated and mutually exclusive. For he speaks of the data a and a, which thought pronounces to be identical, and a and b which thought pronounces to be different, as if they were given one by one prior to any relation between them. Mind comes in afterwards and creates these connections. It passes to and fro between the given facts, spinning its spider-webs of relations; for these relations are nothing but memories of its own transitions, the consciousness of the unity of itself in its movement, and have no objective existence as connections between the facts. What his theory yields to us, therefore, are objective *data* plus subjective connections, the former given, the second made.

It is hardly necessary to indicate that against the assumption of such isolated data, awaiting the connecting activity of thought, all those arguments might be brought forward which have been urged against the associative theory of knowledge. It is sufficient to say that Lotze himself has used these arguments. In his criticism of empiricism he shows, after the manner of Kant, that *a priori* relations of thought enter into all the facts of experience. "The image of a particular form presented in space, the succession in time of the notes in a melody, these too, in every particular and detail of the picture, are no whit less the product of the thinking subject, no whit less, therefore, *"a priori."* [1] And besides the direct criticism of empiricism we might cite his view of the function of thought as a whole. He regards it as the conversion of the associative into the reflective consciousness, or of coincident into inwardly coherent experience: a conversion which he represents as impossible unless the relations which thought finds are already given in the data. Indeed, we have the same movement here as that which was described in the earlier chapters. Having said explicitly that the relation between red and yellow, straight and curved, can exist only so far as we think it, and "by the act of our thinking it," he adds a little later, "we could not so much as bring red and blue under the general name of colour did not that common element exist in them, to our consciousness of which we testify in framing the name."[2] So long as he is establishing the disparity between the products and the data of thought, and insisting upon the independence of reality of the thinking processes, he speaks of *a* and *a*, *a* and *b*, "red and red," "red and yellow" as purely discrete data, and of the relations of

[1] *Logic*, § 326.   [2] See *Logic*, §§ 338, 339.

identity and difference as memories of a mental transition. But when he considers the difficulty of accounting for the correspondence of the results of thought with reality, he makes reality yield relations as well as isolated data. If, for instance, the relations are mere memories of the mind's movement to and fro, why should the relation of *a* and *a* be always pronounced to be identity, and that of *a* and *b* difference? Memories of transitions, consciousness of mental unity in mental activity could not of themselves yield different relations; and Lotze must therefore find the special relation required in each case in the material. But when we bring his views together, and ask how then, if thought makes these relations, or if these relations are memories of mental transitions, they can be also in the material, he draws a distinction. The relations that are given in the material, those which stimulate mind into the appropriate activities, have a different character from those which thought makes. Relations of ideas exist *between* them, relations of things exist *in* them; and the former express less than the latter. Thought holds its ideas apart while relating them; it does not fuse them, and the connection does not affect the terms. The relation being *"between"* them, they are separated, so to speak, by an "interval." But an interval between actual facts or events, which are really connected in such a manner as to "influence" one another, is seen by him to be impossible. In the case of real relations there must be no interstices; the relations must penetrate the terms in such a way as to enter into their constitution and be *within* them. If *a* and *b* are real objects or events, say a cause and effect or agent and patient, their differences must fall within and be a manifestation of a deeper unity; but if they are ideas there is no unity *in* their differences; it is superimposed upon them from without by a mental activity.

But this distinction between real and mental relations seems to be a desperate resort. Why should thought be able to connect the merely different, any more than reality can; and how, especially, could it connect it in such a way as to correspond to reality? Why should thought, any more than reality, be able to leap over an interval? Or what proof can we have that real things cannot be externally related except that such a relation is, in the last resort, unthinkable? And why should it be more intelligible in respect of thoughts than it is with respect to things? Above all, how can the mental relations be regarded as "a weakened form," or as merely "less than" the real relations, when in the one case the relation is "between," or "external," and in the other "within" the terms and constitutive of them? An internal relation does not pass into an external one by a process of weakening, nor can the one serve as a stimulus to the other. In fact, we find that there is such a discrepancy between Lotze's view of thought and his view of reality as to make any correspondence between them unintelligible; for his theory of the relations of thought is mechanical, while his theory of reality is organic.

It is, however, important to bear in mind that this discrepancy *is* between an externally combining thought and an inwardly coherent reality. It exists, in other words, between reality and a thought which is formal—to which every datum, be it a thing, or event, or relation, must be given, and which, when all is given, can at best only establish relations *between* things. But if our criticism is valid, such thought as Lotze describes, which borrows its material from a foreign source, cannot even combine. At each successive stage it lapses into tautology, and Lotze's constant appeal to the material, whether for stimuli to perception, or guidance in inference, classification, and explanation is really an implicit admission that the thought which is unlike reality, and whose activities are not guided by a principle of reality, is helpless. Nevertheless, Lotze will not yield up his view of the formal nature of thought.

I now pass on to the contrast which Lotze endeavours to establish between the process and product of conceiving, and the data given to thought in perceptive experience. It seems sufficient, at first sight, merely to ask the question whether any realities correspond to our general notions. Conceptions are manifestly universal, and actual objects individual. An "animal" as characterless animal, a vertebrate, a mammal, or horse in general, does not exist; and yet in all thinking, strictly so called, we have conceptions of such objects. Here, then, it would seem we have a palpable example of the distinction on which Lotze insists between the products which thought makes, and what is given to it in experience. No one can assert that things in general exist, or deny that the products of thought are general ideas. It is on this contrast between the universality of the products of thought and the individuality of real objects, that Lotze mainly relies to prove his theory. Nevertheless, it seems to me that in this instance also, Lotze has exaggerated a legitimate and useful distinction in thought into a difference in kind, and made it absolute. Once more he treats the perception as particular only, and the conception as universal only; and he assumes that the real object is individual in the sense of being particular. Of course, if this assumption is true, there can be no correspondence between the product of thought and the real object.

Perhaps the clearest way of raising the issue would be to assert the opposite half-truth of Lotze's, and to say that conceptions are not general, and that perceived objects are not particular. We can at least challenge any one to produce any element in the object which is not universal, and any element in the concept which is not particular, and thereby bring out the truth that in every reality, and in every intelligible idea, particular and universal, difference and unity meet. The sensible qualities of objects, the special size, weight, shape, colour, of *this* horse, seem to be particular; and they may not be applicable in *this* conjunction to any other object whatsoever. But, on the other hand, it is manifest that all of these qualities not only are intelligible, but *exist* only in virtue of their relation to other objects and to the self. That is to say, if we abstract from the relations of the object to the system in which it is placed, if we deprive it of all that it has borrowed, nothing remains. *Except their unity*, Lotze might reply. "Everywhere in the flux of thought there remain quite insoluble those individual nuclei, ... which we designate by the name Being."[1] Though each quality of the object must be admitted to be possible only by its relation to other objects, no intelligible object can be conceived as a mere collection of qualities. It has an impervious unity and self-identity as its core and essence, without which the relations could not subsist. In other words, although the qualities can be resolved one by one into relations, the object *itself* cannot be so attenuated without at once passing out of existence and becoming unintelligible. And it seems to me that the answer is valid, so far as it shows that relations, apart from points of sus-

[1] *Mikrokosmus*, Book VIII., chap. i.

pension, are unintelligible.[1] But it is to be noted, on the one hand, that this impervious unity, in which the qualities cohere, is certainly not given in sense, and, on the other hand, that the sensible qualities which sense might be considered to supply, are relations. So that the theory turns round in Lotze's hand; and the contrast which began with attributing the isolated data to sense and the relations to thought, becomes a contrast between an impervious unity behind the qualities, which only thought can yield, and qualities which are impossible except through the relation of objects to each other, which mere sense cannot apprehend. The individual object, in a word, resists the attempt to treat it either as particular or as universal; it is a totality of concrete relations, a unity of universals, and therefore explicable only in the terms of thought and as the work of thought. Now, if we turn to the conception which Lotze contrasts with real objects, we shall find that in some respects at least, it has the same character of concrete thinkable individuality. A conception, say of a horse-in-general, is not a mere indiscriminate collection of contents, but a unity, more or

---

[1] It is evident that relations *plus* points related, however much we insist upon both, cannot solve the problem of their relation. Such a view remains at the mechanical stage of explanation, which leaves the unity, implied even in mechanism, implicit and unexplained. The idea of organism helps us beyond *this* difficulty, even though it brings more difficulties of its own.

less systematic, of consistent thoughts. And its content is specific, at least to the extent that we can distinguish between it and another concept, such as that of an ox-, or an oak-, in-general. Finally, every element in the content is ultimately derived from sense, and explicable only in thought. Wherein, then, lies the difference between the real, or perceived, or experienced object, and the conception? Lotze replies that the elements in the perception are all special and definite, while those in the conception are abstract and universal. The real horse combines *this* colour, with *this* size, *this* shape, *this* weight and particular structure; while the conceived or general horse combines *a* colour with *a* shape, size, weight, and so on. And the fact that the contents of conceptions are ultimately derived from sensuous experience, or that the sensible qualities, apprehended by perception, are possible only in virtue of the relations of objects to objects, does not abolish this distinction. Explanation of the source of particular sensible qualities does not change them into universal entities. Explanation is not elimination, nor does it attenuate the perceptions into conceptions. On the contrary, it leaves the qualities of objects just as they were, namely, particular and specific; and it leaves them equally unchanged, whether they originate in the objects themselves, as they do if the objects are complete or absolute, or are derived from elsewhere and only take temporary embodiment in the objects, as they do if these are finite. The universals of sense, or, if the term be misleading, the real connections between objects which are their qualities, are not abstract but concrete, and they inhere in their fulness only in individual objects. But, as we are told, the very essence of a conception is that it is a combination of universals, each of which is abstract, and each applicable to any object that falls into the class. We must, therefore, conclude that, although the sensible qualities of objects which perception gives are due to their relation to other objects, and explicable only in their connection to the whole system of real things, they are still not universals as the contents of conceptions are. If we indicate them by the term sense-universals, and regard them as given in the data, we must not confuse them with the universals which thought makes.

This distinction, within its own proper limits, is undeniable; but that the distinction is such as to justify us in attributing the contents of perception to the data or material of knowledge, or to reality, and the contents of conception to the activities of a thought which abstracts from sense and proceeds alone on its way, cannot be proved. Each of the universals in a concept is indefinite, and, owing to this indefiniteness, it is applicable to every object of the class and completely true of none. But, on the other hand, no one of them is merely indefinite and general: colour in general is still colour, although it is not necessarily redness, or blueness, or any particular colour. The conception does not, any more than aught else, derive its essential feature from negation, and exist in virtue of what it excludes. The characteristics of a concept lie, after all, in what the universals contain, and all these are, in a manner, as truly particular as the contents of a perception. Colour is a particular quality as contrasted with weight, or size, or shape, although it is universal as compared with redness or blueness. So that the distinction between a conception and a perception is only a difference in degree of definiteness, and it arises neither from the nature of the elements combined, nor from a different combining unity, nor from a difference in their mode of combination; and we cannot attribute the one to a thought which is independent of things, and the other to a perception which is purely or mainly receptive. In fact, perception and conception pass into each other. Any possible element of thought, or any real object presented to it, may be regarded either as a perception or as a conception. Redness, if we contrast it with colour, is a particular perception, but if we contrast it with its own shades of crimson, scarlet, and so on, it is a universal conception. The difference does not lie in the last resort, even in the degree of indefiniteness; for a conception may be more definite than a perception, and contain more elements more explicitly combined. The distinction lies in the fact that in conceiving we are *aware of* the incompleteness and indefiniteness of the mental representation, whereas in perceiving we seem to be apprehending the object as it is. In truth, however, both perceptions and conceptions are incomplete and abstract, and, in that sense, they are both creations of thought, and valid of no real objects. But in the one case the abstraction is conscious, we omit the obvious and aggressive relations of time and space and our sensible affections; while in the other case the abstraction is unconscious, we omit the general laws which scientific or philosophic thought might be able to discover in the object. And, in so far as the abstraction in conception is conscious, the perception is of the two the most abstract, and it omits the elements that are most vitally explanatory of the nature of objects. For conscious abstraction is, in a way, comprehension; we exclude only what is irrelevant to our immediate purpose in order to confine our attention to other elements that we regard as constitutive. And the shadow of what we exclude lingers on what is allowed to remain. In perceiving we seem to be dealing with the particular, the ultimate, and real, only because the synthetic and analytic activities of thought have not been consciously applied to the object. But immediately these activities are exercised, the object will reveal itself as a unity of universal qualities, every one of which becomes a class attribute predicable of other objects and entirely true of none. In fine, perceptive thought seems to give the whole reality only because it is ignorant of the problems present in its objects; while conception seems to give mere thoughts because the abstraction of spatial and temporal elements is as obvious as it is, in many cases, comparatively insignificant to the true understanding of things. The perceptive presentation of the world is manifestly not fuller and truer than that of the sciences and of philosophy, but more abstract and less valid. Its apparent superior correspondence to reality is due merely to the absence of reflection. No one is so sure that he perceives facts and immediately grasps reality, as he is who has never been made aware of their inner complexity, or of their relation to his intelligence. There is nothing so secure as ignorance. In fact, we have in this sense of certainty and self-confidence of ordinary consciousness the counterpart of the self-sufficiency of the morally undeveloped consciousness. The implicit trust in perception, like the simple moral contentment of the child, is due to the fact that the unity of consciousness has not been broken or disturbed by the emergence of the ideal which reveals the imperfection and incompleteness of the elementary forms of our intellectual and moral life.

This view of the relation of perception and conception may be justified to some extent by the consideration that there are two ways in which we may ascend to universals. One is easy and broad, and leads to the extinction of thought. Its highest universal is pure being, which means nothing in particular, and it is reached by the process of omitting the content. The other way is the difficult way of scientific and philosophic thought, which seeks universals that are concrete and in which the specific content persists and is explained. The goal of this method is a principle which is the source of the reality and the truth of the world. Now Lotze is quite aware of this distinction, and he employs it in discriminating between Classification and Explanation.[1] Nevertheless, the contrast between real or perceived objects and the conceptions which are the products of thought is valid only if we take conception in the sense which he definitely condemns, namely, as a process of omission.[2] No doubt the thought which abstracts becomes the less true of reality the emptier it becomes, and inasmuch as all conception is abstraction, at least from our sensibility, all conceptions are untrue. This is the aspect on which Lotze insists. But the other aspect he is prone to ignore, the aspect, namely, that the emptier a thought is, or the more it is conceptual in this abstract sense, the less it is a *thought*. But, in reality, the thought and its object gradually vanish together, and throughout the whole movement of abstraction we are departing from real thought just as truly as we are departing from actual objects.

[1] See chapter v.   [2] See *Logic*, § 23.

So that the correspondence between reality and thought remains unbroken, even when we regard conception as an abstracting process directed towards an empty universal. The apparent disparity between real things and the thought product arises not from what thought makes, but from what it omits and excludes. On the other hand, to the degree in which we correct the abstraction and complete the thought, to that degree the reality for us grows in significance. In fact, everywhere in our experience reality and living thought always develop together. And it is only by confining our attention to the abstract side of the process of conceiving, and by forgetting that abstraction extinguishes thought no less than reality, that conception comes to wear the appearance of being a mere mental creation, less true than that which perception yields.

Thus the contrast which Lotze strives to institute between the product of thought in conceiving and the given reality fails, even when we regard conception as a process of omitting differences. It fails still more obviously if we take conception in its higher sense, in which alone it is employed in the endeavour to comprehend facts and has real value as thought. That contrast fails not only because no reality whatsoever is given apart from thought, and conception enters into perception, but also because perception enters into conception. The reality which we are said to "encounter in perception" is *carried over into* conception in all effective or genuine thought, and it guides that process. No doubt, as I have already admitted, the sensuous elements seem to disappear in conception; but that disappearance is never complete, neither does it take place at all except in the case of data which are recognized as alien to the immediate purpose of our investigation. The irrelevant elements in ordinary investigation into the nature of objects are the time, place, and manner in which objects affect our sensibility, and the absence of these elements has been taken as the characteristic of all conception. In ordinary perception, on the other hand, these sensible relations between objects and ourselves constitute the readiest criteria for distinguishing between reality and illusion. Nevertheless, I should hesitate to say that we "encounter reality in perception," and *not* in conception. The consciousness of loss of contact with reality can come when perception in itself is clear enough, as for instance, when on waking from a deep sleep in a strange room we fail to connect what we see with our past experience. Indeed, it always comes when the continuity of consciousness seems to be suspended, as in recovery from a swoon. It is, I conclude, not in perception as such that we encounter reality. *The consciousness of reality is the consciousness of the unity of our psychical life.* And consequently, the omission of these sensuous elements would not involve loss of contact with reality, except where these elements, as in ordinary life, are the most relevant to our immediate intelligent purposes.

But omission is, in any case, a misleading term. I do not conceive that the scientific investigator who is intent on discovering the physical laws of colour leaves the sensible world behind him. He omits and leaves to the psychologist and the physiologist the problem of the relation of the coloured object to the sentient being, but he carries with him into his apprehension of motion its sensuous evidence. And, in a similar way, each of the other sciences carries up into its theory the sensuous aspect of the fact whose explanation it is seeking. In so far as the sciences deal merely with such aspects, they are all abstract and untrue, and their laws are mere creations of the mind. In this respect there are no facts corresponding to the general conceptions of any one of the sciences; and all the sciences are hypothetical because they begin by mutilating the object "encountered in perception." But in so far as each does explain an aspect of reality it carries up that aspect into its ultimate laws. The physicist, it is true, does not have a sensation of blueness when he detects the number of the vibrations per second which is its physical condition; but the *sensation of blueness was no part of his datum*. His datum was purely physical, and an abstraction. What *was* a part of his datum he carries with him to the solution, and it finds its expression in the law. For the law is no empty abstraction, but a law of the data, distinguishable from the laws of other data. Each law finds its own character in the content, the universal manifesting itself in the system of particulars—quantity in mathematics, matter and motion and space in physics, morphological phenomena in biology, and so on. If perception seems to give reality, and scientific explanation by universal laws only abstractions, that comes, not from the fact that when we explain we leave the reality encountered in perception behind us and enter into an adjectival world, but from the fact that science, because its aim is to explain, takes up only one aspect at a time; while perception sets complex problems for all the sciences. But as little as the known-unknown of perception is the ideal of knowledge, so little is its object reality. The ideal of knowledge would be reached in the re-combination of the aspects (every one of which, as a real content, *lives* in the *forms* of the sciences) into a science of sciences which reveals a concrete universal principle; and it is then, and then only that thought would reach the real. Conception and science and thought seem to be merely "hypothetical," and perception alone seems to "encounter" reality, only because the abstraction in the one case is conscious and in the other unconscious. Neither conception nor perception is true, but perception is the less true; neither is entirely false, nor the invention of the mind set to work by itself, but reality guides both processes, and uses thought in all its forms as the vehicle for expressing itself. Logical conception proceeding along the *via negativa* of abstraction is, I admit, unlike reality both as a process and product; but logical conception is the logician's invention. Living thought proceeds after another fashion and does not omit by explaining, but articulates the indefinite into a system.

Before passing on to the consideration of Lotze's arguments for the subjectivity of judgment and inference, I have one more remark to make. Lotze speaks as if objective or valid truth can be obtained only from the hill-top, or, to translate his metaphor, as if necessarily coherent truth can only be given as the last result of thinking. Indeed, as Lotze admits, prior to the emergence of thought, the question of the truth or untruth of our experiences cannot arise, both being alike impossible to a purely associative consciousness. But this is as much as to say that, apart from thought and its necessary connections, we have no criterion of reality. Reality cannot be given at the beginning, nor can it be given at all except to a consciousness which connects its contents by means of relations of thought. *For reality is itself related to thought, and cannot be set against it in mere contrast.* Nevertheless, such is the ambiguity of Lotze's treatment of the elementary processes and the primary data of our intelligent life, that what is thus *below* the distinction of truth and error, reality and illusion, is erected into a criterion, by reference to which thought and its activities are pronounced to be merely subjective. No doubt Lotze insists that subjectivity does not imply illusiveness; but, on the other hand, he has failed, and necessarily failed, to prove his conviction. It is because thought fails to give facts that he has recourse to feeling; and his proof that thought does not give facts, but ideas and ideal connections, rests on the contrast between thought and its products on the one hand, and what is given to it on the other. And yet, what is given is neither true nor false! The question thus arises, what does Lotze mean by reality? Is reality given before thought begins its work, or after it has completed it? Is it given at the base of the hill, or from the hill-top? Lotze is sufficiently explicit as to the pure subjectivity of the arbitrary ways *from* the one *to* the other; but he is not explicit as to the beginning and the end of the process. For if reality is so given by experience or perception as to serve for the *criterion* of the processes and products of thought, on what grounds can it be denied that these are supererogatory? If perception gives the real, why should we undergo the labour of reflection? And, on the other hand, if reality is not given until thought has completed its work and climbed to the hill-top, how can its processes be condemned by reference to a criterion which thought itself constitutes? The fact is that Lotze uses "reality" in two inconsistent ways. It is now what is given at the beginning, now what is reached at the end; it is now perceived, or even *felt*, it is now attained, in part, by the reflective processes of science and philosophy; it is now the starting point, and now the far-off goal of our intelligent life. We might try to avoid this difficulty by saying that while reality is given in perception, it is not given *as perceived*. But this will not serve the end of Lotze; for unless it is given as perceived, then it cannot serve as the criterion for thought. The reality sinks into a mere word which means less than "something." If, on the other hand, it is not given *as* perceived or felt, then, I presume, it is either given as thought or not given at all. But if it is given as thought then the perception or feeling which has least of the characteristics of thought, or, on Lotze's theory, none of them, is the least true. Lotze's implicit assumption, which really gives its basis to his whole theory of the subjectivity of thought, is the sensational hypothesis of a reality immediately given in the sensuous consciousness; but the sceptical issues of such a hypothesis, to which Lotze is not blind, and the condemnation of the whole labour of reflective thought, and of the whole of the principles and methods of science and philosophy which it involves, force the acknowledgment from him that reality is given, to the degree in which it is given, only from the hill-top, as the result of thought. But this, in turn, implies the idealistic view of the nature of reality; it implies, that is to say, the repudiation of all reality *except* that which is given in thought. Reality is on this view the thinkable, or in other words, the rational; in fact it is thought, unless we presume that thought can think a something other than itself, which we cannot in any manner characterize. Lotze wavers between these views. When he remembers that the associative or merely perceptive consciousness is incapable alike of truth and error, and that reality and unreality come in only with the objectifying and systematizing activities of thought, the reality seems not to be given but to be sought after, and sought after by thought. When he has in his mind the formal character of thought, as he defines it, and the emptiness of its forms, he looks back to perception and immediacy for reality; and by contrast with these he pronounces the activities of thought subjective, and regards them as artificial means whereby we endeavour, by a process which is radically self-stultifying, to escape relativity and reach fact. Both theories cannot be true. Nor is there any way of escaping the contradiction except by conceiving reality, as indeed, given in perception, but also as given ever more fully as we develop its content by means of thought. But I pass on to the remaining forms of thought, namely, Judgment and Inference.

The arguments by which Lotze tries to prove

that Judgment and Inference are unlike real objects, and that reality takes no part in the process of forming them, or that these activities are merely subjective movements of our spirit whereby it endeavours to escape from its eccentric position, are, in the last resort, the same as those which we have just examined in dealing with Conception. They are based upon the same fundamental assumption regarding the nature of thought. It is held that its work is to combine, that the connections it forms are purely its own additions to fact, instigated indeed by objects, but none the less unreal as they stand. Just as "a and a, a and b, red and red, red and yellow" are first given, and just as thought moving to and fro between them and remembering its own transitions forms the purely ideal connections of identity or difference; so there are *given* to judgment two ideas, and it adds a constant connection, namely, the copula "*is*"; and there are *given* to inference two judgments, and it proceeds to form a third judgment by means of them.

Now, that a judgment consists of two ideas *plus* a relation is not true, although logic may find two ideas and one connection, and, indeed, many more, in any judgment which it pleases to analyze. Nor (2) is it true that a judgment consists of reality given in the subject, *plus* ideality or validity, or an adjectival entity in the predicate. Nor (3) do we add a copula which is an abstract "is." On the contrary, we begin in judgment with the copula which is a universal, and whose character varies with every object on which thought happens to be engaged.[1] If we start with the presupposition that judgment is a combining function, then the difference between its process and the relation of real events is undeniable. If we start with the view that thought seizes upon an indefinite reality and articulates it into a system, this insurmountable discrepancy disappears. The reality expands with the thinking process and guides it. Thought is at no point formal or out of "contact" with reality, and reality is at no point *not* ideal. The whole issue thus turns upon the nature of the act of Judgment.

Now, I have already criticised this first view and endeavoured to show that formal or combinatory thought ends in being tautologous and helpless. It cannot connect what is *given* as different. The highest forms of inference fell back into syllogistic thought, whose tautology is explicit; and the Disjunctive and Hypothetical Judgments were as little

---

[1] This view of the concrete copula is implied in the whole treatment of the hypothetical judgment and of reasoning in Mr. Bosanquet's great work on Logic; and it constitutes, if I may venture an opinion, the main advance towards a completer idealism, and a fuller reconciliation of reality and ideality, of fact and truth, which Mr. Bosanquet's *Logic* makes upon Mr. Bradley's. But, for the explicit expression of this view as the true starting point of knowledge, I am indebted to Mr. Edward Caird. It is found to underlie his whole criticism of Kant, and it gives him his point of departure and regulating principle in his account of the Evolution of Religion.

capable of uniting differences as the Categorical. It remains now to indicate the opposite view. On this view thought takes its departure from a single fact or a single idea, or rather from both; for the fact must be presented to thought before thought can start from it, that is to say, it must be an idea, and the idea must be *of* a fact, else it will be empty of all meaning. Indeed, it is because the datum of thought must thus be both ideal and real that the only form of thought which is capable of expressing it is the Judgment. For the judgment, as distinguished from the concept, gives this internal schism; and inference gives no more. And because every object of thought must have these two aspects, *i.e.*, must be both objective and subjective, all the products of thought are judgments. We cannot get beneath judgment while remaining within the intelligible world. The cry, "Wolf!" is a judgment; for, if it is understood, it is an idea that points to an object; and even the Interjection, "Alas!" or "Hurrah!" is a judgment, for it indicates an object of thought, namely, the state of consciousness of the person who utters it. And, on the other hand, the analysis of the most abstruse and concrete products of advanced thought would, of course, show that they consist of judgments.

If this is true then the combinatory view of judgment, as given by Lotze, is manifestly not correct. The idea that is presented as the subject and that which is given in the predicate are already judgments; they are both intelligible and both facts; each of them is both ideal and real. And consequently judgment is not the combination of two ideas. On the contrary, judgment is necessary to form *one* idea, and it never in one operation forms more than one. Nor is the reality given first in the subject and then characterized in the predicate; that is to say, we cannot regard the subject as pure reality and the predicate as pure ideality, nor have we first a substantive and then an adjective. For the reality that is said to be given in the subject is given also as ideal, or as known, *so far*. It is not there unless it is given, and it is not given except as ideal. There is no " that " which is not also a " what," and even a " something " has some meaning with the complete elimination of which it would vanish. The object of thought disappears with the activity of thought, and the activity with the object. In other words, thought cannot begin its movement except at the instigation of reality, and the only reality that can excite its activity must be given to it, and, therefore, be so far ideal. In a mere "that" both reality and ideality are at the vanishing point. What we cannot characterize except indefinitely, we cannot assert to exist except tentatively.

On this question of the priority of reality *in any sense* to ideality there depend the most important issues, and, indeed, the issue on which we are here engaged, namely, the adjectival nature of thought and its unlikeness to reality; for Lotze *presupposes* that the data are given prior to their ideal combination by thought. If only we could catch a judgment in the making, it might help us to determine this issue. Such a judgment in the making was, as we have seen, given by Lotze in the Impersonal Judgments: "It rains," "It is unpleasant." Now, in these instances, the process is, I believe, that of further characterizing a "something"; in other words, it is a process of discovering distinctions within an indefinite subject. There is not connection but development of content, and thought proceeds not by aggregation but by evolution.

Nevertheless, it may be urged, the reality seems to be given, however indefinitely, in the subject, and predication seems to be its ideal extension. That is to say, the reality is supplied, and what thought adds seems to be an adjective, valid indeed, but not real. The "that" seems to be given before the "what"; and the "that" seems to be *given*, while the "what" seems to be *made*. I reply that, in any case, the unity of the act of judgment is exposed in this process, and the judgment is not the combination of two ideas—of an "it" with "unpleasantness"—by means of a third element, namely, the copula "is." We have not grasped the "it" until the judgment is complete, and during the whole process we have been engaged, not with two objects, but with one; we have not been combining but evolving. But further examination will show, I believe, that the reality is not given in the subject, but in the judgment as a whole, or, in other words, in the "something" which is articulated into subject and predicate, neither of which is prior to the other. In other words, judgment does not consist in the application of a conception to a perception, nor in the subsumption of a perception under a conception. Perception and conception, reality and ideality, are given only together; or in other words, their unity is prior to the difference, though it reveals its character only in the differences.

Let me endeavour to illustrate this view that the real or perceptive element is not given first in the subject, and the adjectival or conceptual superadded in the predicate. I write the word "Peter," and the reader, by the very fact of understanding the word, instantaneously forms a judgment. That judgment indicates a certain reality characterized in a certain way, and which is both a "that" and a "what." What then is "the reality" thus "given in the subject?" The answer will probably be that it is a person, possibly the apostle from the shores of the Sea of Galilee. But I complete the sentence and write, "Peter is a Greek word meaning a rock." And immediately the original "reality" in the reader's mind is absolutely rejected, and another substituted in its place. Now, this seems to me to imply that the reality cannot be said to have been there *before* the complete judgment; and that it would not have appeared to be there except for the fact that we form judgments immediately on the first hearing of the subject, and anticipate the expression of it in the complete act of judging. I shall illustrate this by one more example. I set down the words "The three brothers." Once more a judgment is instantaneously formed, although in being formed, it is held in hand as reversible, and the mind has not rested in a *complete* judgment; that is to say, it has not completely grasped the reality before the act of judgment, (which is single although it takes time to perform,) is finished. When the words, "The three brothers," are spoken the reality which is called up before the mind, though with the possibility of its rejection, is probably, three persons. But I proceed: "The three brothers is the name of a hiring boat that plies on the Menai Straits." Once more the originally assumed reality is entirely rejected and another substituted, when the judgment is complete.

If in this way we can really detect the process of judgment it seems to be impossible to say that the reality is given in the subject and that we then attach an ideal content to it, or combine another idea with it. That there was an idea and a reality when the mere subject was given is undeniable; the reality could not be given except as ideal, and there is no thought except judgment. But that one idea is given in its completeness, and that another idea is joined to it by an external copula seems to me to be untenable. Throughout the act of judgment we deal with one content, and the reality of that content, no less than its meaning, is only given when this single but progressive act of thought is finished. The reality is from beginning to end involved in the meaning, it grows with the growth of the meaning, and it also guides the process of evolving the meaning by means of judgment.

Lotze is no doubt right in insisting that real objects are not related to one another as the ideas are connected in a judgment, *if* judgment consists of two ideas first given separately and then connected by a copula. But this difference might be taken as an indication of the necessity of reviewing the theory of judgment, instead of as a reason for asserting a discrepancy between that function of thought which is employed in all knowledge, and the objects which, after all, as Lotze confesses, we ultimately reach by means of it. The discrepancy, however, lies once more between reality and a thought which combines externally, deriving its activities solely from itself and moving in obedience to private laws of its own in formal abstraction from its data. But that thought, as we have tried to prove, is neither living nor real thought; for external combination is impossible, and thought severed from real content is absolutely helpless. External combinations of subject *plus* predicate *plus* copula are, indeed, unlike the relations of objects in the real world; but living thought issues in no such external combinations. It deals with a universal which by its instrumentality sunders into subject and predicate and remains nevertheless a single concrete totality, or systematic unity of differences.

Now it is evident that this view of judgment would reverse the whole treatment of thought by Lotze; for it strikes at the root of his conception of its combinatory function, and repudiates entirely the separation of ideality and reality. To establish it we should be obliged to attempt a task beyond our power and present purpose, namely, that of following in detail the process by which the content of thought, or reality, enters vitally into and dominates the thinking process in all its forms. We should have to follow the view so admirably expounded by Mr. Bosanquet, according to which the real content manifests itself even in hypothetical judgments, where the thought sequence, or the necessary connection is shown to issue from the reality presupposed in the protasis, and in disjunctive judgments in which the reality first shows itself as explicitly systematic. In a similar way we should have to elaborate the view already suggested, that inference also is the evolution of a single content, and try to show that while thought obeys laws which are universal, each *proof* derives its character from its material, and is completely cogent only if that material shows itself as a unity of differences, or a systematic totality whose evidence lies in the necessary mutual implication of its constitutive elements.[1]

But there is a grave objection to this intimate identification of reality and thought which we cannot thus pass over. This view we have suggested seems to imply that things themselves change with our process of comprehending them. But it seems to be undeniably plain that reality is not one thing when the process of thinking begins and another when it ends. Even if it be admitted that *for us* the reality expands with its explanation, or that conception, judgment, and inference are the processes whereby the indefinite content gradually realizes itself in thought as a systematic whole which contains explicit differences explicitly combined in a unity by necessary relations, the question still arises, Is not such an expansion merely the expansion of a subjective datum? Is it not the original *idea of* reality that has moved with our thought? Surely reality itself, as Lotze contends, is indifferent to our activities. No one can hold that real objects actually participate in these processes. Did the earth begin to go round the sun when the modern astronomical theory was discovered? Or did the plants and animals first form a systematic kingdom when Darwin wrote his Origin of Species?

[1] See above, chap. vii.

I at once admit the negative. Such a preposterous identification of the real movement of events with the dialectical movement of our thought cannot be held. Nor would it have been attributed to idealistic writers except for the presupposition, already criticised, that thought begins with ideas and must determine reality in correspondence to its subjective contents. But another view is possible. The correspondence between the real and ideal, which not even the Sceptic can utterly deny, may conceivably arise in two ways. *Our thought may determine reality, or reality may determine our thought.* On the first view reality would come to be in the act of thinking it. And it is this first view alone which Lotze considers. This is the view he attributes to Idealists; and it is against giving to thought a power adequate to make reality, or to convert the phenomena of a subjective consciousness, or a world of ideas into actual facts that he directs his whole polemic. Neither in his criticism of Idealism nor in the exposition of his own theory does he conceive any other than a subjective starting point for knowledge. Consequently he obtains objects at all only by "objectifying" and "positing" states of consciousness, and his ultimate account of them still leaves them subjective phenomena. He asserts indeed that they are valid of reality; but he neither accounted for that validity, nor showed any such way of conceiving thought and reality as to make their co-operation in producing knowledge intelligible. His assertion of "validity" is therefore purely dogmatic, and he has in the last resort to trust in a faith which his philosophy cannot justify. Now, unless the criticism we have advanced is fundamentally erroneous, neither thought nor feeling nor intuition can correct the error of Lotze's original assumption, namely, that knowledge begins with an inner world of subjective states, and then strives to find a way outwards. Such an outlet into the world of facts we deemed impossible, and its possibility is certainly not demonstrated by Lotze: we are absolutely confined to the spectacle of an inner play of changing states, and even these we cannot know without, in the very act of knowing, converting them into objects. Knowledge is both subjective and objective, and every object of knowledge is both presented to thought and by thought, is both real and ideal. It is the theory that endeavours to step from thoughts to things which takes a *mauvais pas* that no logic can justify.

Now, it was in the consciousness of the impassable barrier which intercepts all movement from within outwards, or from ideality to reality, that Idealism took its rise. Convinced of the self-contradictory scepticism that awaits a theory which starts from a subjective origin, it is as frankly realistic as is ordinary consciousness, or Materialism; and, without hesitation, it conceives that, in all his thinking, however inadequate it may be, man thinks of objects. But it refuses to define these objects in such a manner as to make the problem of thinking them insoluble; that is to say, it denies the ordinary assumption that reality implies the exclusion of the ideal. Starting from the fact, to which all the knowledge we have seems to bear witness, and with the denial of which the fact of knowledge is unaccountable, namely, that its object is both subjective and objective, it refuses to partition real being into two elements, and to make over reality to things and ideality to thought. It finds that knowledge is the self-revelation of reality in thought, and that our thought is the instrument of that self-revelation. And it thus escapes the impossible task which a subjective view of the origin of knowledge inevitably brings both to Lotze and to the Sceptics whose arguments he failed to meet, namely, that of showing how the thought of man can so determine reality that objects shall correspond to ideas. Its problem is to show how reality determines our thinking, or, put in a logical form, how the *content* of conception, judgment, and reasoning guides the reflective processes.

I may, in concluding, be allowed to illustrate this point by a reference to Kant. Kant conceived that the cardinal error of Associationism lay "in the assumption that our cognition must conform to objects." "Let us then," he says, "make the experiment whether we may not be more successful in Metaphysics, if we assume that the objects must conform to our cognition."[1] He consequently endeavoured to discover the nature of reality from the conditions of its intelligibility, and in doing so he constructed the world of objects, step by step, on the plan of the world of knowledge. But he did not thereby discover anything more than the *conditions* of a world intelligible to us. That it actually existed could not be proved by any such process. On these premises reality must remain hypothetical, and the content of our knowledge through and through phenomenal. In a word, the subjective origin of Kant's speculative effort rendered it a vain and impossible endeavour to reach things as they are, or things in themselves, which, so far from "conforming to our cognition," remained absolutely beyond its reach as unknowable and empty entities. What Kant succeeded in demonstrating was that "our cognition does not conform to objects" *if objects are to be regarded as they were conceived by Hume and the Associationists*, that is to say, if they are conceived as independent facts and events really disconnected, though outwardly and contingently combined in our knowledge by means of purely mental relations. He showed, as against his predecessors, that the only Nature which could be knowable by us is a Nature which is systematic,

---

[1] Preface to the Second Edition of the *Critique of Pure Reason*.

and which owes its systematic character to a principle that is analogous to the supreme unity of self-consciousness.[1]

Now Idealists have accepted this reconstruction of Nature from the hands of Kant, and they start from the assumption which Kant's process of proof seems to have justified, namely, that reality is intelligible only as a rational system in which, as in an organic whole, a single principle lives and everywhere manifests itself. And they have made this conception of the systematic and rational coherence of reality their starting point, in such a manner that they do not doubt, any more than men of science do, that the endeavour of thought will lead to truth, or that reality will yield its treasures to the enquiring intellect. The uncertainty and suspicion of intelligence, which must characterize every theory that makes the subjective side of knowledge its starting point and represents the processes of thinking as an inward movement of a spirit left to itself, is found to have no better justification than that violent "divorce of thing and thought" which every effort after knowledge ignores and which all acquired knowledge, whether empirical or reasoned, contradicts. Hence Idealists return once more to the attitude of ordinary consciousness and of science, and commit their thinking to the guidance of

---

[1] That he conceived that unity as formal is undeniable. But, important as this point is, I may pass it over in this discussion.

fact. They may even be said to have returned, in one sense, to the attitude of Hume and his predecessors, and to be engaged in solving the problem "how our cognition conforms to objects."

But, taught by Kant, they conceive these objects, which constitute the data of thought and dominate its processes, in a manner fundamentally different from Hume. The reality which is *given* in perception, and which is given no less in every act of thought, is no longer a collection of independent, mutually exclusive, or even unrelated objects and elements, but a rational system. It is, therefore, to that system that they commit themselves. But to commit themselves to a rational system is, so to speak, to commit reason to the charge of reason. The conformity of cognition to objects is its conformity to objects which are themselves conceived as manifestations of an intelligent or spiritual principle. From this point of view the Idealist may, not less than the Materialist, regard man as a natural product, and not less than the Associationist, regard mind as the recipient of truth, and its activities as governed by facts. But on the other hand, the nature whose product he is conceived to be is a Nature which is spiritual, and the facts which are pressed upon mind by its natural environment, are themselves rational. Nor is there any enslavement of intelligence, if it is subordinated only to intelligence. Mind may freely communicate itself to mind. Neither by making himself an instrument of the Good that is working in the world, nor by making himself the vehicle of its truth, does man give away his freedom, or eliminate his spiritual nature. On the contrary, it is by that path that he realizes himself.

From this point of view, the correspondence between knowlege and reality may prove to be intelligible. Reality will not, indeed, change with our comprehension of it, nor will objects and events become connected *pari passu* with the concatenation of our thoughts into judgments and inferences. But it will guide these processes step by step, and reveal itself ever more fully as our knowledge advances. For, in one sense, reality is there at the beginning. Without it thought could make no advance, and, set to work *in vacuo*, it could not even spin its "spider-webs" of mental relations. In another sense, reality is not present to thought even at its best. Man aspires after truth as he aspires after goodness, and we cannot assert that he ever reaches them. Set, as we know him, at the point of collision between evil and good, error and truth, having process and evolution as the very essence and inner necessity of his life, a complete truth is as unattainable to him as complete goodness. Nevertheless, he does not fail utterly; incomplete knowledge is still knowledge, as the least good is still good. And that which stands between him and failure is just this fact of his vital ontological relation in all his intelligent life to the Reality which lives and moves in all things, revealing itself everywhere, but most completely, so far as human experience shows, in the spiritual life of Man.

THE END

www.ingramcontent.com/pod-product-compliance
Lightning Source LLC
Chambersburg PA
CBHW032020220426
43664CB00006B/310